# KEYS TO A
# POWERFUL
# VOCABULARY

## Level 1

# KEYS TO A POWERFUL VOCABULARY

## Level 1

### THIRD EDITION

## Janet Maker
*Los Angeles Trade-Technical College*

## Minnette Lenier
*Los Angeles Pierce College*

Prentice Hall
Englewood Cliffs, New Jersey 07632

**Library of Congress Cataloging-in-Publication Data**

Maker, Janet.
    Keys to a powerful vocabulary : level I / Janet Maker, Minnette
Lenier.—3rd ed.
      p.  cm.
    Includes index.
    ISBN 0-13-668948-5
    1. Vocabulary.  I. Lenier, Minnette.  II. Title.
PE1449.M33  1994
428.1—dc20                          93-10922
                                        CIP

Pronunciation guide and art on pages 4, 10, 14, 17, 19, 24, 30, 34, 36, 41, 55, 62, 64, 69, 80, 83, 85, 90, 100, 102, 104, 109, 126, 128, 130, 135, 144, 146, 148, 153, 161, 163, 165, 170, 177, 180, 183, 189, 201, 204, 206, 212, 221, 222, 227, 228, 231, 237, and 238 reprinted with permission from *Webster's New World Dictionary*, Third College Edition. Copyright © 1988 by Simon & Schuster.

Art on pages 74, 76, 95, and 97 from Minnette Lenier and Janet Maker, *Get It All Together*, Set A, 1978, cards A-7, B-13, B-21, C-13. By permission of Opportunities for Learning, Inc., Chatsworth, California.

Thesaurus excerpts in Chapters 11 and 12 are from *The New American Roget's College Thesaurus* by Philip D. Morehead and Andrew T. Morehead. Copyright ©1958, 1962 by Albert H. Morehead. Copyright ©1978, 1985, renewed 1986 by Philip D. Morehead and Andrew T. Morehead. Used by permission of Dutton Signet, a division of Penguin Books USA Inc.

Acquisitions editor: Carol Wada
Editorial assistant: Joan Polk
Editorial/production supervision and
   interior design: Mary McDonald
Copy editor: Durrae Johanek
Cover design:Wendy Alling Judy
Prepress buyer: Herb Klein
Manufacturing buyer: Bob Anderson

© 1994, 1991, 1983 by Prentice-Hall, Inc.
A Paramount Communications Company
Englewood Cliffs, New Jersey 07632

Printed in the United States of America
10  9  8  7

ISBN 0-13-668948-5

Prentice-Hall International (UK) Limited, *London*
Prentice-Hall of Australia Pty. Limited, *Sydney*
Prentice-Hall Canada Inc., *Toronto*
Prentice-Hall Hispanoamericana, S.A., *Mexico*
Prentice-Hall of India Private Limited, *New Delhi*
Prentice-Hall of Japan, Inc., *Tokyo*
Simon & Schuster Asia Pte. Ltd., *Singapore*
Editora Prentice-Hall do Brasil, Ltda., *Rio de Janeiro*

# CONTENTS

# PREFACE

*Keys to a Powerful Vocabulary* was written with three major purposes in mind. First, we wanted to teach the words most essential for college students. The words in this book were chosen because they appear very frequently in college textbooks. Essential words were also suggested by our students and by other instructors.

Secondly, we wanted the book to teach the skills necessary for students to improve their vocabularies on their own—use of context, word memory techniques, dictionary, word parts, etymology, thesaurus, and usage.

Our third purpose was to make students excited about words. We know that vocabulary has often been presented in school in painful ways: long, boring lists of words. We tried to make this book fun, to communicate to students the enjoyment of words that we feel. The exercises involve interesting information, stories, and a variety of activities—sentences using words in context; matching words with synonyms, antonyms, definitions, and etymologies; filling in word parts; analogies; crossword puzzles; and completing open-ended sentences.

The book is designed so that students can progress at their own rates. We begin with a pretest and end with a posttest so students can evaluate their progress. The exercises are self-checking, with the answers in the back of the book. Chapters 3 through 12 contain reviews of words in previous chapters, as an aid to memory. Halfway through the book we review all the words in Chapters 1 through 6, and there is a final review of words in Chapters 1 through 12 in the back of the book, immediately before the posttest. These reviews are included to assist those students who are using the book as a text to prepare for midterm and final exams. The new edition expands the Review Words section in each chapter to include definitions and context sentences. A new Progress Chart appears in the back of the book.

# ACKNOWLEDGMENTS

For their creative and/or editorial assistance we wish to thank Sallie Brown, Bill Broderick, Jules Lenier, Anne-Kristin Noer, Claudia Gumbiner, and Carolyn Taffel, and also Carol Wada, and Phil Miller at Prentice Hall.

For assistance with field testing and/or research, thanks to Barbara Scheibel, the hundreds of instructors and students who responded to our endless surveys on words, and the Prentice Hall representatives who convinced the instructors to respond.

A special thanks to Bill Proctor, who created some of the drawings in this book.

Thank you to the reviewers: Dr. Javier Ayala, University of Texas at Brownsville; Paulette Diamond, Queensborough Community College; Diane B. Tingle, Delaware Technical and Community College; and Jo Devine, University of Alaska at Juneau.

Pronunciations of words are from *Webster's New World Dictionary of the American Language,* Pocket-size Edition (Simon & Schuster, 1990). Synonym entries in Chapter 12 are based on *Webster's New World Dictionary of the American Language,* Third College Edition (Simon & Schuster, 1988). Many of the obscure facts in the book are from the *Guinness Book of World Records* and *Ripley's Believe It or Not.*

# chapter 1

# INTRODUCTION

Scientists believe that Cro-Magnon man might have uttered his first "words" about 40,000 B.C. Ever since then, words have been used to express how we think and feel. Without the right word it is hard to say what we mean. For example, if we did not have a word for this animal

we would have to refer to it as "a leaping, plant-eating mammal native to Australia and neighboring islands, with short forelegs, strong, large hind legs, and a long, thick tail; the female has a pouch, or marsupium, in front, for her young."[1] Fortunately, we can just say it's a *kangaroo.*

But how did we get the word *kangaroo?* Where do words start? Later in this book you'll learn that words come from many places, including other languages. No one can say for sure how *kangaroo* was coined, but it is widely believed that one of the first explorers of Australia, when he saw his first kangaroo, pointed to it and asked his native guide, "What is that?" "Kangaroo," the guide replied. So the word came from the language of the Australian natives. Years later it was discovered that the word *kangaroo* meant "I don't know."

Words stand for ideas. The more you know, the more things you can think and talk about. For example, it's said that the Eskimo language has 17 different words to describe types of snow. Most of us don't even know 17 types exist; about all we can say is that snow can be powdery, packed, or slushy. But snow is so important to the Eskimos' lives that they have a word for each different type.

Words come into existence to satisfy a need and they leave the language when they are no longer useful. Our language is alive and changing. Every year new words are added to the dictionary and others are classified as archaic (no longer used). Ten years ago you would not have found entries for *E-mail, liposuction,* or *spin doctor.* The average person no longer knows the meaning of *spondulix* (money) or *buncombe* (meaningless chatter).

Why increase your vocabulary? It's practical! A long word can often take the place of many little words. For example, if you couldn't say "His sister is an etymologist," you would have to say, "His sister is an expert in tracing the beginning and future development of a word, word part, or phrase back as far as possible in its own language and to its source in modern or earlier languages."

So you see, having a good vocabulary allows you to think about a wide range of ideas and to communicate them with exactness. It also helps you under-

[1]Victoria Neufeldt, Editor-in-Chief, *Webster's New World Dictionary,* Pocket Edition (New York: Simon & Schuster, 1990) p. 600. Copyright © 1990 by Simon & Schuster, Inc.

stand the ideas of writers and speakers so that you can easily understand the material in textbooks and get good grades on tests.

The question is, how do we learn and remember words? In this book you will learn more than 300 words that are frequently used in college classes. You will also discover *how* to learn those words and the other words you will need in your life.

## Methods of Learning Vocabulary

This book is organized to help you learn vocabulary as quickly and efficiently as possible. As an example, we will trace for you the different methods of learning the word *supercilious*.

**supercilious:** full of or characterized by pride or scorn; haughty

### *Word Memory (Chapter 2)*

To help you associate the word *supercilious* with its meaning, you could picture a man eating his supper on the ceiling because he thinks he's superior to everybody else.

### *Using the Context (Chapter 3)*

"His supercilious manner made the people he worked with feel inferior." The sentence gives you a good clue to the meaning.

## Getting the Most from Your Dictionary (Chapter 4)

*Main entry*  *Pronunciation*  *Parts of speech*

*Etymology* ——

**su·per·cil·i·ous** (soo′pər sil′ē əs) *adj.* [< L. *super*, above + *cilium*, eyelid, hence (in allusion to raised eyebrows) haughtiness] disdainful or contemptuous; haughty

*Definitions*

## Suffixes, Prefixes, and Roots (Chapters 5–9)

**supercilious:** super = over; cilium = eyelid; ous = full of

The word parts refer to the facial expression associated with excessive pride or scorn—raised eyebrows.

## Word Histories (Chapter 10)

The word *supercilious* comes from Latin. *Cilium* in Latin means eyelid, and *super-cilium* means eyebrow (over the eyelid).

## Thesaurus (Chapter 11)

Synonyms (similar words) of *supercilious:* haughty, proud, scornful, vain, snobbish, stuck up
Antonyms (opposite words) of *supercilious:* overly humble, "yes man," flatterer

## Using Words Correctly (Chapter 12)

Shades of meaning: When would you use *supercilious* rather than *proud, haughty, insolent, overbearing,* or *disdainful?*

—**proud** is the broadest term in this comparison, ranging from reasonable pride to an exaggerated opinion of one's importance [too *proud* to beg, *proud* as a peacock]; **haughty** implies such consciousness of high station, rank, etc. as is displayed in scorn of those one considers beneath one [a *haughty* dowager]; **insolent,** in this connection, implies both haughtiness and lack of respect esp. as demonstrated in behavior or speech that insults others [she has an *insolent* disregard for her servant's feelings]; **overbearing** implies extreme, domineering insolence [an *overbearing* supervisor]; **supercilious** stresses an aloof, scornful manner toward others [a *supercilious* intellectual snob]; **disdainful** implies even stronger and more apparent feelings of scorn for that which is regarded as beneath one.[2]

[2]Based on *Webster's New World Dictionary, Third College Edition* (Victoria Neufeldt, Editor-in-Chief) (New York: Simon & Schuster, 1988), p. 1082.

## Getting Started

Because students differ in their vocabulary needs, each chapter contains three lists of words: Review Words, New Words, and Advanced Words. The Review Words are 10 words you should already know. We include them in case some of them are unfamiliar. The New Words are the 20 main words you will be studying in that chapter. Advanced Words are 10 more difficult words. We include them for those students ready for more advanced work. Following is a self-checking quiz to help you measure your present vocabulary. Circle the closest definition for each word, and then check your answers in the back of the book.

Name _____

## PRETEST

Circle the word that is closest in meaning to the numbered word.

1. apathy    a. interest   b. dislike   c. fright   d. unconcern

2. endeavor    a. try   b. desire   c. resist   d. develop

3. default    a. fail to do something   b. accept blame   c. criticize   d. blame someone else

4. fallacy    a. incorrect idea   b. true belief   c. happy ending   d. good idea

5. unscrupulous    a. dishonest   b. very careful   c. depressed   d. disappointed

6. compulsory    a. unnecessary   b. fast   c. required   d. genuine

7. integrity    a. kindness   b. doubt   c. honesty   d. talent

8. shrewd    a. difficult   b. innocent   c. clever   d. rich

9. ambiguous    a. very large   b. unclear   c. helpful   d. certain

10. chronic    a. brief   b. painful   c. expensive   d. long-lasting

11. obsolete    a. new   b. used   c. old-fashioned   d. artistic

12. desolate    a. busy   b. solid   c. happy   d. deserted

13. apparatus    a. ideas   b. machinery   c. parts   d. extras

14. intrigue    a. exposure   b. scheme   c. boredom   d. conclusion

15. derivation    a. source   b. end   c. middle   d. style

16. fluency    a. awkwardness   b. flow   c. channel   d. pattern

17. intimidate    a. accept   b. relieve   c. frighten   d. admire

18. obligatory    a. required   b. optional   c. legal   d. introductory

19. equitable    a. essential   b. silent   c. fair   d. sudden

20. reliance    a. trust   b. risk   c. belief   d. thought

21. unbiased    a. unfair   b. gentle   c. fair   d. rough

22. atypical       a. ordinary   b. unusual   c. in a good mood   d. in a bad mood

23. entice         a. explain   b. lure   c. avoid   d. attack

24. irrational     a. unreasonable   b. sensible   c. practical   d. defensive

25. misconstrue    a. mislead   b. prove   c. believe   d. misunderstand

26. degenerate     a. defend   b. deteriorate   c. decorate   d. define

27. avert          a. accompany   b. change   c. prevent   d. advise

28. jurisdiction   a. twelve people   b. police state   c. legal power   d. government

29. irrevocable    a. irregular   b. noisy   c. unchangeable   d. reversible

30. inconspicuous  a. illegal   b. hidden   c. obvious   d. striking

31. proficient     a. intelligent   b. troublesome   c. embarrassed   d. skilled

32. obstinate      a. helpful   b. angry   c. stubborn   d. stingy

33. stagnant       a. standing still   b. moving around   c. acting   d. refusing

34. superficial    a. on the surface   b. lying hidden   c. overdone   d. giving shelter

35. simulate       a. produce   b. imitate   c. accept   d. join

36. depose         a. keep   b. remove   c. promote   d. return

37. attain         a. attempt   b. maintain   c. dream of   d. reach

38. recipient      a. giver   b. robber   c. lender   d. receiver

39. inconceivable  a. unimaginable   b. surprising   c. interesting   d. real

40. pertinent      a. serious   b. appropriate   c. unique   d. strange

41. accessible     a. lost   b. unavailable   c. too much   d. approachable

42. dismal         a. absent   b. sick   c. gloomy   d. present

43. fanatic        a. extremist   b. moron   c. fighter   d. bore

44. chaos          a. order   b. confusion   c. war   d. peace

45. bizarre        a. interesting   b. suspicious   c. strange   d. frightening

46. vice           a. evil   b. good   c. tool   d. lawyer

47. jeopardy       a. risk   b. fear   c. doubt   d. disinterest

48. somber         a. gloomy   b. loud   c. boring   d. bright

49. dupe           a. murder   b. deceive   c. influence   d. gather

50. infer          a. hint   b. prove   c. accept   d. conclude

Check your answers in the back of the book.
Fill in your score here _____

Record your score on the Progress Chart on page 260.

## The Meaning of Your Score

If you scored:

Below 20 correct:     You may want to concentrate on the Review Words as well as on the New Words.

20–29 correct:     Your vocabulary is average for the New Words in this book.

30–50 correct:     You may want to concentrate on the Advanced Words as well as on the New Words.

*Note:* Students scoring above 40 might wish to take the pretest in *Keys to a Powerful Vocabulary, Level II.*

# chapter 2
# WORD MEMORY

© 1980 "Drabble" is reprinted by permission of UFS, Inc.

There are more than a million words in the English language. If you are the average American, you probably know about 40,000 of them. However, since you are a college student you will need to learn new words at a much faster rate than the average American in order to understand the ideas presented in your classes. Large numbers of new words are difficult to remember. The purpose of this chapter is to teach you some techniques to help you remember the words you will learn both in this book and in your other reading.

## Four Memory Techniques

- Pronounce the word aloud.
- Give the word meaning.
- Use mnemonic devices.
- Review often.

1. *Pronounce the word aloud.* Unfortunately, this is sometimes easier said than done. English spelling often fails to indicate the pronunciation of a word, as described in the following poem:

### Hints on Pronunciation for Foreigners[1]

I take it you already know
Of tough and bough and cough and dough?
Others may stumble but not you,
On hiccough, thorough, laugh, and through.
Well done! And now you wish, perhaps,
To learn of less familiar traps?

Beware of heard, a dreadful word
That looks like bread and sounds like bird,
And dead: it's said like bed, not bead—
For goodness' sake don't call it "deed"!
Watch out for meat and great and threat
(They rhyme with suite and straight and debt.)

A moth is not a moth in mother
Nor both in bother, broth in brother
And here is not a match for there
Nor dear and fear for bear and pear,
And then there's dose and rose and lose—
Just look them up—and goose and choose,
And cork and work and card and ward,
And font and front and word and sword,
And do and go and thwart and cart—
Come, come, I've hardly made a start!
A dreadful language? Man alive.
I'd mastered it when I was five.

T.S.W.
(only initials of writer known)

[1]From Carol Chomsky's *Reading, Writing and Phonology*. In M. Wolf, M. K. McQuillen, and E. Radwin (eds.), "Thought and Language/Language and Reading," *Harvard Educational Review*, 1980.

Because of the peculiarities of English spelling, it is important to understand the use of the dictionary pronunciation guide. The New Words presented in each chapter of this book have the following pronunciation guide at the bottom of the page:

fat, āpe, cär; ten, ēven; is, bīte; gō, hôrn, tōōl, look; oil, out; up, fʉr; get; joy; yet; chin; she; thin, *then*; zh, leisure; ŋ, ring; ə for *a* in *ago, e* in *agent, i* in *sanity, o* in *comply, u* in *focus;* ' as in *able* (ā'b'l)

For example, the word *exert* is pronounced **eg zʉrt'**:

*e* is pronounced as in *egg*.

*g* is pronounced as in *get*.

*z* does not appear on the guide because it has only one possible pronunciation.

*ʉr* is pronounced as in *fur*.

*t* does not appear on the guide because there is only one way you can pronounce it.

Putting the sounds together, we see that *eg* rhymes with *leg* and *zʉrt* rhymes with *hurt*, equaling **eg zʉrt'**. The accent mark over the second syllable (zʉrt') means that you put the heavy stress on that syllable. When there are two accent marks, the heavier one receives more stress than the lighter one.

One symbol that often gives students problems is the *schwa*. It occurs only in unaccented syllables, is written ə, and is always pronounced the same way: an "uh" sound. There are about 25 different ways the schwa can be spelled in words. Here are some examples, with the spelling of schwa in italics.

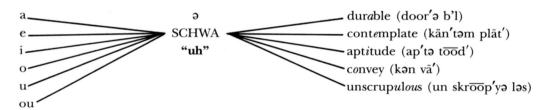

a ——
e ——
i ——
o ——
u ——
ou ——

ə
SCHWA
"**uh**"

—— dur*a*ble (door'ə b'l)
—— cont*e*mplate (kän'təm plāt')
—— apt*i*tude (ap'tə tōōd')
—— c*o*nvey (kən vā')
—— unscrup*ulou*s (un skrōōp'yə ləs)

As you can see, it doesn't matter whether the schwa is spelled as *a, e, i, o, u, ou,* or other spellings. It's still pronounced "uh."

For practice with the pronunciation guide, use it to translate the three proverbs below into English spelling:

a. ev'rē kloud haz ə sil'vər lī'niŋ

Translation _____

b. ə wächt pät nev'ər boilz

Translation _____

c. ə pen'ē sāvd iz ə pen'ē ʉrnd

Translation _____

Check your answers in the back of the book.

Some dictionaries have slightly different symbols in their pronunciation guides, but the symbols are always explained by the use of key words. If the guide is not at the bottom of the page, it will be in the front of the dictionary.

2. *Give the word meaning.* After you have pronounced the word correctly, you should concentrate on what it means. Reading a complicated definition in the dictionary is not usually enough to make sure that you will understand and remember it. You will thoroughly understand a meaning only if you can define it in your own words and then use it as part of your vocabulary. Therefore, when you are trying to learn a new word, you should restate the definition in your own words and use the word in a meaningful sentence.

3. *Use mnemonic devices.* Mnemonic devices are tricks that aid memory. The word *mnemonic* comes from the name of the Greek goddess of memory, Mnemosyne. Three mnemonic devices are presented below that you can use to memorize vocabulary; you can also make up your own.

a. *Word Association:* Sometimes you can associate a new word with a word you already know that gives a clue to the meaning. For example, you could associate *fallacy,* which refers to an untrue idea or an error in reasoning with *false.* To remember *subsequent,* which means coming after (following in time, or place, or order, think of "in sequence after each other").

b. *Visual Association:* It's always easier to remember things that are visually exciting. For example, to remember that *arid* means dry, try to picture a large can of Arid[2] deodorant with the motto "Arid keeps you dry." To remember *escalate,* you might picture yourself riding on a department store escalator going up. To remember *ordeal* (a difficult experience), you might picture a gangster with a gun at your head ordering you to make a deal.

[2]The deodorant is actually spelled Arrid.

c. *Rhyming:* Some people find it easier to remember sounds than pictures. For example, if you want to remember that a *hoax* is a practical joke, you might think of the phrase "A hoax fools folks." Or to remember that *absurd* means foolish, you might think of the phrase "Absurd as a polka-dotted bird." For *endeavor,* you could try "People who endeavor try forever."

4. *Review often.* Getting the word into your memory isn't the end of the story. You also have to keep it there. The only way to prevent forgetting is to review what you have learned. One way of reviewing is to use the new information. In the case of vocabulary, use the new words, both in your reading and in your speaking. Another method is to use flash cards for review.

In each chapter of this book are practice exercises for reviewing the words you have learned. If, after you have completed the exercises, you still aren't sure you will remember the word, put it on a *flash card.* A flash card is a blank file card. Put the word and its pronunciation on one side. On the other side, write the definition and perhaps a sentence that gives the meaning of the word:

apathy
ap'ə thē

lack of emotion
Instead of feeling excited when
I saw my ex-husband, I felt
only apathy.

Always carry 10 to 20 cards in your pocket or purse so you can use them at odd moments: for example, standing in line, waiting for gas, eating lunch alone. Test yourself by looking at the word and trying to remember the meaning; then turn the card over and check yourself. The next time you review the cards, use the backs: Read the definition and see if you know the word. You should also try to spell the word so that you will be able to use it in writing. Don't be discouraged if you forget the word. The average person needs about seven self-testing sessions to thoroughly master a new word. The sessions should be spaced several hours or days apart. When you feel that you have mastered the word, put the card in another pile at home that you review less often so that the pile you carry with you won't keep getting larger.

# REVIEW WORDS

**absurd** (ab surd′, ab zurd′) *adj.*   so unreasonable as to be ridiculous

**contemplate** (kän′təm plāt′) *v.*   1. to look at or think about deeply for a long time   2. to expect or intend

**convey** (kən vā′) *v.*   1. to take from one place to another; transport; carry   2. to transmit

**cope** (kōp) *v.*   1. to fight or contend (with) successfully   2. to deal with problems, etc.

**hostile** (häs′təl) *adj.*   1. of or characteristic of an enemy   2. unfriendly

**negligent** (neg′lə jent) *adj.*   1. habitually failing to do the required thing; neglectful   2. careless

**negotiate** (ni gō′shē ät′) *v.*   1. to discuss with a view to reaching agreement   2. to succeed in crossing, passing, etc.   3. to bargain

**neurotic** (noo rät′ik) *adj.*   of, characteristic of, or having a mental disorder characterized by anxiety, compulsions, phobias, etc.; overly anxious—*n.*   a person who is characterized by anxiety, compulsions, phobias, etc.

**ordeal** (ôr dēl′, ōr′dēl′) *n.*   any difficult or painful experience

**unique** (yoo nēk′) *adj.*   1. one and only; sole   2. without like or equal   3. very unusual

fat, āpe, cär; ten, ēven; is, bīte; gō, hôrn, tool, look; oil, out; up, fur; get; joy; yet; chin; she; thin, *th*en; zh, leisure; ŋ, ring; ə for *a* in *ago, e* in *agent, i* in *sanity, o* in *comply, u* in *focus;* ′ as in *able* (ā′b'l)

Read the following list of review words. Then in each space below write the word that best completes that sentence. Check your answers in the back of the book.

| | | | | |
|---|---|---|---|---|
| absurd | convey | hostile | negotiate | ordeal |
| contemplate | cope | negligent | neurotic | unique |

1.  For some children the first day of school is an _____ .

2.  It is difficult for a shy person to _____ feelings.

3.  Wearing a bathing suit in freezing weather is _____ .

4.  One reason unions came into existence was to _____ group contracts.

5.  During the 1800s, while there were some _____ tribes, most Native Americans are remembered as being peaceful.

6.  An adult who continually sucks his or her thumb is _____ , and probably needs to seek therapy.

7.  A person usually finds it difficult to _____ with the death of a beloved pet.

8.  A _____ parent may lose custody of his or her children.

9.  The 530.2 carat diamond called the Star of Africa is _____ ; no other diamond is as large.

10. Some people _____ the past year on New Year's Day.

## EXERCISE 2: REVIEW WORDS

I. For each of the following words, read the dictionary definition and then write the definition in your own words, and write a sentence using that word. Sample answers are provided at the back of the book.

1. absurd

   a. Definition _____

   b. Sentence _____

2. cope

   a. Definition _____

   b. Sentence _____

3. negotiate

   a. Definition _____

   b. Sentence _____

4. ordeal

   a. Definition _____

   b. Sentence _____

5. unique

   a. Definition _____

   b. Sentence _____

II. For each of the following words, make up a mnemonic device, such as a word association, a visual association, or a rhyme. See the back of the book for sample answers.

1. contemplate _____

2. convey _____

3. hostile _____

4. negligent _____

5. neurotic _____

# NEW WORDS I

Below is the first list of New Words for this chapter. Make up a mnemonic device for each one and compare yours with our samples in the back of the book.

**commemorate** (kə mem′ə rāt′) *v.*   1. to honor the memory of, as by ceremony   2. to keep alive the memory of; serve as a memorial to

Mnemonic _____

**default** (di fôlt′) *n.*   1. failure to do something or be somewhere when required or expected, such as failure to pay money due, failure to appear in court, failure to take part in or finish a contest—*v.*   1. to fail to do, pay, finish, etc. (something) when required   2. to lose (a contest, etc.) by failing to appear, to do, to pay, to finish, etc.; to forfeit

Mnemonic _____

**detest** (di test′) *v.*   to dislike very much; hate

Mnemonic _____

**durable** (door′ə b'l) *adj.*   1. lasting in spite of hard wear or much use   2. lasting a long time

Mnemonic _____

**evade** (ē vād′) *v.*   1. to cleverly avoid or escape something [to *evade* the hunters]   2. to avoid doing or answering directly; get around; get out of [to *evade* a question, to *evade* payment of a tax]

Mnemonic _____

**exert** (eg zʉrt′) *v.*   1. to put forth or use energetically; put into action or use [to *exert* strength, influence, etc.]   2. to try hard   3. to bring to bear, especially with sustained effort or lasting effect [to *exert* an influence on the company's policy]

Mnemonic _____

**frigid** (frij′id) *adj.*   1. extremely cold; without heat or warmth   2. without warmth of feeling or manner; stiff and formal

Mnemonic _____

**notorious** (nō tôr′ē əs) *adj.*   widely known in a negative way; having a bad reputation

Mnemonic _____

**spontaneous** (spän tā′nē əs) *adj.*   1. acting without thinking   2. occurring without apparent cause

Mnemonic _____

**unscrupulous** (un′skrōōp′yə ləs) *adj.*   dishonest

Mnemonic _____

fat, āpe, cär; ten, ēven; is, bīte; gō, hôrn, tōōl, look; oil, out; up, fʉr; get; joy; yet; chin; she; thin, *th*en; zh, leisure; ŋ, ring; ə for *a* in *ago*, *e* in *agent*, *i* in *sanity*, *o* in *comply*, *u* in *focus*; ′ as in *able* (ā′b'l)

## EXERCISE 3: FILL-IN

Read the following list of words. Then in the spaces below write the word that best completes each sentence. Check your answer in the back of the book.

| | | | | |
|---|---|---|---|---|
| commemorate | detest | evaded | frigid | spontaneously |
| default | durable | exerts | notorious | unscrupulous |

1.  Levi Strauss first made his pants out of tent canvas so they would be more

    _____ than regular cloth trousers.

2.  People who _____ coffee will not like mocha ice cream because it is flavored with coffee.

3.  Some people believe that the full moon _____ strange influences over people, like driving them temporarily insane.

4.  To _____ on a loan hurts your credit rating.

5.  Al Capone, the _____ gangster of the 1920s, had a sterling silver toilet seat engraved with his initials.

6.  Unlike most people living in _____ climates, one man in Alaska wears nothing heavier than a T-shirt all year.

7.  King Charles IX of France encouraged pickpockets to practice their

    _____ trade during his parties because it amused him to watch the expert thieves steal his guests' jewelry, money and even swords without the victims' knowledge. Worst of all, he allowed the thieves to keep what they stole.

8.  On November 13, 1982, a memorial was dedicated in Washington, D.C. to

    _____ the American soldiers who were killed or listed as missing during the Vietnam War.

9.  If we did not breathe _____, we might die in our sleep.

10. Vincenzo Peruggia, an employee of the Louvre Museum who stole the Mona Lisa in

    August 1911, _____ police for two years. He was finally arrested when he attempted to sell the painting to the Italian Government for $95,000.

# NEW WORDS II

Make up a good sentence using each of the New Words below.

**aptitude** (ap′tə tōōd′) *n.*   ability or talent

Sentence _____

**arid** (ar′id) *adj.*   dry and barren

Sentence _____

**concise** (kən sīs′) *adj.*   brief and to the point; short and clear

Sentence _____

**drastic** (dras′tik) *adj.*   having a strong or violent effect; harsh; severe; extreme

Sentence _____

**endeavor** (in dev′ər) *v.*   to try; to make a serious attempt—*n.*   a serious attempt or effort

Sentence _____

**escalate** (es′kə lāt′) *v.*   1. to rise as on an escalator   2. to get bigger step by step, as from a
limited or local conflict into a general, esp. nuclear, war   3. to grow or increase
rapidly, as prices or wages

Sentence _____

**fallacy** (fal′ə sē) *n.*   1. false or mistaken idea, opinion, etc.; error   2. an error in reasoning

Sentence _____

**hoax** (hōks) *n.*   a trick or fraud, esp. one meant as a practical joke

Sentence _____

**pending** (pen′diŋ) *adj.*   1. not decided, determined, or established [a *pending* lawsuit, patent
*pending*]   2. about to happen—*prep.*   during; while awaiting; until

Sentence _____

**subsequent** (sub′si kw′nt) *adj.*   coming after; following in time, place, or order

Sentence _____

fat, āpe, cär; ten, ēven; is, bīte; gō, hôrn, tōōl, look; oil, out; up, fᵘr; get; joy; yet; chin; she; thin, *th*en; zh, leisure; ŋ, ring; ə for *a* in *ago, e* in *agent, i* in *sanity, o* in
*comply, u* in *focus;* ′ as in *able* (ā′b'l)

Circle the letter before the word or phrase that best defines the italicized word in each sentence. Check your answers in the back of the book.

1. Mozart revealed his *aptitude* for music at an early age.

   a. desire   b. talent   c. distaste   d. need

2. Blidet Amor, a village in the Sahara Desert, is constructed only of dried mud and would be destroyed by rain if it weren't for the *arid* climate.

   a. mild   b. dry   c. harsh   d. cold

3. Victor Hugo thought he had written the most *concise* letter in the world when, in order to find out how his new book *Les Miserables* was selling, he sent his publisher the letter "?". However, the equally brief reply was "!".

   a. funny but important   b. long and silly   c. rambling and detailed   d. short and clear

4. Some countries still have such *drastic* punishments for crimes as cutting off a person's hand for stealing.

   a. stupid   b. expensive   c. extreme   d. minor

5. *Endeavoring* to get close enough to kill while hunting, some American Indians tried to look like deer by wearing skins and antlers.

   a. attempting   b. praying   c. dressing   d. shooting

6. Since the 1980s, violent crimes in the United States have been *escalating*.

   a. stopping   b. prosecuted   c. lessening   d. increasing

7. Historically, visitors to the Church of St. Menoux in France believed the *fallacy* that they could cure their headaches by sticking their heads into a hole in the stone altar.

   a. good idea   b. false idea   c. truth   d. children's story

8. A recent U.F.O. sighting in Texas turned out to be a *hoax*.

   a. comedy   b. trick   c. robbery   d. curse

9. *Pending* further research, doctors cannot be certain of the effects of vitamins on cancer.

   a. awaiting   b. completing   c. avoiding   d. limiting

10. Many people attend college *subsequent to* finishing high school.

    a. following   b. along with   c. before   d. in order to

## EXERCISE 5: TRUE-FALSE

Place a *T* or an *F* in the space provided. Check your answers in the back of the book.

_____ 1. A hero deserves to be *commemorated*.

_____ 2. Some *notorious* people are wanted by the police.

_____ 3. When a lawsuit is *pending*, its outcome is undecided.

_____ 4. You can trust an *unscrupulous* person.

_____ 5. When you have an *aptitude* for something you can't do it.

## EXERCISE 6: ANALOGIES

A word analogy is a puzzle in which two sets of words are compared. The two words in the first set have some kind of relationship to each other. You have to recognize the relationship in order to fill in the blank in the second set. Analogies use the mathematical symbols :, which means *is to*, and ::, which means *as*. For example:

      night  :  day  ::  dark  :  _____

This example reads: night *is to* day *as* dark *is to* _____.
You must decide on the relationship of the first two words. *Night* and *day* are opposites. Therefore, the word in the blank must be the opposite of *dark*. The answer is *light*.

    There are two kinds of relationships in the analogies below. The words mean either the same thing or are opposites. If the words are synonyms, write *S* in the blank before each number. If they are antonyms, write *A*. Fill in the blanks and check your answers in the back of the book.

_____ 1. unique : common ::
arid : _____

    a. tough  b. dry  c. wet  d. desert

_____ 2. absurd : ridiculous ::
fallacy : _____

    a. truth  b. dishonesty  c. falsehood
d. sadness

_____ 3. cope : deal ::
default : _____

    a. pay  b. heat  c. steal  d. forfeit

_____ 4. negotiate : bargain ::
frigid : _____

    a. hot  b. cold  c. dry  d. old

_____ 5. convey : withhold ::
concise : _____

    a. to the point  b. rambling
c. interesting  d. creative

# ADVANCED WORDS

**avid** (av′id) *adj.*   1. having a strong desire; greedy [*avid* for power]   2. eager and enthusiastic [an *avid* reader of books]

**belligerent** (bə lij′ər ənt) *adj.*   1. warlike   2. ready to fight or quarrel [a *belligerent* tone]

**defunct** (di fuŋkt′) *adj.*   no longer existing; dead or extinct

**dubious** (doo′bē əs) *adj.*   1. causing doubt; vague [a *dubious* remark]   2. feeling doubt; hesitating   3. with the outcome undecided or hanging in the balance [a *dubious* battle]   4. rousing suspicion; questionable; shady [a *dubious* character]

**feasible** (fē′zə b'l) *adj.*   1. capable of being done; possible [a *feasible* scheme]   2. within reason; likely [a *feasible* story]   3. suitable [land *feasible* for cultivation]

**guise** (gīz) *n.*   1. manner or way, customary behavior or manner   2. manner of dress   3. a false or deceiving outward appearance [under the *guise* of friendship]

**hypocrite** (hip′ə krit) *n.*   a person who pretends to be what he is not or who pretends to feel what he doesn't feel

**irate** (ī rāt′) *adj.*   very angry

**juncture** (junk′chər) *n.*   1. a joining or being joined   2. a point or line of joining or connection; joint, as of two bones, or a seam   3. a point of time   4. a particular or critical moment in the development of events; a crisis

**lethal** (lē′thəl) *adj.*   1. causing or capable of causing death; fatal or deadly   2. having to do with death

fat, āpe, cär; ten, ēven; is, bīte; gō, hôrn, tool, look; oil, out; up, fur; get; joy; yet; chin; she; thin, *th*en; zh, leisure; ŋ, ring; ə for *a* in *ago, e* in *agent, i* in *sanity, o* in *comply, u* in *focus;* ' as in *able* (ā′b'l)

# EXERCISE 10: ADVANCED WORDS IN CONTEXT

Use the Advanced Words to fill in the blanks in the sentences that follow. Check your answer in the back of the book.

| avid | defunct | feasible | hypocrite | juncture |
| belligerent | dubious | guise | irate | lethal |

1.  It may not seem _____, but the Siamese twins, Chang and Eng, who were joined at the chest, each married. One fathered 10 children and the other fathered 12.

2.  It would have taken several _____ lobster eaters to finish the 42 lb., 7 oz. North American lobster now on display at the Museum of Science in Boston.

3.  If you are a sophomore in college, you have the _____ distinction of being both wise and foolish. The word comes from the Greek roots *sophos,* meaning wise, and *moros,* meaning foolish.

4.  A person who asks for charitable donations from others but never makes a contribution is a _____.

5.  Japanese who eat the "deadly puffer fish", a delicacy served in the finest restaurants, hope the cook has carefully cut out the skin, muscles, and internal organs where the _____ poison is stored.

6.  Under the _____ of still being loyal to the Revolutionary Army forces, General Benedict Arnold took the defense plans of Fort West Point and gave them to the British army.

7.  The bombing of Pearl Harbor was a _____ act that caused the United States to declare war against Japan.

8.  The _____ of the Union Pacific and Central Pacific railroads, which created the first transcontinental railroad in the United States, was marked with a golden spike on May 10, 1869, in Promontory, Utah.

9.  With the establishment of the United Nations, the earlier League of Nations became officially _____.

10. A father whose teenage son crashes his new car may well be _____.

It is not enough just to learn the words in this book. Your needs will be different from the needs of other students, since you will come into contact with different words in your classes and in your life. Each chapter in this book has a page on which you are asked to write ten words that you believe you need to learn. You may have seen them in your textbooks, in newspapers or magazines, or in other sources. Try to choose words that occur often rather than words you will probably rarely see. Write your first ten words in the spaces provided below. Then pronounce each word, put the definition in your own words, use the word in a sentence, and put it on a flash card for regular review.

1. _____

2. _____

3. _____

4. _____

5. _____

6. _____

7. _____

8. _____

9. _____

10. _____

# chapter 3

# USING THE CONTEXT

Bill Proctor

Did you guess the meaning of *conjecture* in the cartoon? We are sure that you guessed it meant *guess*. If you did guess the meaning, you used context. In the last chapter we mentioned that you probably know about 40,000 words. Did you ever think about how you learned them? Did you look up all 40,000 in the dictionary? Most people don't look up very many unfamiliar words. Using the dictionary is time-consuming, and you don't always have a dictionary handy when you see a new word. Also, definitions without examples are hard to remember and use correctly. For example, the woman in the cartoon is using the word *conjecture* according to the way it's defined in the dictionary rather than the way people really use it. We will discuss this problem in Chapter 12.

The easiest, most common way to learn and to remember new words is through context. When you were learning to talk, you learned the word *cookie* because your parents used the word while you were eating one. You formed a mental association between the word and the context (eating the cookie). You probably learned to read the word by seeing it printed on a box that you knew contained cookies. Again, the situation provided the context. After you learned to read, you were able to figure out the meanings of new words by using the surrounding sentence or paragraph as context. The easiest way to use the context in reading is to look at the words surrounding the unfamiliar one and make a guess as to what the word means.

## Types of Context Clues

Your success at guessing the meaning of an unfamiliar word depends on the amount and kind of the clues present in the sentence or paragraph and on your ability to recognize them. Inability to recognize context clues can result in depending on the dictionary for meanings or just skipping the word, hoping that it will not interfere with the meaning of what you are reading. When the context clues are not sufficient, you have no choice but to use the dictionary; however, looking up words does break your train of thought and slows you down. The method of just skipping over unfamiliar words can be acceptable when getting the exact meaning isn't important; however, it may get you in trouble when you try it with textbooks.

The italicized words in the sentences below are taken from the New Words for this chapter, so they probably will not be familiar to you. Use the context to figure out their meanings, and circle the letter of the closest definition.

1. In most colleges, at least one course in English is *compulsory,* or required, for a degree.

   a. optional   b. suggested   c. needed   d. desirable

   The answer is *c*. The context in this sentence gave you the **definition** of the word *compulsory*. The definition can be either a *synonym*, as in the sample above, or it can consist of several words.

2. Some rich people keep their real jewels in the safe and wear *replicas* in public.

   a. originals   b. copies   c. drawings   d. plans

The answer is *b*. The context of the sentence provided the clue by using **contrast.** In other words, you knew from the sentence that the meaning of the word *replicas* had to contrast with real jewels.

3. There is an old saying that people from Missouri never believe what they read, are never convinced by what they hear, and always doubt what they haven't personally experienced—in short, when someone says "I'm from Missouri," it means she's *skeptical.*

   a. doubting   b. trusting   c. stupid   d. clever

   The answer is *a*. In this case the context provided a **summary** clue to the meaning of the word *skeptical. Skeptical* summed up all the ideas that went before.

4. *Ethnic* groups living in the United States, such as the Poles and Italians, enrich American society.

   a. political   b. small   c. cultural   d. major

   The answer is *c*. In this case the words *Poles* and *Italians* offer **examples** of ethnic groups.

5. The more *intricate* a puzzle is, the harder it is to solve.

   a. complicated   b. simple   c. interesting   d. dull

   The answer is *a*. In this example, our experience with solving puzzles gives the clue to meaning; this is called an **experience** clue.

# REVIEW WORDS

**analysis** (ə nal′ə sis′) *n.*   1. a breaking up of a whole into its parts to find out their nature; a breakdown   2. a statement of the results of this   3. an investigation

**calamity** (kə lam′ə tē) *n.*   a great misfortune, disaster

**deduction** (de duk′shən) *n.*   1. a reduction; an amount taken off   2. reasoning from the general to the specific   3. a conclusion from logical reasoning

**imply** (im plī′) *v.*   1. to have as a necessary part, condition, etc.   2. to indicate indirectly; hint; suggest

**maneuver** (mə nōō′vər) *n.*   1. a planned and controlled movement of troops, warships, etc.   2. a skillful or shrewd move—*v.*   to manage or plan skillfully

**media** (mē′dē ə) *n.*   all the means of communication, as newspapers, radio, etc.

**precise** (prē sīs′, pri sīs′) *adj.*   1. accurately stated; definite   2. minutely exact   3. strict; scrupulous

**preliminary** (prē lim′ə ner′ē, pri lim′ə ner′e) *adj.*   leading up to the main action, etc.; introductory—*n.*   a first step, procedure, etc.

**random** (ran′dəm) *adj.*   purposeless; unplanned

**solemn** (säl′əm) *adj.*   1. sacred   2. formal   3. serious; grave; earnest

---

fat, āpe, cär; ten, ēven; is, bīte; gō, hôrn, tōōl, look; oil, out; up, fʉr; get; joy; yet; chin; she; thin, *th*en; zh, leisure; ŋ, ring; ə for *a* in *ago, e* in *agent, i* in *sanity, o* in *comply, u* in *focus;* ′ as in *able* (ā′b′l)

Read the following list of Review Words. Then in each space below write the word that best completes that sentence. Check your answers in the back of the book.

analysis      deduction      maneuver      precise      random
calamity      imply      media      preliminary      solemn

1. In Bingo, the numbers are chosen at _____ .

2. It is important to know how to _____ a car when you go into a skid.

3. The mass _____ include radio, television and newspapers.

4. A graduation is usually a _____ event followed by celebration.

5. In some states if you are stopped by a police officer for driving under the influence of alcohol, you do not have to agree to a breath test _____ .

6. An Olympic level ice skater must be capable of very _____ movements on the ice.

7. In 1992, Hurricane Andrew, which resulted in billions of dollars in property loss, was a _____ for the State of Florida.

8. If a telephone call which you did not make appears on your telephone bill, you should request the telephone company to make a _____ on your next bill.

9. In many contests, you must enter the _____ rounds before you can enter the final contest.

10. Many soap commercials on television _____ that if you use a particular product, you will be more attractive to the opposite sex.

Use the context to fill in the blanks in the following mystery story with words from the Review list below. Then solve the mystery.

| | | | | |
|---|---|---|---|---|
| analysis | deduction | maneuver | precise | random |
| calamity | imply | media | preliminary | solemn |

**The Case of the Missing Sword**

Inspector Keane of Scotland Yard was investigating the theft of a jeweled sword stolen from the home of Lord Farnsworth. The crime had not yet been reported to the news _____. Lord Farnsworth considered the theft a

1

_____, not only because of the sword's value but also because it had

2

been given to one of his ancestors by Queen Elizabeth I as a reward for loyal service to the crown. The mood was _____ as Inspector Keane began. The

3

_____ investigation revealed the following facts:

4

1. Only Lord Farnsworth and his butler, Jeeves, had been in the house that evening.

2. Lord Farnsworth usually kept the sword locked in the safe in his study. He had taken it out earlier to admire it and, instead of returning it to the safe, had been careless enough to leave it on his desk when he left his study at about 7:00 P.M.

3. Both Lord Farnsworth and Jeeves had heard the sound of glass breaking. Jeeves, a very _____ person, had glanced at the clock and noted that it was

5

exactly 9:50 P.M.

4. Lord Farnsworth arrived in the study a few minutes later, having first searched for his pistol in his dresser drawers. He was the first to arrive in the study; he had passed Jeeves's room on the way.

5. Upon entering the study, Lord Farnsworth found _____ destruc-

6

tion of books, papers, and furniture in the room. The window was broken, and there were fragments of glass scattered on the lawn outside. All the windows and doors to the house were locked, and none appeared to have been disturbed.

After an _____ of the facts and some thoughtful

7

_____, Inspector Keane said, "All the facts _____

8                                                                         9

that the crime was a clever _____ by the butler. A search of Jeeves's

10

room revealed the sword in his bureau drawer. How did Keane know that the butler did it?

**Solution**

One clue was that the broken glass was outside the house. This meant that the window must have been broken from the *inside.* Also, Jeeves's room was closer to the study than Lord Farnsworth's was, yet it took him longer to arrive even though Lord Farnsworth had spent several minutes searching for his pistol. Keane deduced that Jeeves had stolen the sword, broken the window to make it appear that the room had been entered from outside, then returned to his room to hide the sword.

Check the answers in the back of the book. If any of the Review Words are unfamiliar to you, use the methods discussed in Chapter 2 to make them part of your vocabulary.

# NEW WORDS I

For each of the New Words that you don't already know, use the four memory techniques described in Chapter 2.

**assess** (ə ses′) *v.*  1. to set a value on; to judge the worth or importance of  2. to impose a fine, tax, etc. on

**attain** (ə tān′) *v.*  1. to gain through effort; accomplish; achieve  2. to reach or come to; arrive at [he *attained* the age of 90]

**bland** (bland) *adj.*  1. mild  2. dull; boring

**compulsory** (kəm pul′sər ē) *adj.*  must be done; required

**ethnic** (eth′nik) *adj.*  having to do with cultural or racial groups

**integrity** (in teg′rə tē) *n.*  1. honesty and sincerity  2. wholeness; unbrokenness

**invaluable** (in val′yoo ə b'l) *adj.*  extremely valuable; having value too great to measure; priceless

**naive** (nä ēv′) *adj.*  1. genuinely, sometimes foolishly, simple; childlike; innocent  2. not suspicious

**ponder** (pän′dər) *v.*  to weigh mentally; think deeply about; consider carefully; deliberate; meditate

**skeptical** (skep′ti k'l) *adj.*  not easily convinced; doubting; questioning

fat, āpe, cär; ten, ēven; is, bīte; gō, hôrn, tool, look; oil, out; up, fur; get; joy; yet; chin; she; thin, then; zh, leisure; ŋ, ring; ə for *a* in *ago*, *e* in *agent*, *i* in *sanity*, *o* in *comply*, *u* in *focus*; ' as in *able* (ā′b'l)

## EXERCISE 3: FILL-IN

Read the following list of words. Then in each space below write the word that best completes that sentence. Check your answers in the back of the book.

| assess | bland | ethnic | invaluable | pondering |
| attain | compulsory | integrity | naive | skeptical |

1. The _____ objects from the tomb of King Tut are worth many times more than the gold and jewels that were used to create them.

2. One hundred years ago, young brides were so _____ that they believed babies were brought by storks.

3. No one knows what the character portrayed in Rodin's famous statue is _____.

4. When they _____ manhood, the young men of Yule Island in New Guinea wear earrings made of 13 shells.

5. Patients recovering from major surgery are usually given a _____ diet including gelatin, clear soup and liquids.

6. It is difficult to _____ the wealth of the world's richest people. As J. Paul Getty once said "If you can count your millions, you are not a billionaire."

7. The story that George Washington admitted to chopping down the cherry tree was used to illustrate his _____.

8. Most people are _____ about the story that Aeschylus, the ancient Greek poet, was killed when a tortoise fell out of the sky and struck him, but we might believe that he was struck and killed by a meteorite.

9. It is not _____ that a picture of a U.S. President appear on all U.S. paper money. In fact, the $10,000 bill has the picture of former Secretary of the Treasury Samuel Chase on the front.

10. Some people think of chop suey as an _____ food of the Chinese; actually, it was created by a restaurant owner in California as a way to get rid of leftovers.

**ambiguous** (am big′yoo wəs) *adj.*   1. having two or more possible meanings   2. not clear; indefinite; uncertain; vague

**chronic** (krän′ik) *adj.*   1. lasting a long time or coming back often: said of a disease   2. having had an ailment for a long time [a *chronic* patient]   3. continuing indefinitely; constant [a *chronic* worry]

**dilemma** (di lem′ə) *n.*   a choice between two unpleasant situations

**exempt** (eg zempt′) *v.*   to free from a duty or rule—*adj.*   not required to follow a rule, duty, etc. expected of others

**implicit** (im plis′it) *adj.*   1. suggested or to be understood though not plainly expressed; implied   2. necessarily or naturally involved though not plainly apparent or expressed; essentially a part or condition   3. without reservation or doubt; unquestioning; absolute

**intricate** (in′tri kit) *adj.*   1. hard to follow or understand because of puzzling parts, details, or relationships [an *intricate* problem]   2. full of detail [an *intricate* lace pattern]

**plight** (plīt) *n.*   an awkward, sad, or dangerous situation

**replica** (rep′li kə) *n.*   a very close copy

**shrewd** (shro͞od) *adj.*   clever or sharp in practical matters

**venture** (ven′chər) *n.*   1. a risky or dangerous undertaking, especially in business   2. something on which a risk is taken—*v.*   1. to expose to danger, risk, or chance of loss   2. to express at the risk of criticism or objection [to *venture* an opinion]

fat, āpe, cär; ten, ēven; is, bīte; gō, hôrn, to͞ol, look; oil, out; up, fʉr; get; joy; yet; chin; she; thin, *th*en; zh, leisure; ŋ, ring; ə for *a* in *ago, e* in *agent, i* in *sanity, o* in *comply, u* in *focus;* ' as in *able* (ā′b'l)

Circle the letter before the word or phrase that best defines the italicized word in each sentence. Check your answers in the back of the book.

1. "The girl ran into her friend with a big dog" is an *ambiguous* statement because you can't tell who has the dog.

   a. unclear   b. excellent   c. helpful   d. inaccurate

2. Smokers often develop a *chronic* cough which may not go away even if they stop smoking.

   a. continual   b. infrequent   c. frightening   d. painful

3. In the *dilemma* in which a robber says "your money or your life," you should hand over your money.

   a. easy decision   b. difficult choice   c. unimportant choice   d. pleasant choice

4. In some countries, such as Israel, women are not *exempt from* military service.

   a. included in   b. primary sources of   c. excused from   d. burdened by

5. It is an *implicit* rule that a person should not cheat on tests.

   a. stated   b. understood   c. weak   d. strong

6. Some Native American blankets have *intricate* patterns that take many hours to weave.

   a. involved   b. honest   c. simple   d. random

7. The *plight* of the endangered Nile crocodile has improved since the government authorized the creation of special farms. Eggs from the river bank, which would normally be eaten by wild animals or destroyed by man, can be safely hatched on the farm and the babies returned to the river.

   a. eventual fate   b. past history   c. dangerous circumstances   d. total destruction

8. Miniature trains are often exact *replicas* of full scale originals.

   a. reproductions   b. originals   c. counterfeits   d. mirror images

9. Jean Nicot, from whose name we get the word "nicotine," began a tobacco plantation in France because he was a *shrewd* enough businessman to realize that the plant would become very popular in Europe.

   a. careless   b. clever   c. poor   d. simple

10. If you *venture* driving your vehicle in a blinding rain, you may suffer an automobile accident.

    a. risk   b. avoid   c. fear   d. love

Place a *T* or an *F* in the space provided. Check your answers in the back of the book.

_____  1.  A test should assess students' knowledge.

_____  2.  Implicit assumptions are unstated.

_____  3.  Pondering a problem can help you reach a solution.

_____  4.  "Nothing ventured, nothing gained" means that you should avoid any risks.

_____  5.  All Americans are from the same ethnic group.

Write *S* in the blank if the words are synonyms and *A* if they are antonyms. In each analogy, complete the second set of words, so they have the same relationship as the first. Check your answers in the back of the book.

_____  1.  analysis : investigation ::        a.  keep   b.  run   c.  require   d.  excuse
            exempt : _____

_____  2.  random : orderly ::                a.  solution   b.  problem   c.  example
            dilemma : _____                   d.  troubles

_____  3.  precise : careless ::              a.  innocent   b.  knowing   c.  dumb
            naive : _____                     d.  thoughtless

_____  4.  preliminary : preparatory ::       a.  clear   b.  useful   c.  complicated
            intricate : _____                 d.  simple

_____  5.  solemn : gay ::                    a.  sharp   b.  skillful   c.  fast   d.  stupid
            shrewd : _____

Write the letter of the word that means the opposite of the word in the first column. Check your answers in the back of the book.

_____  1.  compulsory          a.  spicy

_____  2.  chronic             b.  dishonesty

_____  3.  integrity           c.  unnecessary

_____  4.  predicament         d.  sudden

_____  5.  bland               e.  solution

In each group below, circle the word that does not mean what the others mean. Check your answers in the back of the book.

1. ambiguous    vague    certain    undefined
2. attain    accomplish    lose    gain
3. replica    duplicate    reprint    original
4. skeptical    unsure    positive    suspicious
5. invaluable    worthless    valueless    cheap

## EXERCISE 9: SENTENCE COMPLETION

Complete each sentence in your own words. Sample answers are provided in the back of the book.

1. Taking algebra is *compulsory* before _____
   _____.

2. There are many *ethnic* groups in the United States because _____
   _____.

3. Grades help you *assess* your progress in college; however, _____
   _____.

4. Since many people don't like *bland* food, _____
   _____.

5. It is possible to *attain* nearly any goal, provided that _____
   _____.

6. *Implicit* assumptions can be a problem when _____
   _____.

7. Your partner's *integrity* should be above question; otherwise, _____
   _____.

8. *Naive* people can get into trouble, especially _____
   _____.

9. It doesn't pay to *ponder* test questions too much; in fact, _____
   _____.

10. Bob is very *skeptical;* as a result, _____

_____.

11. Sometimes politicians are purposely *ambiguous;* that is, _____

_____.

12. A *chronic* cough can be a symptom of something serious; therefore, _____

_____.

13. I face a serious *dilemma* whenever _____

_____.

14. A counselor's advice can be *invaluable,* primarily _____

_____.

15. I never do *intricate* jigsaw puzzles; instead, _____

_____.

16. There are three reasons for the *plight* of the rhinoceros: first, _____

_____.

17. The *replica* is perfect, except that _____

_____.

18. Lloyd not only makes *shrewd* investment decisions; he also _____

_____.

19. The *venture* was successful due to _____

_____.

20. No one is *exempt* from criticism; consequently, _____

_____.

# ADVANCED WORDS

**adamant** (ad′ə mənt) *n.*  a hard stone or substance that was supposedly unbreakable—*adj.*
1. too hard to be broken  2. not giving in; unyielding  3. relentless  4. inflexible; unbending

**arbitrary** (är′bə trer′ē) *adj.*  1. not fixed by rules but left to one's judgment or choice [*arbitrary* decision, *arbitrary* judgment]  2. based on one's preference, notion, whim, etc.  3. absolute; dictatorial

**coherent** (kō hir′ənt) *adj.*  1. sticking together  2. logically connected; consistent; clearly stated  3. capable of logical, intelligible speech, thought, etc.

**futile** (fyo͞ot′l) *adj.*  1. useless; hopeless; ineffective  2. unimportant

**imperative** (im per′ə tiv) *adj.*  1. necessary; urgent  2. indicating authority or command

**negligible** (neg′li jə b′l) *adj.*  small; unimportant; can be disregarded

**ominous** (äm′ə nəs) *adj.*  threatening; serving as an evil omen

**perpetrate** (pur′pə trāt′) *v.*  1. to do (something evil, criminal, etc.)  2. to commit (a blunder, etc.)

**procrastinate** (prō kras′tə nāt′) *v.*  to put off doing (something unpleasant) until a future time

**tangible** (tan′jə b′l) *adj.*  1. can be touched or felt by touch; having actual form  2. able to be valued [*tangible* assets]  3. can be understood; definite

---

fat, āpe, cär; ten, ēven; is, bīte; gō, hôrn, to͞ol, look; oil, out; up, fur; get; joy; yet; chin; she; thin, *th*en; zh, leisure; ŋ, ring; ə for *a* in *ago, e* in *agent, i* in *sanity, o* in *comply, u* in *focus;* ' as in *able* (ā′b′l)

Use the Advanced Words to fill in the blanks in the sentences that follow. Check your answers in the back of the book.

| | | | | |
|---|---|---|---|---|
| adamantly | coherent | imperative | negligible | procrastinate |
| arbitrary | futile | ominous | perpetrate | tangible |

1. The movement of a glacier over one year may be _____ , perhaps a few inches; however, over hundreds of years, it can move miles.

2. The black clouds were an _____ sign for the people waiting to see the Macy's Thanksgiving Day Parade.

3. If you _____ and do not start a term paper until the day before it is due, you probably will not write a successful paper.

4. Politicians who _____ refuse to change an unpopular stand will usually find themselves out of office.

5. Stanley Mark Rifkin was able to _____ the biggest computer fraud in history by manipulating the computer system of a California bank. He was arrested by the FBI for defrauding the bank of $10.2 million.

6. Intelligence is not enough to ensure success in college. Good study habits are

   _____ .

7. Nixon's _____ decision to invade Cambodia without the knowledge of the American people is considered to be one of the most serious mistakes of his presidency.

8. To be _____ , a paragraph should not include statements off the topic.

9. Ancient chemists, called alchemists, made _____ attempts to change base metals, such as iron, into gold.

10. People who enter the clergy usually are not motivated by _____ rewards.

## EXERCISE 11: OWN WORDS

Find ten unfamiliar words in books, magazines, and newspapers, and write them on the lines below. Try to guess their meanings from the context in which you found them before you look them up in the dictionary. Pronounce each word, put the definition in your own words, use the word in a sentence, make up a mnemonic, and put the word on a flash card for regular review.

1. _____

2. _____

3. _____

4. _____

5. _____

6. _____

7. _____

8. _____

9. _____

10. _____

## EXERCISE 12: CROSSWORD PUZZLE

Following you will find the first crossword puzzle in the book, which reviews the New Words for Chapter 2. Unlike Blondie, you know that you're only allowed to put one letter in each box. But we suggest you use a pencil so you can change your answers if your first thoughts are incorrect. The clues with an asterisk (*) have answers from the New Word list for Chapter 2, so if you need help, you can check the word list on the inside front cover of this book. Check your answers in the back of the book.

### Across

*1. Long lasting
*8. Dry
9. Exclamation (sounds like a letter of the alphabet)
11. Opposite of *ma*
13. Silly
15. Stuck-up person
18. Remain
*19. Like Al Capone or Jesse James
*23. Make an effort
25. Opposite of *out*
26. Dine
28. Exclamation similar to *aha*
30. Farm animal
*33. Dishonest
37. Spanish word for *two*
*38. To fail to do something
39. Plural of *ox*
41. Abbr. for *latitude*
*42. Increase rapidly

### Down

2. Abbr. for *Amateur Athletic Union*
3. What you say when freezing
4. Top for a jar
5. Man's nickname
6. Think about
7. Opposite of *down*
*10. A trick
12. Abbr. for Associate in Science degree
*13. Ability
14. Title of respect
15. Gestapo abbreviation
16. Opposite of *hi*
*17. Try
20. Opposite of *off*
21. Smell
22. Instruments for seeing: micro_____, tele_____
24. Part of the foot
27. Donkey
29. Initials for the Department of Housing and Urban Development
31. Debtor's note
32. Seabird
34. Opposite of *all*
35. First two letters of things like flying saucers
36. Heavenly body
40. Sound of laughter

# chapter 4

# GETTING THE MOST FROM YOUR DICTIONARY

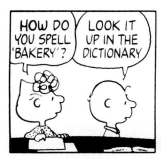

© 1980 "Peanuts" is reprinted by permission of UFS, Inc.

This chapter will help you learn how to use a very effective tool: the dictionary. Everybody knows how to look up definitions, but few people can really use all the valuable material a good dictionary provides. For example, in the dictionary you can quickly find a word's spelling, pronunciation, etymology, and meaning. This chapter is divided into sections dealing with specific techniques for improving your skills. First, we will discuss the structure of the dictionary. Second, we will discuss how to use the dictionary. Finally, we will examine the extra material found at the beginning and end of the dictionary.

## Dictionary Structure

The dictionary is structured so that a maximum amount of information can appear in a minimum amount of space. A pocket dictionary has about 60,000 entries. The largest dictionary, the 12-volume *Oxford English Dictionary,* contains 414,825 words. To use the dictionary effectively, you must understand its structure and its abbreviations. Look at the sample on the opposite page. It's from *Webster's New World Dictionary,* paperback edition.[1]

### Guide Words

At the top of the page you will see two **guide words:** *motion* and *mouth.* These words indicate the first and last words that appear on the page. By using them you can quickly find on which page a word would be located without having to slow down your search to look at all the entries. For example, by using the guide words you would know that *motorize* would be on the page but *mosaic* would not.

### Main Entry

*Main entry*

**mo-tor** (mōt'ər) *n.* [L. *movere,* to move]     **1** anything that produces motion

Each word that is in boldface type on the page is called a **main entry.** Some of the entries have a number next to them. An example is *mount.*

**mount**[1] (mount) *n.* [< L. *mons*] a mountain

The number 1 indicates that there is another main entry below that is spelled the same way but that has significantly different meanings and perhaps origins. English has come from many different sources, and some words that look alike have different histories.

The boldface type in the main entry indicates the **syllabication** and acceptable **spelling.** The syllabication is indicated by dashes in this dictionary sample, but some dictionaries use dots or spaces between syllables. Whether dashes, dots, or spaces are used, the syllabication indicates where you would break the word in writing. If two spellings of the word are given in boldface type, either spelling can

---

[1]Except where otherwise indicated, dictionary excerpts in this chapter are from *Webster's New World Dictionary,* Pocket Edition (Victoria Neufeldt, Editor-in-Chief) (New York: Simon & Schuster, Inc., 1990). Reprinted with permission © 1990 by Simon & Schuster, Inc.

**Main entries**

**Idiomatic expressions**

**Etymology**

**Definitions**

**Usage**

**Main entry without a full pronunciation (see * below)**

**Part of speech**

**Unusual spellings**

**Word used in context**

**Cross-reference**

**Pronunciation**

**Spellings of different forms of the word**

**Multiple entry**

motion     385     mouth

**mo·tion** (mō′shən) *n.* [< L. *movere*, to move] **1** a moving from one place to another; movement **2** a moving of a part of the body; specif., a gesture **3** a proposal formally made in an assembly —*vi.* to make a meaningful movement of the hand, etc.; gesture —*vt.* to direct by a meaningful gesture —go through the motions to do something as from habit, without enthusiasm, enjoyment, etc. —in motion moving —**mo′tion·less** *adj.*

**motion picture** FILM (*n.* 4)

**motion sickness** nausea, vomiting, etc. caused by the motion of a car, boat, etc.

**mo·ti·vate** (mōt′ə vāt′) *vt.* **-vat′ed, -vat′ing** to provide with, or affect as, a motive; incite —**mo′ti·va′tion** *n.*

**mo·tive** (mōt′iv) *n.* [< L. *movere*, to move] **1** an inner drive, impulse, etc. that causes one to act; incentive **2** MOTIF (sense 1) —*adj.* of or causing motion

**-mo·tive** (mōt′iv) *combining form* moving, of motion [*automotive*]

**mot·ley** (mät′lē) *adj.* [< ?] **1** of many colors **2** of many different or clashing elements [*a motley group*]

**mo·to·cross** (mō′tō krôs′) *n.* [Fr.] a cross-country race for lightweight motorcycles

**mo·tor** (mōt′ər) *n.* [L. < *movere*, to move] **1** anything that produces motion **2** an engine; esp., an internal-combustion engine **3** a machine for converting electric energy into mechanical energy —*adj.* **1** producing motion **2** of or powered by a motor **3** of, by, or for motor vehicles **4** of or involving muscular movements —*vi.* to travel by automobile

**mo·tor·bike′** *n.* [Colloq.] **1** a motor-driven bicycle **2** a light motorcycle

**mo·tor·boat′** *n.* a motor-driven boat, esp. a small one

**mo·tor·cade** (-kād′) *n.* [MOTOR + -CADE] an automobile procession

**mo·tor·car′** *n.* an automobile

**mo·tor·cy·cle** (-sī′kəl) *n.* a two-wheeled vehicle propelled by an internal-combustion engine

**motor home** a motor vehicle with a truck chassis, outfitted as a traveling home

**mo·tor·ist** (mōt′ər ist) *n.* one who drives an automobile or travels by automobile

**mo·tor·ize** (-īz′) *vt.* **-ized′, -iz′ing** to equip with a motor or with motor-driven vehicles

**motor vehicle** an automotive vehicle, esp. an automobile, truck, or bus

**mot·tle** (mät′'l) *vt.* **-tled, -tling** [< MOTLEY] to mark with blotches, etc. of different colors —**mot′tled** *adj.*

**mot·to** (mät′ō) *n., pl.* **-toes** or **-tos** [It., a word] a word or saying that expresses the goals, ideals, etc., as of a nation

**mould** (mōld) *n., vt., vi.,* chiefly *Brit., etc.* sp. of MOLD[1], MOLD[2], MOLD[3]

**mould·ing** *n.* chiefly *Brit., etc.* sp. of MOLDING

**moul·dy** (mōl′dē) *adj.* chiefly *Brit., etc.* sp. of MOLDY

**moult** (mōlt) *vi.* chiefly *Brit.* sp. of MOLT

**mound** (mound) *n.* [< ? MDu *mond,* protection] a heap or bank of earth, sand, etc. —*vt.* to heap up

**mount**[1] (mount) *n.* [< L. *mons*] a mountain

**mount**[2] (mount) *vi.* [< L. *mons,* mountain] **1** to climb; ascend **2** to climb up on something, as a horse **3** to increase in amount —*vt.* **1** to go up; ascend [*to mount stairs*] **2** to get up on (a horse, platform, etc.) **3** to provide with horses [*mounted* police] **4** to place or fix (a jewel, picture, etc.) on or in the proper support, backing, etc. **5** to arrange (a dead animal, etc.) for exhibition **6** to place (a gun) into proper position for use **7** to prepare for and undertake (an expedition, etc.) —*n.* **1** a mounting **2** a horse, etc. for riding **3** the support, setting, etc. on or in which a thing is mounted

**moun·tain** (mount′'n) *n.* [ult. < L. *mons*] **1** a natural raised part of the earth, larger than a hill **2** a large pile, amount, etc. —*adj.* of or in mountains

**moun·tain·eer′** (-ir′) *n.* **1** one who lives in a mountainous region **2** a mountain climber

**mountain goat** a long-haired, goatlike antelope of the Rocky Mountains

**mountain lion** COUGAR

**moun′tain·ous** *adj.* **1** full of mountains **2** like a mountain; esp., huge

**mountain sickness** weakness, nausea, etc. caused by thin air at high altitudes

**Mountain State** any of the eight States of the W U.S. through which the Rocky Mountains pass; Mont., Ida., Wyo., Nev., Utah, Colo., Ariz., & N. Mex.

**moun·te·bank** (mount′ə baŋk′) *n.* [It. *montambanco,* lit., mounted on a bench: orig. a person on a bench selling quack medicines] a charlatan or quack

**mount′ing** *n.* something serving as a backing, support, setting, etc.

**mourn** (môrn) *vi., vt.* [OE *murnan*] **1** to feel or express sorrow for (something regrettable) **2** to grieve for (someone who has died) —**mourn′er** *n.*

**mourn′ful** *adj.* **1** feeling or expressing grief or sorrow **2** causing sorrow

**mourn′ing** *n.* **1** the expression of grief, esp. at someone's death **2** black clothes, etc., worn as such an expression **3** the period during which one mourns

**mouse** (mous; *for v. also* mouz) *pl.* **mice** [OE *mus*] **1** any of many small rodents, esp. a species that commonly infests buildings **2** a timid person **3** [Slang] a black eye **4** a hand-held device for controlling the video display of a computer —*vi.* **moused, mous′ing** to hunt mice

**mousse** (mōos) *n.* [Fr., foam] **1** a light, chilled dessert made with egg white, whipped cream, etc. **2** an aerosol foam used to keep hair in place, etc.

**mous·tache** (mus′tash′, məs tash′) *n. var. of* MUSTACHE

**mous·y** (mous′ē, mouz′-) *adj.* **-i·er, -i·est** of or like a mouse; specif., quiet, timid, drab, etc. Also **mous′ey** — **mous′i·ness** *n.*

**mouth** (mouth; *for v.* mouth) *n., pl.* **mouths** (mouthz) [OE *muth*] **1** the opening in the head through which food is taken in and sounds are made **2** any opening

*The main entry has accent marks if a full pronunciation is not given.

be used. For example, *catalog* and *catalogue* are both acceptable spellings in *Webster's*. You can usually assume that the more common spelling appears first. If a spelling is marked *Brit.*, as with the word *mould*, it is not a standard spelling for Americans.

> **mould** (mōld) ***n.***, ***vt.***, ***vi.*** *chiefly Brit., etc. sp. of* MOLD¹,
>     MOLD², MOLD³
> **mould'ing** ***n.*** *chiefly Brit., etc. sp. of* MOLDING
> **moul-dy** (mōl'dē) ***adj.*** *chiefly Brit., etc. sp. of* MOLDY
> **moult** (mōlt) ***vi.*** *chiefly Brit. sp. of* MOLT

## Pronunciation

After the entry you will find the **pronunciation.** The symbols used are those found in the pronunciation key at the bottom of the page or in the front of the book. The use of this guide was explained in Chapter 2, and you have been using it to pronounce the New Words and Advanced Words in each chapter. The symbols differ slightly in different dictionaries, so you should familiarize yourself with the key used in the dictionary you will be using.

    Sometimes you will see only a portion of a pronunciation. An example is the entry for *motorcade*.

*Partial pronunciation*

> **mo'tor-cade'** (-kād') ***n.*** [MOTOR + -CADE] an automobile
>     procession

This happens when the first part of the word is identical to the pronunciation in the previous main entry. If you look at the pronunciation of *motor* and add the pronunciation for *-cade* you will get the full pronunciation, which is (mōt'ər kād').

    If the word is pronounced more than one way, both pronunciations are given. An example is the entry for *phenomenon*.

*Multiple pronunciations*

> **phe-nom-e-non** (fi näm'ə nän', -nən) ***n.***, ***pl.*** **-na** (-nə); also,
>     esp. for 2 & usually for 3, **-nons'** [< Gr. *phainesthai*,
>     appear]    **1** any observable fact or event that can be
>     scientifically

The first three syllables in either pronunciation are the same (fi näm'ə) but the last syllable can be pronounced differently (nän or nən). The last "o" in the word could be pronounced as the vowel in *on* (nän) or as the schwa ("uh") (nən). Sometimes multiple pronunciations are used because the word can be used as more than one part of speech. For example, the word *refund* is pronounced with the accent on the first syllable (rē'fund) when it is a noun, as in "I am getting a tax refund this year." But when the word is used as a verb, as in "I asked them to refund my money because I was unhappy with the product," the accent is on the second syllable (ri fund').

## Part of Speech

*Part of speech*

> **mo-tor** (mōt'ər) ***n.*** [L. < *movere*, to move]    **1** anything
>     that produces motion    **2** an engine; esp., an internal-
>     combustion engine

The part of speech follows the pronunciation. A few of the symbols you will see are

| n. | = | noun | a word that names a person, place, or thing |
| v. | = | verb | a word that indicates action |
| vt. | = | transitive verb | action that is received by a person or thing— "I threw the ball" |
| vi. | = | intransitive verb | action that is not received by a person or thing— "I *live* in a house" |
| adj. | = | adjective | a word that modifies a noun |
| adv. | = | adverb | a word that modifies verbs, adjectives, or other adverbs |

When the word can be used as more than one part of speech, the most common way the word is used is usually presented first with its definitions following. Then the next part of speech and its definitions are given. Here is the full entry for *motor*. Notice that it can be used as a noun, an adjective, or a verb.

> **mo-tor** (mōt′ər) *n.* [L. < *movere*, to move] **1** anything that produces motion **2** an engine; esp., an internal-combustion engine **3** a machine for converting electrical energy into mechanical energy —*adj.* **1** producing motion **2** of or powered by a motor **3** of, by, or for motor vehicles **4** of or involving muscular movements —*vi.* to travel by automobile

*Parts of speech*

## Etymology

> **mo-tor** (mōt′ər) *n.* [L. < *movere*, to move] **1** anything that produces

*— Etymology*

After the pronunciation and part of speech comes the **etymology,** or origin of the word. The symbol < means "derived from." You may find letters such as L. for Latin, Fr. for French, OE for Old English, and so forth. These indicate the language in which the word originated. A complete list of abbreviations is located at the front of the dictionary. In our sample you will see there are no etymologies for *motorboat,* *motorcade* or *motorist* because they are all based on *motor.* If you looked on the same page in the dictionary you would find that *motor* comes from the Latin word *movere.* If it is not known where a word originated you will find a "?" within the brackets. This is what you would find for *motley:*

> **mot-ley** (mät′lē) *adj.* [< ?] **1** of many colors **2** of many different or clashing elements [*a motley* group]

## Definitions

> **mo-tor** (mōt′ər) *n.* [L. < *movere*, to move] **1** anything that produces motion **2** an engine; esp., an internal-combustion engine **3** a machine for converting electrical energy into mechanical energy —*adj.* **1** producing motion **2** of or powered by a motor **3** of, by, or for motor vehicles **4** of or involving muscular movements —*vi.* to travel by automobile

*Definitions*

Some words have more than one definition. If there is more than one definition under a part of speech, each definition is numbered in boldface type. For example, the word *motor* has three noun definitions, four adjective definitions, and one verb definition. The more common words have even more definitions. For example, the word *set* has 50 noun definitions, 128 verb definitions, and 10 adjective definitions. Although all 188 definitions could be found in an unabridged edition, they would not all be found in your pocket dictionary. Some definitions also put the word in context in a phrase.

> **mount**[2] (mount) *vi.* [< L. *mons*, mountain]  **1** to climb; ascend  **2** to climb up on something, as a horse  **3** to increase in amount —*vt.*  **1** to go up; ascend [*to mount* stairs]  **2** to get up on (a horse, platform, etc.)  **3** to provide with horses [*mounted* police]

If there is a technical definition, you will see the technical field indicated. For example, *motile* has one definition from biology.

> **mo·tile** (mōt'l) *adj.* [< L. *movere*, to move] *Biol.* capable of or exhibiting spontaneous motion —**mo·til'i·ty** *n.*

Sometimes, instead of a definition, an entry refers you to a *cross-reference*. For example, *mountain lion* refers you to *cougar*, where you have the following entry:

> **cou·gar** (kōō'gər) *n.* [< Amind (Brazil)] a large, powerful, tawny wild cat
>
> **mountain lion** *same as* COUGAR

## Usage

In addition to the definitions, you will see the English **usage** indicated if it is different from the conventional usage acceptable in formal writing. In brackets before a definition you may find terms like *slang, colloq., archaic,* and *obs.* A *slang* word is very informal and should not be used in writing assignments. Slang terms can be either new words or old words to which new meanings are attached. For example, *nerd* and *peel rubber* are slang expressions. *Colloquial* (*colloq.*) expressions are used in conversation and informal writing but not in term papers or formal letters. In our sample, *motorbike* is colloquial. An *archaic* or *obsolete* (*obs.*) word or definition is one that was used in the past but is rarely or never used today. Examples are *rivage* (shore) and *mislike* (dislike).

An *idiomatic* expression is a phrase in which the words do not have their ordinary meaning. For example, the words *cool* and *not hot* would have similar definitions, but "you're cool" and "you're not so hot" could cause quite a bit of trouble if you thought they meant the same thing. These expressions are put in boldface type and defined under the main entry. In our sample, under the entry *motion,* "go through the motions" is in dark type because the word *motion* is used idiomatically.

> **mo·tion** (mō'shən) *n.* [< L. *movere*, to move]  **1** a moving from one place to another; movement  **2** a moving of a part of the body; specif., a gesture  **3** a proposal formally made in an assembly —*vi.* to make a meaningful movement of the hand, etc. —*vt.* to direct by a meaningful gesture **go through the motions** to do something mechanically, without real meaning —**in motion** moving —**mo'tion·less** *adj.*

*Idiomatic usage*

To check your understanding of the dictionary's structure, fill in the proper terms for each of the numbered dictionary parts. Check your answers in the back of the book.

8.

**ahem**                    13                    **air mass**

1.

**a-hem** (ə hem') *interj.* a cough, etc. made to get someone's attention, etc.

**-a-hol-ic** (ə häl'ik) *combining form* one preoccupied with (something specified)

**a-hoy** (ə hoi') *interj.* a call used in hailing [ship *ahoy*]

**aid** (ād) *vt., vi.* [< L. *ad-*, to + *juvare*, to help] to help; assist —*n.*    **1** help or assistance    **2** a helper

2.

**aide** (ād) *n.* [Fr.]    **1** an assistant    **2** an aide-de-camp

**aide-de-camp** or **aid-de-camp** (ād'də kamp') *n., pl.* **aides'-** or **aids'-** [Fr.] a military officer serving as an assistant to a superior

3.

**AIDS** (ādz) *n.* [*A(cquired) I(mmune) D(eficiency) S(yndrome)*] a condition of deficiency of certain leukocytes, resulting in infections, cancer, etc.

**ai-grette** or **ai-gret** (ā gret', ā'gret') *n.* [see EGRET] a bunch of the long, white, showy plumes of the egret

4.

**ail** (āl) *vt.* [OE *eglian*, to trouble] to cause pain and trouble to —*vi.* to be in poor health

**ai-le-ron** (ā'lə rän') *n.* [Fr. < L. *ala*, wing] a pilot-controlled airfoil at the trailing edge of an airplane wing, for controlling rolling

5.

**ail-ment** (āl'mənt) *n.* a mild illness

**aim** (ām) *vt.* [< L. *ad-*, to + *aestimare*, to estimate]    **1** to direct (a weapon, blow, etc.) so as to hit    **2** to direct (one's efforts)    **3** to intend —*n.*    **1** an aiming    **2** the ability to hit a target    **3** intention —**take aim** to aim a weapon, etc.

6.

**aim'less** *adj.* having no purpose —**aim'-less-ly** *adv.* — **aim'less-ness** *n.*

**ain't** (ānt) [< *amn't*, contr. of *am not*] [Colloq.] am not: also a dialectal or substandard contraction for *is not*, *are not*, *has not*, and *have not*

7.

**air'-cooled'** *adj.* cooled by having air passed over, into, or through it

9.

**air'craft'** *n., pl.* **-craft'** any machine for traveling through the air

**aircraft carrier** a warship with a large, flat deck, for carrying aircraft

**air'drop'** *n.* the dropping of supplies, troops, etc. from an aircraft in flight —**air'drop'** *vt.*

**Aire-dale** (er'dāl') *n.* [after *Airedale*, valley in England] a large terrier with a wiry coat

10.

**air'field'** *n.* a field where aircraft can take off and land

**air'foil'** *n.* a wing, rudder, etc. of an aircraft

**air force** the aviation branch of a country's armed forces

**air gun** a gun or gunlike device operated by compressed air

**air'head'** *n.* [Slang] a frivolous, silly, and ignorant person

**air lane** a route for travel by air; airway

**air'lift'** *n.* a system of transporting troops, supplies, etc. by aircraft —*vt.* to transport by airlift

**air'line'** *n.* a system or company for moving freight and passengers by aircraft —*adj.* of or on an airline

11.

**air'lin'er** *n.* a large airline-operated aircraft for carrying passengers

**air lock** an airtight compartment, with adjustable air pressure, between places of unequal air pressure

12.

**air'mail'** *n.* mail transported by air; esp., in the U.S., mail going overseas by air Also sp. air mail —*adj.* of or for mail sent by air —*vt.* to send (mail) by air

**air'man** (-mən) *n., pl.* **-men**    **1** an aviator    **2** an enlisted person in the U.S. Air Force

**air mass** *Meteorol.* a huge, uniform body of air having the properties of its place of origin

1. _____          7. _____
2. _____          8. _____
3. _____          9. _____
4. _____          10. _____
5. _____          11. _____
6. _____          12. _____

## Using the Dictionary

### *Finding the Main Entry*

If you don't find a main entry for a word, look under its base word. For example, *motivation* is found under *motivate*.

**mo-ti-vate** (mōt'ə vāt') *vt.* **-vat'ed, -vat'ing** to provide with, or affect as, a motive; incite —**mo'ti-va'tion** *n.*

If you can't find a word you are looking for, try another spelling. For example, try *weird* for *wierd* or *sheriff* for *sherif*. If that fails, try rhyming the first syllable of the word you want with a familiar word you know how to spell. This should give you some alternate spellings for the beginning of the word. For example, the first syllable of *hurdle* sounds like *her,* but if you look under *herdle* you will not find the word. If you try rhyming the first syllable, you will find it also rhymes with *fur* and *shirt.* These are logical alternate spellings for the first part of the word. If rhyming fails and you have tried a few alternate spellings, you can always ask someone for the spelling. However, you should try to find the word yourself first. Otherwise, you'll never improve your guessing ability. After you find the spelling of a word that you couldn't locate, write the spelling and say the word aloud so you will remember it.

Recently a student could not find a main entry for each of the following words. The word was either misspelled or it was part of another main entry. Use a dictionary to look up each entry. If you don't find a main entry for the word, look for its base. If the base is not a main entry, the word may be misspelled and you should try the methods suggested above to locate the word. After you have found the word, put the main entry in the space provided.

1. fearless _____
2. cieling _____
3. currently _____
4. insincerity _____
5. ilegal _____

6. kendergarten _____
7. lable _____
8. lisence _____
9. neice _____
10. massiveness _____

Check your answers in the back of the book.

### *Understanding the Definitions*

Once you have found the entry, the second step is understanding the word's definitions. Don't be frustrated when you find a word that is defined by another word you don't understand. If, for example, you are looking up *terse,* you may find a definition such as

> **terse** (tʉrs) *adj.* **ters′er, ters′est** [L. *tersus,* wiped off] free
> of superfluous words; concise; succinct

Perhaps you don't understand the words *superfluous, concise,* and *succinct. Superfluous* is defined as

> **su-per′-flu-ous** (sə pʉr′flōō əs, soo-) *adj.* [< L. *super-,*
> above + *fluere,* to flow] excessive or unnecessary

Therefore, *terse* means free of unnecessary words. *Concise* means

> **con-cise** (kən sīs′) *adj.* [< L. *com-,* intens. + *caedere,* to
> cut] brief and to the point; terse

Therefore, *terse* means brief and to the point. *Succinct* means

> **suc-cinct** (sək siŋkt′) *adj.* [< L. *sub-,* under + *cingere,* to
> gird] clear and brief; terse

Therefore, *terse* means clear and brief.

### Using the Pronunciation Guide

To test your understanding of how to use the pronunciation guide to cope with words that have more than one pronunciation, use the pronunciation guide below to complete the following exercise. Use your dictionary for help. Check your answers in the back of the book.

fat, āpe, cär; ten, ēven; is, bīte; gō, hôrn, tōōl, look; oil, out; up, fʉr; get; joy; yet; chin; she; thin, *then*; zh, leisure; ŋ, ring; ə for *a* in *ago*, *e* in *agent*, *i* in *sanity*, *o* in *comply*, *u* in *focus*; ' as in *able* (ā'b'l)

1. Fill in the definitions in your own words.
   refuse   a.  ri fyo͞oz' _____
            b.  ref'yo͞os _____

2. Circle one of the following pronunciations for the word *record* to complete each of the sentences below.
   a. Music lovers usually have good *record* collections.
      (ri kôrd'    rek'ərd)
   b. I decided to tape *record* the lecture covering the final exam.
      (ri kôrd'    rek'ərd)

3. Fill in the correct parts of speech.
   present   a.  prez''nt _____
             b.  pri zent' _____

### Choosing the Correct Definition

When you come to a word with several meanings, such as *bar,* you have to use the context in which the word appeared in order to choose the correct definition. Using the following entry for *bar,* place the number of the correct definition on the line before each of the following sentences. The first one has been done for you. Use the part of speech to help you choose the correct definition. Check your answers in the back of the book.

> **bar** (bar) *n.* [< ML. *barra*]   **1** any long, narrow piece of wood, metal, etc., often used as a barrier, lever, etc.   **2** an oblong piece, as of soap   **3** anything that obstructs or hinders   **4** a band or strip   **5** a law court, esp. that part, enclosed by a railing, where the lawyers sit   **6** lawyers collectively   the legal   profession   **8** a counter, as for serving alcoholic drinks   **9** a place with such a counter   **10** *Music a)* a vertical line dividing a staff into measures *b)* a measure —*vt.* **barred, bar'ring**   **1** to fasten with a bar   **2** to obstruct; close   **3** to oppose   **4** to exclude —*prep.* excluding [the best, *bar* none] —**cross the bar** to die

_10 b_ a. When the conductor is rehearsing an orchestra, he or she tells them at what bar
noun        to begin.

_____ b. In most states you must be 21 before you can enter a bar.
noun

_____ c. The door was nearly impossible to break in because a bar of wood had been
noun        nailed across it.

_____ d. The price of chocolate is increasing so rapidly that few people can remember
noun        when a Hershey Bar cost 5¢.

_____ e. Law students must pass an examination before they can be admitted to the bar.
noun

_____ f. At one time women were barred from certain jobs because of their sex.
verb

_____ g. Our path was barred by the tree that had fallen during the thunderstorm.
verb

When you look up a word, make a habit of checking the pronunciations, etymology, and all the meanings. Try to put the definition in your own words and use the word in a sentence. Doing this will help you remember the word and make it a part of your vocabulary.

## Additional Material in Dictionaries

Most dictionaries include extra material at the beginning and end. Just a few examples from a selection of dictionaries include

All the nations in the world

Populations and places in the United States and Canada

Foreign words and phrases

Colleges and universities in the United States and Canada

Proofreaders' marks

Tables of weights and measures

Knowing what extra material your dictionary contains could save you a trip to the library to look up the same information.

**acute** (ə kyo͞ot′) *adj.*   1. sharp-pointed   2. keen of mind   3. sensitive   4. severe (as pain)   5. severe (but not chronic)   6. very serious

**appropriate** (ə prō′prē āt′) *v.*   1. to take for one's own use, often improperly   2. to set aside (money, etc.) for a specific use—*adj.*   (ə prō′prē it) suitable; fit; proper

**complex** (käm′pleks, kəm pleks′) *adj.*   1. consisting of two or more related parts   2. complicated—*n.*   (käm′pleks)   1. a complicated whole   2. a unified grouping, as of buildings

**contemporary** (kən tem′pə rer′ē) *adj.*   1. living or occurring in the same period   2. of about the same age   3. modern

**deliberate** (di lib′ər it) *adj.*   1. carefully thought out; premeditated   2. not rash or hasty   3. unhurried—*v.*   (di lib′ər āt′) to consider carefully

**elaborate** (ē lab′ər it, i lab′ər it) *adj.*   developed in great detail; complicated —*v.*   (ē lab′ə rāt, i lab′ə rāt′)   1. to work out in great detail   2. to add more details (usually with on or upon)

**invalid** (in′və lid) *adj.*   weak and sickly—*n.*   one who is ill or disabled—*adj.*   (in val′id) untrue

**minute** (min′it) *n.*   1. the sixtieth part of an hour or of a degree of an arc   2. a moment   3. a specific point in time   4. [pl.] an official record of a meeting, etc.—*adj.*   (mī no͞ot′)   1. very small   2. of little importance   3. of or attentive to tiny details; precise

**parallel** (par′ə lel′) *adj.*   1. extending in the same direction and at a constant distance apart, so as never to meet   2. similar or corresponding—*n.*   1. lines that remain an equal distance apart   2. any comparison showing likeness   3. any of the imaginary lines on a map or globe indicating latitude to the equator and representing degrees of latitude—*v.*   1. to be equally distant from   2. to compare   3. to match; equal

**terminal** (tʉr′mə n'l) *adj.*   1. of, at, or forming the end or extremity   2. concluding; final   3. close to causing death, as cancer   4. of or at the end of a transportation line—*n.*   1. an end; extremity   2. a connective point on an electric circuit   3. either end of a transportation line, or a main station on it

fat, āpe, cär; ten, ēven; is, bīte; gō, hôrn, to͞ol, look; oil, out; up, fʉr; get; joy; yet; chin; she; thin, *th*en; zh, leisure; ŋ, ring; ə for *a* in *ago, e* in *agent, i* in *sanity, o* in *comply, u* in *focus;* ′ as in *able* (ā′b'l)

Read the following list of Review Words. Then in each space below write the word that best completes that sentence. Check your answers in the back of the book.

| | | | | |
|---|---|---|---|---|
| acute | complex | deliberate | invalid | parallels |
| appropriate | contemporaries | elaborate | minute | terminal |

1. Hitler, Churchill, Stalin and Franklin Delano Roosevelt were _____ .

2. The _____ eggs created in Russia by Faberge were decorated with many jewels.

3. Disney's Epcot Center consists of a _____ of several buildings which are international in character.

4. President Franklin D. Roosevelt never wanted to be viewed as an _____ ; therefore he never allowed anyone to photograph him in his wheelchair.

5. An _____ illness such as appendicitis requires hospitalization.

6. The _____ between Shakespeare's *Romeo and Juliet* and the modern musical *West Side Story* are obvious.

7. Some dollhouse furniture has such _____ detail that some of the tiny trim has to be painted with a magnifying glass.

8. Because of the possibility of early detection, breast cancer is no longer always a _____ illness.

9. After the 1992 Los Angeles riots, the federal government decided to _____ federal relief funds to the hardest hit areas.

10. In a professional chess match, there is a timer that limits the amount of time a player can _____ .

Each of the Review Words below has more than one pronunciation. Read each sentence aloud, then circle the pronunciation for the word as you used it. If necessary you can use a dictionary. Check your answers in the back of the book.

1. The law permitting apartment house owners to refuse to rent their apartments to families was ruled *invalid* in California.

   (in val′id       in′və lid)

2. Chopin's *Minute Waltz* was never meant to be played in 60 seconds.

   (min′it       mī n$\overline{oo}$t′)

3. The judge told the jury to *deliberate* before deciding on a verdict.

   (di lib′ər it       di lib′ər āt′)

4. The Celestial Suite at the Astroworld Hotel in Houston, Texas, has *elaborate* furnishings, including an indoor swimming pool with a Jacuzzi; it costs $2,500 a day!

   (ē lab′ər it       ē lab′ə rāt′)

5. In 1890, Congress had to *appropriate* $400 million to run the country, which is a small amount compared to the nearly $600 billion that is appropriated now.

   (ə prō′prē āt′       ə prō′prē it)

6. The teacher decided to further *elaborate* on the causes of the Revolutionary War.

   (ē lab′ər it       ē lab′ə rāt′)

7. To be seen by the naked eye, what seems to be a *minute* speck on the sun (called a sunspot) must actually have an area of about 500 million square miles.

   (min′it       mī n$\overline{oo}$t′)

8. Refusing to become an *invalid* when he was crippled by polio, Franklin D. Roosevelt continued in politics to become governor of New York and then president of the United States.

   (in val′id       in′və lid)

9. If an invitation says "black tie," it is *appropriate* for a man to wear a tuxedo.

   (ə prō′prē āt′       ə prō′prē it)

10. The detectives believed that the fire was the result of a *deliberate* attempt to burn the building down, probably for the insurance money.

   (di lib′ər it       di lib′ər āt′)

The Review Words below have multiple meanings. There are two sentences for each word. Read each sentence, then identify which dictionary meaning would best describe how the word is used, listing the number of the definition in the space provided. Be careful to choose a definition under the correct part of speech; the part of speech is provided below each space. Check your answers in the back of the book.

> **a-cute** (ə kyōōt′) **adj.** [< L. *acuere*, sharpen]  **1** sharp-pointed  **2** keen of mind  **3** sensitive [*acute* hearing]  **4** severe, as pain  **5** severe but not chronic [an *acute* disease]  **6** very serious  **7** less than 90° [*acute* angles]

_____    a.    A thief named Peletier probably suffered *acute* neck pain on April 22, 1792, when
adj.          he became the first person to be beheaded with the guillotine.

_____    b.    A German woman named Veronica Seider is reported to have vision 20 times
adj.          more *acute* than normal; she can identify people more than a mile away.

> **ter-mi-nal** (tʉr′ mə nəl) **adj.** [L. *terminalis*]  **1** of, at, or forming the end or extremity  **2** concluding; final  **3** close to causing death [*terminal* cancer]  **4** of or at the end of a transportation line —**n.**  **1** an end; extremity  **2** a connective point on an electric circuit  **3** either end of a transportation line, or a main station on it  **4** a device, usually with a keyboard and video display, for putting data in, or getting it from, a computer

_____    a.    The biggest railroad *terminal* in the world is Grand Central Station, New York City;
noun        it covers 48 acres.

_____    b.    Today many hospitals have begun to offer personal counseling to patients with
adj.          *terminal* illnesses and their families.

> **con-tem-po-rar-y** (kən tem′pə rer′ē) **adj.** [< L. *com-*, with + *tempus*, time]  **1** living or happening in the same period  **2** of about the same age  **3** modern —**n.**, *pl.* **-ies** one living in the same period as another or others

_____    a.    Modern research indicates that man and dinosaurs were never *contemporaries*.
noun

_____    b.    Television has finally begun to deal with *contemporary* issues, such as sexual
adj.          problems, abortion, and child abuse.

> **par-al-lel** (par′ə lel′) **adj.** [< Gr. *para-*, side by side + *allēlos*, one another]  **1** extending in the same direction and at a constant distance apart, so as never to meet  **2** similar or corresponding —**n.**  **1** a parallel line, surface, etc.  **2** any person or thing similar to another; counterpart  **3** any comparison showing likeness  **4** any of the imaginary lines parallel to the equator and representing degrees of latitude: in full parallel of latitude —**vt.** **-leled′** or **-lelled′**, **-lel′ing** or **-lel′ling**  **1** to be parallel with [the road *parallels* the river]  **2** to compare  **3** to match; equal—**par′al-lel′ism′** (-iz′əm)

**adj.**    a.   *Parallel* lines, such as railroad tracks, seem to come closer together as you look farther into the distance.

**noun**    b.   Some historians attempt to draw *parallels* between the economic events leading to World War I and those leading to World War II.

> **com-plex** (kəm pleks′; *also, and for* **n.** *always,* käm′pleks)
> **adj.** [< L. *com-*, with + *plectere*, to weave]
> **1** consisting of two or more related parts   **2** compli-
> cated —**n.**   **1** a complex whole   **2** a unified group-
> ing, as of buildings   **3** *Psychoanalysis a)* a group of
> mostly unconscious impulses, etc. strongly influencing
> behavior *b)* loosely, an obsession

**noun**    a.   Today some people work in large business *complexes* having as many as 1,000 offices.

**adj.**    b.   Willem Klein is called the human computer because he can solve very *complex* mathematical problems, such as finding the 23rd root of a 200-digit number, in his head.

## EXERCISE 4: USING THE DICTIONARY

1. Fill in the following information from the dictionary you are using.

a.   Title _____

b.   Copyright date _____

c.   Hard cover or paperback _____

2. Use your dictionary to change the part of speech of each of the words below. Some of the new words will be in the same main entry as the base words; others will have their own entries. The first one has been done for you. Check your answers in the back of the book.

a.   invalid   _____*invalidate*_____     d.   deliberate   _____
                    verb                                           noun

b.   elaborate   _____     e.   terminal   _____
                    noun                                           verb

c.   minute   _____
                 adverb

3. Using the dictionary, find what these abbreviations mean. On the first line fill in the word that the following abbreviations stand for. On the second line write their definitions. The first one has been done for you. Check your answers in the back of the book.

a.   etc.   _____*et cetera*_____     _____*and so forth*_____

b.   i.e.   _____     _____

c.   e.g.   _____     _____

d.   et al.   _____     _____

e.   R.S.V.P.   _____     _____

4. Interpreting the meaning of symbols used in entries helps you make the most of your dictionary. Find out what each of the symbols below means. Look at the abbreviations list at the front of your dictionary if you can't guess the meaning from the entry. Check your answers in the back of the book.

a. Circle (1) or (2).
The [v-] in the entry at right indicates that
*vandal* means: _____
(1) a member of a Germanic tribe?
(which is capitalized)
(2) a person who destroys things?
(which is not capitalized)

**Van-dal** (van′ dəl) *n.*    **1** a member of a Germanic people who sacked Rome (455 A.D.)    **2** [v-] one who maliciously destroys property, esp. works of art

b. What does [see fol.] mean here? _____

**fan-tas-tic** (fan tas′tik) *adj.* [see fol.]    **1** imaginary; unreal    **2** grotesque; odd    **3** extravagant    **4** incredible —**fan-tas′ti-cal-ly** *adv.* —**fan-tas′ti-cal-ness** *n.*
**fan-ta-sy** (fant′ə sē) *n., pl.* -**sies** [< Gr. *phainein,* to show]    **1** imagination or fancy    **2** an illusion or reverie    **3** fiction portraying highly IMAGINATIVE (sense 2) characters or settings

c. Basing your answer on the directions in the *ice hockey* entry, circle the meaning in the *hockey* entry that refers to ice hockey.

**ice hockey** *same as* HOCKEY (sense 1)

**hock-ey** (häk′ē) *n.* [prob. < OFr *hoquet,* bent stick]    **1** a team game played on ice skates, with curved sticks and a hard rubber disk (*puck*)    **2** a similar game played on foot on a field, with a small ball

d. What does [ON] mean in this entry? _____

**boon¹** (bo͞on) *n.* [ON, *bon,* petition] a welcome benefit; blessing

e. What does *pl.* mean in this entry? _____

**fi-as-co** (fē as′kō) *n., pl.* -**coes, -cos** [Fr. < It.] a complete, ridiculous failure

This is an acrostic. The number below each space in the clues tells you where to fill in that letter in the Mystery Saying below. To answer the questions, you will need to look up the key words in a dictionary. Then write the answers in the spaces provided. Write the same letter in each space having a matching number. Not all paperback dictionaries contain all the answers; you may have to use more than one dictionary. For some of the answers, you may have to refer to the lists at the back of the dictionary. Check your answers in the back of the book.

1. First name of President McKinley

   __ __ __ __ __ __ __
   10  6  12  12  6  1  4

2. Origin of sag

   __ __ __ __ __ __ __ __ __ __ __
   14  2  1  7  15  6  7  1  11  6  1  7

3. Cloven is the past participle of what verb?

   __ __ __ __ __ __
   2  12  13  1  11  13

4. The Druids were priests for this group

   __ __ __ __ __
   2  13  12  8  14

5. Country of which La Paz is the capital

   __ __ __ __ __ __ __
   5  3  12  6  11  6  1

6. Meaning of the Latin word *ego*

   __ __ __ __
   14  13  12  9

**Mystery Saying: A Definition of Love**

__    __ __ __ __ __ __ __ __ __ __
1     2  3  4  5  6  7  1  8  6  3  7

__ __    __ __ __    __ __ __ __ __ __
3  9     8  10  3     11  3  10  13  12  14

__ __ __    __ __ __ __ __ __ __ __ __ __
8  10  3     2  3  7  14  3  7  1  7  8  14

__ __ __    __ __ __    __ __ __ __ __
1  7  15     8  10  3     9  3  3  12  14

# NEW WORDS I

The first ten words presented in this chapter are words with multiple meanings.

**abstract** (ab strakt′, ab′strakt) *adj.*   1. not material, not concrete, not tangible or actual [beauty is an *abstract* word]   2. not practical or applied   3. concerning art that is not realistic—*n.*  (ab′strakt) a summary of a book, article, speech, etc.—*v.*  (ab′strakt, ab strakt′)   1. to form a general idea from particular instances   2. to summarize

**aggravate** (ag′rə vāt′) *v.*   1. to make worse   2. to annoy

**attribute** (ə trib′yōōt) *v.*   1. to give credit to a source [the quotation is *attributed* to Aristotle]   2. to credit as a quality or characteristic unique to one—*n.*  (a′trə byōōt′) a characteristic or quality of a person or thing

**compensate** (käm′pən sāt′) *v.*   1. to make up for   2. to pay

**consistency** (kən sist′ən sē) *n.*   1. the condition of holding together; firmness or thickness   2. agreement, harmony, logical connection [arguments lacking *consistency*]   3. condition of remaining the same; agreement with what has already been done

**foil** (foil) *v.*   1. to keep from being successful; frustrate—*n.*   1. a very thin sheet of metal   2. the metal coating on the back of a mirror   3. a person or thing that sets off or heightens the effect of another person or thing by contrast   4. a long, thin fencing sword with a button on the point to prevent injury

**intimate** (in′tə mit) *adj.*   1. private; personal [one's *intimate* feelings]   2. close, friendly [an *intimate* friend]—*n.*  close friend—*v.*  (in′tə māt′)  to hint or imply

**intrigue** (in trēg′) *v.*   1. to carry on a secret love affair   2. to plot or scheme secretly   3. to excite interest or curiosity; fascinate [the puzzle *intrigued* her]—*n.*  (in trēg′, in′trēg)   1. secret plot or plotting   2. secret love affair

**liberal** (lib′ər əl, lib′rəl) *adj.*   1. generous   2. plentiful [a *liberal* reward]   3. broad-minded   4. favoring reform or progress—*n.*   1. a person or group favoring liberalism

**objective** (əb jek′tiv, äb jek′tiv) *adj.*   1. based on facts; real [an *objective* painting, description, etc.]   2. not affected by personal feelings or prejudice; fair; impersonal [an *objective* point]   3. dealing with things external to the mind rather than thoughts   4. a kind of test, as a multiple choice or true-false test, that has a single answer—*n.* something aimed at; a goal

fat, āpe, cär; ten, ēven; is, bīte; gō, hôrn, tōōl, look; oil, out; up, fur; get; joy; yet; chin; she; thin, *then*; zh, leisure; ŋ, ring; ə for *a* in *ago, e* in *agent, i* in *sanity, o* in *comply, u* in *focus;* ′ as in *able* (ā′b′l)

Below are ten words with more than one meaning from your New Words list. First, fill in the word that belongs in each sentence below. Second, using the definitions on your New Words list, write the number of the proper definition in the blank in front of the number. To help you find the right definition, we have provided the part of speech below that blank. The first one is done for you. Check your answers in the back of the book.

abstract                attributed          consistency         intimate        liberal
aggravate               compensate          foil                intrigued       objective

_____*1*_____   1. Smoking can ____*aggravate*____ a cough.
verb

_____   2. The legend of Hamlet, which is often _____ to Shakespeare,
verb            actually can be traced back hundreds of years before.

_____   3. Some psychologists have claimed that Napoleon's desire to build an empire was
verb            an attempt to _____ for his small height.

_____   4. No one wants _____ details of his or her personal life
adj.            printed in the newspapers.

_____   5. The runny _____ of soft-boiled eggs causes some people to
noun            refuse to eat them.

_____   6. The police of New York City tried unsuccessfully to _____ a
verb            thief who stole 15,000 books from the public library. This was the largest theft of
                books ever reported.

_____   7. Many people are surprised that what seems like a _____
adj.            portion of cream cheese has the same number calories as a small pat of butter.

_____   8. The invention of the seismograph provided an accurate and
adj.            _____ measure of the strength and length of an earthquake.

_____   9. The Pledge of Allegiance, which children recite from memory, contains
noun            _____ ideas like "liberty and justice for all" that even adults
                find hard to understand.

_____  10. A young child can be more _____ by an empty box than by
verb            the expensive toy that came in it.

# NEW WORDS II

These ten words are either words frequently used in dictionary entries or words that have unusual plurals.

**abridge** (ə brij′) *v.*   1. to reduce in scope, extent, etc.; shorten   2. to shorten by using fewer words but keeping the main contents; condense   3. to lessen people's rights, authority, etc.

**apparatus** (ap′ə rat′əs, ap′ə rāt′əs) *n.*   1. the instruments, tools, materials, etc. needed for a specific use.   2. a device or machine for a specific use

**archaic** (är kā′ik) *adj.*   1. belonging to an earlier period; ancient   2. out-of-date; old-fashioned   3. that which is no longer used except for special purposes, as in poetry or church rituals ["thou" is an *archaic* word for "you"]

**colloquial** (kə lō′kwē əl) *adj.*   1. having to do with, or like, conversation; conversational   2. using words, phrases, and idioms characteristic of informal speech and writing

**criterion** (krī tir′ē ən) *n.*   a standard, rule, or test by which something can be judged; measure of value

**data** (dāt′ə, dat′a) *n.pl.*   information; facts or figures from which conclusions can be drawn

**derivation** (der′ə vā′shən) *n.*   1. source or origin   2. etymology

**obsolete** (äb′sə lēt′) *adj.*   1. no longer used   2. out of date

**phenomenon** (fi näm′ə nän′, fi näm′ə nən) *n.*   1. a scientific fact   2. an unusual occurrence

**thesis** (thē′sis) *n.*   1. a statement maintained or defended in an argument   2. a formal and lengthy research paper, especially one written in partial fulfillment of the requirements for a master's degree

fat, āpe, cär; ten, ēven; is, bīte; gō, hôrn, to͞ol, look; oil, out; up, fur; get; joy; yet; chin; she; thin, *th*en; zh, leisure; ŋ, ring; ə for *a* in *ago, e* in *agent, i* in *sanity, o* in *comply, u* in *focus;* ' as in *able* (ā′b'l)

Circle the letter before the word or phrase that best defines the italicized word in each sentence. Check your answers in the back of the book.

1. *Reader's Digest* is one of our most popular magazines because its *abridged* versions of books and magazine articles take very little time to read.

   a. completed   b. interesting   c. complicated   d. shortened

2. For safety reasons, no trapeze artist in the circus would perform on a piece of *apparatus* that had not been carefully checked beforehand.

   a. equipment   b. rope   c. music   d. evidence

3. An *archaic* name for Halloween is "Nutcrack Night." On that evening nuts were thrown into a fire to see if a lover were true. If the nuts burst, he or she was not to be trusted.

   a. idealistic   b. old-fashioned   c. interesting   d. impractical

4. *Colloquial* phrases such as "you're a nice kid" should not be used on college term papers.

   a. strange   b. informal   c. important   d. current

5. Many experts think the most difficult event to judge in the Winter Olympics is figure skating. This is because the *criteria* for scoring mistakes are so complex.

   a. irregularities   b. ideas   c. standards   d. judgements

6. Interpol, the International Criminal Police Organization, enables its member nations to exchange vital *data* concerning criminals around the world.

   a. gossip   b. theories   c. evidence   d. signs

7. The *derivation* of the word "gypsy" is "Egypt." In early times people mistakenly believed that the wandering tribes came from that country when, in fact, today they are believed to have come from northwestern India.

   a. opposite   b. origins   c. spelling   d. meaning

8. Edison's invention of the electric light bulb made lighting houses with gas lamps *obsolete*.

   a. practical   b. silly   c. fashionable   d. outdated

9. A famous natural *phenomenon* is the geyser Old Faithful in Yellowstone National Park. It erupts every 66 to 70 minutes on the average, rarely varying more than 35 minutes either way.

   a. disaster   b. experiment   c. occurrence   d. volcano

10. Descarte's *thesis*, "I think; therefore, I am," argues that thinking is proof of existence.

    a. question   b. major argument   c. example   d. trial

## EXERCISE 8: IRREGULAR PLURALS

If the word below is singular, write its plural in the blank; if the word is plural, write its singular in the blank. Use a dictionary if you need help. Check your answers in the back of the book.

1. criterion     _____

2. data     _____

3. thesis     _____

4. phenomenon     _____

5. apparatus     _____

## EXERCISE 9: TRUE-FALSE

Place a *T* or an *F* in the space provided. Check your answers in the back of the book.

_____ 1. A book that is abridged leaves nothing out.

_____ 2. One garden apparatus is a shovel.

_____ 3. You should not use slang in a formal paper, such as a master's thesis.

_____ 4. An obsolete thing is useful.

_____ 5. A phenomenon is an unusual event.

## EXERCISE 10: ANALOGIES

Write *S* in the blank if the words are synonyms and *A* if they are antonyms. In the blank write the letter of the word that best completes each analogy. Check your answers in the back of the book.

_____ 1. complex : involved ::
objective : _____
    a. thought   b. fear   c. subjective
    d. goal

_____ 2. contemporary : recent ::
attribute : _____
    a. personality   b. characteristic
    c. difference   d. weight

_____ 3. minute : huge ::
intimate : _____
    a. public   b. forbidden   c. threatened
    d. private

_____ 4. elaborate : complicated ::
intrigue : _____
    a. story   b. conspiracy   c. attempt
    d. mistake

_____ 5. appropriate : improper ::
abstract : _____
    a. concrete   b. abandoned   c. unrealistic
    d. sad

## EXERCISE 11: MATCHING MEANINGS

Write the letter of the word that means the opposite of the word in the first column.
Check your answers in the back of the book.

_____ 1. aggravate              a.  formal

_____ 2. colloquial             b.  changeableness

_____ 3. compensate             c.  stingy

_____ 4. consistency            d.  soothe

_____ 5. liberal                e.  default

## EXERCISE 12: WORD CONTRASTS

In each group below, circle the word that does not mean what the others mean.
Check your answers in the back of the book.

1.  archaic      contemporary      obsolete      antique

2.  data      statistics      facts      theories

3.  derivation      origin      ending      roots

4.  foil      ruin      frustrate      assist

5.  criterion      rule      guess      measurement

## EXERCISE 13: SENTENCE COMPLETION

Complete each sentence in your own words. Sample answers are provided in the
back of the book.

1.  You might want to read an *abridged* novel if _____
    _____.

2.  Whenever you look at an *abstract* painting, _____
    _____.

3.  Spicy food can *aggravate* an ulcer; however, _____
    _____.

4.  Modern hospitals must have expensive *apparatus;* for example, _____
    _____.

5.  The *archaic* language we find in old books sounds strange because _____
    _____.

6. Beauty is an *attribute* most women fear losing; thus _____

_____ .

7. Idioms are *colloquial;* for example, _____

_____ .

8. Some employers try to *compensate* their workers when _____

_____ .

9. If there is not *consistency* in disciplining a child, _____

_____ .

10. Although teachers may have specific *criteria* in mind when grading an essay test, _____

_____ .

11. Whenever you collect *data* for a term paper, _____

_____ .

12. When you look up the *derivation* of a word, _____

_____ .

13. If you hear a burglar, you should call 911 instead of trying to *foil* the robbery because _____

_____ .

14. You may tell your best friends your *intimate* secrets; nevertheless, _____

_____ .

15. Unless a book is *intriguing,* _____

_____ .

16. We want to eat a *liberal* portion from each of the four basic food groups every day because

_____ .

17. Although you may not know your specific *objectives* before you finish college, _____

_____ .

18. Even though using gas for home lighting is *obsolete,* _____

_____ .

19. The Beatles were a *phenomenon* in the 1960s, yet _____

_____ .

20. Until you develop a *thesis* for your term paper, _____

_____ .

# ADVANCED WORDS

**cite** (sīt) *v.*   1. summon before a court of law   2. quote   3. mention for example or proof   4. mention especially because of outstanding service

**collateral** (kə lat'ər əl) *adj.*   1. extra or additional   2. having a minor relationship   3. security or guarantee for repayment of a loan—*n.*   anything, such as stocks or bonds, that secures or guarantees a debt

**defer** (di fur') *v.*   1. to put off to a future time; delay   2. to give in to the wish or judgment of another, as in showing respect; yield

**deluge** (del'yo͞oj) *n.*   1. a great flood   2. a heavy rainfall   3. an overwhelming rush of anything—*v.*   1. to flood   2. to overwhelm or overrun

**denomination** (di näm'ə nā'shən) *n.*   1. a unit of value [coins of different *denominations*]   2. the name of a group   3. a particular religious group or church

**derelict** (der'ə likt') *adj.*   1. deserted by the owner; abandoned   2. neglectful of duty; negligent—*n.*   1. property (especially a ship deserted at sea) that has been abandoned   2. a bum

**desolate** (des'ə lit) *adj.*   1. alone; deserted   2. miserable—*v.*   (des'ə lāt)   1. to desert   2. to ruin

**mode** (mōd) *n.*   1. a way of doing   2. customary usage   3. current fashion or style   4. the number that occurs most frequently in a given series

**perennial** (pə ren'ē əl) *adj.*   1. lasting more than a year   2. long lasting [a *perennial* youth]   3. growing every year—*n.*   a plant that grows every year

**precipitate** (pri sip'ə tāt') *v.*   1. cause [*precipitate* a crisis]   2. hasten the occurrence of   3. throw headlong; hurl downward   4. separate a solid from a solution   5. rain or snow

fat, āpe, cär; ten, ēven; is, bīte; gō, hôrn, to͞ol, look; oil, out; up, fur; get; joy; yet; chin; she; thin, *th*en; zh, leisure; ŋ, ring; ə for *a* in *ago, e* in *agent, i* in *sanity, o* in *comply, u* in *focus;* ' as in *able* (ā'b'l)

Use the Advanced Words to fill in the blanks in the sentences that follow. Check your answers in the back of the book.

| cited | defer | denomination | desolate | perennial |
|-------|-------|--------------|----------|-----------|
| collateral | deluge | derelict | mode | precipitated |

1. Edward Ebzery of Brisbane, Australia, is probably the man _____ for and convicted of the most crimes, having been arrested 1433 times for drunkenness.

2. Once the lush tropical islands of Hawaii were _____, having no plants, animals or people.

3. In 1969, the U.S. Treasury announced that no bill with a _____ higher than $100 would be printed.

4. It is still the _____ in Great Britain to send upper class children to boarding schools instead of educating them nearby.

5. The greatest _____ recorded in a twenty-four hour period, 73.62 inches of rain, flooded an island in the Indian Ocean on March 15–16, 1952.

6. The assassination of Austrian Archduke Ferdinand by a Serbian gunman in 1914 _____ World War I.

7. The British company that owned the "unsinkable" *Titanic* was _____ in failing to provide enough lifeboats; this resulted in the death of 1,517 people when the boat hit an iceberg and sank.

8. Shylock demanded a pound of Antonio's flesh as _____ for a loan in Shakespeare's play, *The Merchant of Venice.*

9. The largest flowering plant is a Chinese wisteria, a _____ planted in 1892 that now weighs over 250 tons and covers over one acre.

10. At Christmas, some merchants agree to _____ until February payments on merchandise bought in December.

Fill in the puzzle below in pencil. The clues with an asterisk (*) refer to words on New Words lists in previous chapters. You can also check the word list on the inside front cover of this book. Check your answers in the back of the book.

**Across**

1. Abbr. for *before Christ*
3. A metal container for cooking
6. Round baked dessert
9. Actor Sir Laurence Olivier's monogram
10. Abbr. for *line* or *lane*
11. Abbr. for *Habeus Corpus Act*
13. Abbr. for *mountain*
*14. Not clear; vague
15. Patriot Patrick Henry's monogram
16. Abbr. for *notary public*
17. Antonym of *stop*
18. Same as 10 across
19. Abbr. for *Dutch*
20. Where bees make their home
21. Roman numeral for 2
22. Abbr. for *ton*
23. Signal for help
25. Abbr. for *cubic centimeter*
26. Abbr. for *Social Security Administration*
28. Openings in fences
29. Antonym of *cool*
30. Abbr. for *atomic*
*31. Copy
35. Abbr. for *New York*
37. Apparatus for chopping trees
*38. Priceless
43. I am; he _____
*44. Difficult choice
45. To declare untrue
46. Antonym of *arid*
47. Rock that contains minerals, such as iron
48. Abbr. for *extraterrestrial*

**Down**

*1. Not spicy
*2. Must be done; required
*3. A sad or dangerous situation
4. Antonym of *stopping*
5. Abbr. for *intensive care unit*
*7. Suggested; not clearly expressed

*8. Having to do with cultural or racial groups
11. Truthful
*12. To evaluate
24. Abbr. for *Old English*
26. Detective Holmes's monograph
27. Past tense of *eat*
30. Abbr. for *Alabama*
*32. To think deeply about
33. The country whose capital is Rome

*34. To free from a rule or duty; not eligible
*35. simple and childlike
36. Chess, checkers, and cards, e.g.
37. Abbr. for *aluminum*
39. Where grapes grow
40. Explorer Lief Erikson's monogram
41. Abbr. for *United Mine Workers*
42. Used with a ball
45. "I _____," said the bride.

From your readings in books, magazines, newspapers, and textbooks, select ten words that you want to learn; choose words you are likely to see again. Write your words on the lines below. Look up each word in the dictionary. First, look at the pronunciation and try to pronounce the word. Next, put the definition in your own words. Then, use the word in a sentence or make up a mnemonic device to help you remember the meaning of the word. Finally, put the word on the front of a flash card with the sentence or mnemonic at the bottom. Put the definition on the back. Review your words regularly.

1. _____

2. _____

3. _____

4. _____

5. _____

6. _____

7. _____

8. _____

9. _____

10. _____

# chapter 5

# SUFFIXES

We have looked at the meanings of words based on their use in sentences. Now we are going to look at their meanings based on how the words are constructed. One of the most useful ways to figure out the meanings of unfamiliar words is to break the words down into parts called roots, prefixes, and suffixes. The **root** is the basic core of the word. **Prefixes** are added to the beginnings of words to change their meanings. For example, *unscrupulous* means the opposite of *scrupulous* because the prefix *un* means *not*. **Suffixes** are word endings and can be attached to whole words, as in price*less,* or to parts of words, as in archa*ic*. Suffixes will be discussed in this chapter. Chapter 6 will cover the common prefixes, and Chapters 7, 8, and 9 will cover 15 useful **roots**.

Knowing the most commonly used word parts will help you understand hundreds of new words. For example, the difficult word *vociferous* can be easily understood when broken down into its parts:

| Word Part | Definition | Examples |
|---|---|---|
| voc | call, voice | voice, vocal, vocabulary |
| fer | carry, bear | ferry, transfer, refer |
| ous | full of, like | famous, glorious, synonymous |

It refers to a voice (*voc*), which is full of (*ous*) loudness, or which carries (*fer*) a long way; therefore, the word means loud and noisy.

You can see that knowing how to divide and conquer words can be very helpful. Just knowing how to recognize suffixes can help solve several word mysteries. For example, you may not realize it but you already know the words *exemplify, deprivation, quizzical, problematical,* and *fibrous.* Below we have separated the base word and the suffixes.

| Word | Base | | Suffix | Suffix Meaning |
|---|---|---|---|---|
| exemplify | example | + | fy | make or do |
| deprivation | deprive | + | tion | state or quality of |
| quizzical | quiz | + | ic, al | like |
| problematical | problem | + | ic, al | like |
| fibrous | fiber | + | ous | full of, like |

To test your knowledge of suffixes, fill in the missing endings in the mystery below. Check your answers in the back of the book.

**The Case of the Mysterious Call**

Inspect_____ Keane quick_____ put down the telephone re-
ceiv_____. Exact_____ ten minutes later he was being driv_____ to an
unknown destina_____. It was difficult to see anything in the fogg_____
weather. Within twenty minutes Keane had lost his sense of direct_____ as they
drove through the desol_____ Engl_____ countryside. "Where are we?" he
asked the driv_____. "I was told not to tell you anything," his compan_____
responded, with a dread_____ chuckle. It was the kind of sound he had so often

heard when involved in one of his fam_____ cases. Maybe this was a trap, and his
<br>14
friend's telephoned plea that he was urgent_____ needed was the bait. As Keane
<br>15
began to comtempl_____ his predica_____, the driver sudden_____
<br>16 17 18
stopped the car. "Here we are, sir." Keane looked out and saw an old mansion with a
large wood_____ door. His heart skipped a beat as he left the car. He wished he
<br>19
had brought his revolv_____ as he remembered the urgen_____ of this
<br>20 21
friend's call and now saw his destination. Keane knocked on the mass_____ door
<br>22
and the butl_____ prompt_____ answered.
<br>23 24
      Obvious_____ the man had been waiting for him. Once again he was
<br>25
fear_____ that danger was present. As he stepped inside the dark house, the
<br>26
gigant_____ door slammed shut with a nois_____ bang. Now he had no
<br>27 28
choice. He followed the butler down an end_____ corrid_____ until the
<br>29 30
man stopped. Apparent_____ they were in front of the libr_____. Keane
<br>31 32
cautious_____ stepped into the black_____. Sudden_____ the lights
<br>33 34 35
were thrown on by someone, and to Keane's astonish_____ a dozen of his most
<br>36
intim_____ friends yelled, "Happy Birthday, Inspector!"
<br>37

      As you can see from the story, suffixes are used very often. They don't usually change the meaning of the base very much. Their main function is to change a word to a different part of speech, that is, to make the word do a different job in the sentence. For example, in the sentence "King Kong filled the natives with terror," the base word *terror* is used as a noun. To use it as a verb, we would have to say "King Kong terrified the natives," or "King Kong terrorized the natives." We formed the verb from the noun by adding the suffixes *-ify* and *-ize*. Common suffixes can change base words or roots into nouns, adjectives, verbs, and adverbs.

      If you need a review of the basic parts of speech, please refer to Chapter 4, pages 48–49.

## Types of Suffixes

### *Suffixes That Form Nouns*

| Base | Suffix | Noun |
| --- | --- | --- |
| exert, include | **tion, sion, ion** | exertion, inclusion |
| pass | **age** | passage |
| rely, obsolete | **ance, ence** | reliance, obsolescence |
| intimate | **cy** | intimacy |
| skeptic | **ism** | skepticism |
| retire | **ment** | retirement |
| quiet | **tude** | quietude |
| press | **ure** | pressure |
| unique | **ness** | uniqueness |
| absurd | **ity** | absurdity |

The following suffixes form nouns and also change the meaning to indicate a person or thing that does something.

| Base | Suffix | Noun |
|------|--------|------|
| music | (i)an | musician |
| negotiate, jest, lie | or, er, ar | negotiator, jester, liar |
| alarm | ist | alarmist |

## Suffixes That Form Adjectives

| Base | Suffix | Meaning | Adjective |
|------|--------|---------|-----------|
| detest, flex | able, ible | able to be, worthy of being | detestable, flexible |
| magnet | ic | | magnetic |
| wool | en | | woolen |
| East | ern | | Eastern |
| fever | ish | | feverish |
| skeptic | al | like, relating to | skeptical |
| grime, friend | y, ly | | grimy, friendly |
| Europe | an | | European |
| finance | ial | | financial |
| create | ive | | creative |
| synonym | ous, ious | full of, like | synonymous |
| right | eous | | righteous |
| purpose | less | without | purposeless |

## Suffixes That Form Nouns or Adjectives

| Base | Suffix | Meaning | Noun and Adjective |
|------|--------|---------|--------------------|
| spoon, plenty | ful | fullness; full of | spoonful (noun) plentiful (adj.) |
| assist, absorb | ant, ent | a person or thing that; that has, shows or does | assistant (noun) absorbent (adj.) |
| custom, rob | ary, ory, ery, ry | a person or thing connected with, or a place for; relating to, connected with | customary (adj.) robbery (noun) |

MY TEACHER ONCE TOLD ME MY PLAYING STYLE WOULD SOME DAY REVOLUTIONIZE MODERN MUSIC!

WHAT I'VE HEARD YOU PLAY SO FAR IS PRETTY REVOLTING!

## Suffixes That Form Verbs

| Base | Suffix | Verb |
|------|--------|------|
| glory | **ify** | glorify |
| emphasis | **ize, ise** | emphasize |
| haste | **en** | hasten |
| invalid | **ate** | invalidate |

## One Suffix That Forms Adverbs

| Base | Suffix | Adverb |
|------|--------|--------|
| random | **ly** | randomly |

## Spelling Changes

You probably noticed in the examples above that there are often spelling changes when suffixes are added to base words. Although all spelling principles in English have exceptions, following are a few of the most useful. For practice, fill in the blanks following each rule, and check your answers in the back of the book.

1.  If a single final consonant in a base has a single vowel before it and is in a single syllable or stressed syllable, double the consonant before a suffix beginning with a vowel.

single vowel   single final consonant

trans + MIT + er = transmiTTer

stressed syllable   vowel

In filling in the following blanks, double the final consonant only if the word meets all four criteria:

(1)   The base has a *single* consonant at the end.

(2)   There is a *single* vowel before the final consonant.

(3)   The vowel-consonant combination occurs in the final *stressed* syllable.

(4)   The suffix begins with a *vowel.*

a.   solemn + ity = _____

b.   omit + ing = _____

c.   bit + en = _____

d.   unique + ness = _____

e.   occur + ence = _____

2. If a base ends in silent *e*, drop the *e* before adding a suffix that begins with a vowel.

$$\underset{\downarrow}{\text{silent } e} \quad \underset{\downarrow}{\text{vowel}}$$
$$\text{passive} + \text{ity} = \text{passivity}$$

a. acute + ness = _____

b. futile + ity = _____

c. liberal + ism = _____

d. cope + ing = _____

e. precise + ion = _____

3. When the last two letters of a base are consonant + *y*, change the *y* to *i* before adding a suffix, unless the suffix begins with *i*.

consonant  y

fallacy + ous = fallacious

a. copy + er = _____

b. study + ing = _____

c. library + an = _____

d. annoy + ance = _____

e. pity + ful = _____

4. *able-ible*
When a base is a complete word, the suffix *-able* is usually added. When the base is part of a word, *-ible* is usually added. Add *-able* or *-ible* to the following bases.

a. poss _____

b. employ _____

c. detest _____

d. invis _____

e. break _____

5. *ary-ery; ant-ent; ance-ence*

There is no clear-cut rule for remembering which of these suffixes to use. You will need to memorize each case individually using mnemonic devices. For example, to distinguish station*ary* (not moving) from station*ery* (writing paper), you might associate the word st*a*ble with station*a*ry because they both contain the letter *a* and have similar meanings. Following are five words ending in one of these suffixes. Make up a mnemonic device for remembering the spelling for each and write it in the blank space.

a. bravery _____

b. secretary _____

c. defendant _____

d. adjacent _____

e. coincidence _____

## EXERCISE 1: BASE WORDS

Below are ten words from earlier chapters in this book. First, underline the suffix in each word. Then, on the blank lines, write the base word that remains after each suffix is removed. Some of the words will require spelling changes. If you need help, use your dictionary. Check your answers in the back of the book.

1. derivation _____

2. spontaneously _____

3. deduction _____

4. skeptical _____

5. conspiracy _____

6. coherent _____

7. consistency _____

8. compulsory _____

9. citation _____

10. objective _____

# REVIEW WORDS

**ancestry** (an′ses′trē) *n.*    1. family descent    2. all one's ancestors

**brutality** (broo tal′ə tē) *n.*    harshness or cruelty

**decisive** (də sī′siv) *adj.*    1. conclusive    2. showing decision    3. crucial; critically important

**exemplify** (eg zem′plə fī′) *v.*    to show by example

**frequency** (frē′kwən sē) *n.*    1. the number of times any event recurs in a given period    2. the number of cycles per unit of time

**offensive** (ə fens′iv) *adj.*    1. attacking or for attack    2. unpleasant; disgusting    3. insulting—*n.*    attitude or position of attack

**priceless** (prīs′lis) *adj.*    of very great value; invaluable; inestimable

**priority** (prī ôr′ə tē) *n.*    1. coming before in time or order, rank, importance    2. a preceding right to get by or do something before others    3. something given attention before something else

**stabilize** (stā′bə līz′) *v.*    1. to make firm    2. to keep from changing    3. to give steadiness (to a plane or ship)

**temperament** (tem′prə mənt) *n.*    1. one's natural disposition; nature    2. a nature that is excitable, moody, etc.

---

fat, āpe, cär; ten, ēven; is, bīte; gō, hôrn, tool, look; oil, out; up, fʉr; get; joy; yet; chin; she; thin, *th*en; zh, leisure; ŋ, ring; ə for *a* in *ago, e* in *agent, i* in *sanity, o* in *comply, u* in *focus;* ' as in *able* (ā′b'l)

Read the following list of Review Words. Then in each space below write the word that best completes the sentence.

| | | | | |
|---|---|---|---|---|
| ancestry | decisive | frequency | priceless | stabilize |
| brutality | exemplify | offensive | priority | temperament |

1. The _____ of rain determines the underground water table.

2. A _____ Picasso painting which had been stolen over ten years ago was recently found by the F.B.I. during a drug raid.

3. Training wheels on a youngster's bicycle are added to _____ it until the child learns to ride on two wheels.

4. A male employer who makes _____ personal remarks to a female employee may be sued for sexual harassment.

5. Some people consider scientific experimentation on animals a form of

_____ .

6. In an emergency room, the patients are treated in a _____ based on the seriousness of their injuries, not their time of arrival.

7. Any colt of the Kentucky Derby winner Secretariat or his offspring is very valuable because of his or her _____ .

8. Miss America is supposed to _____ the best qualities of American womanhood.

9. The destruction of the Berlin Wall was a _____ step toward the reuniting of East Germany and West Germany.

10. Only dogs of a calm _____ should be allowed around small children.

## EXERCISE 3: REVIEW WORDS

Below are the Review Words for this chapter. Using your knowledge of suffixes, change each of them to the part of speech given below each blank. If you need help, use your dictionary. Check your answers in the back of the book.

1.  frequency _____
    adverb

2.  decisive _____
    noun

3.  priceless _____
    noun

4.  brutality _____
    adjective

5.  ancestry _____
    adjective

6.  offensive _____
    verb

7.  temperament _____
    adjective

8.  priority _____
    adjective

9.  exemplify _____
    noun

10. stabilize _____
    adjective

## EXERCISE 4: ADDING SUFFIXES

Add the suffixes to the five base words below. Use your spelling rules as guides. Check your answers in the back of the book.

1.  desolate + ion _____

2.  attain + able _____

3.  escalate + or _____

4.  convey + ance _____

5.  rely + ant _____

## EXERCISE 5: CHECKING SPELLING

Some of the words below are spelled incorrectly. Using your suffix spelling rules as guides, find the incorrectly spelled words and write them correctly in the blanks. Check your answers in the back of the book.

1.  preferible _____

2.  slippery _____

3.  confinment _____

4.  acquaintance _____

5.  permissable _____

6.  skinnyness _____

7.  futility _____

8.  propeler _____

9.  civillize _____

10. booster _____

# NEW WORDS I

**acquisition** (ak′wə zish′ən) *n.*    1. something gained by one's own efforts    2. something gotten as one's own

**authoritarian** (ə thôr′ə ter′ē ən) *adj.*    requiring unquestioning obedience to authority, as that of a dictator—*n.*    a person who believes in or practices such obedience

**consolidate** (kən säl′ə dāt′) *v.*    1. to combine into one; unite    2. to make or become strong or stable [the troops *consolidated* their position]

**deprivation** (dep′rə vā′shən) *n.*    1. having something taken away or kept away    2. a loss

**fluency** (floo′ən sē) *n.*    the ability to speak or write smoothly or effortlessly

**graphic** (graf′ik) *adj.*    describing or being described in vivid detail; vivid

**laborious** (lə bôr′ē əs) *adj.*    involving or calling for much hard work; difficult

**methodical** (mə thäd′i k'l) *adj.*    characterized by method; orderly; systematic

**monetary** (män′ə ter′ē) *adj.*    1. of or connected with money    2. of the coinage or currency of a country

**nonpartisan** (nän pär′tə z'n) *adj.*    not controlled or influenced by any single political party

fat, āpe, cär; ten, ēven; is, bīte; gō, hôrn, tool, look; oil, out; up, fur; get; joy; yet; chin; she; thin, *th*en; zh, leisure; ŋ, ring; ə for *a* in *ago*, *e* in *agent*, *i* in *sanity*, *o* in *comply*, *u* in *focus*; ′ as in *able* (ā′b'l)

Fill in the correct word to complete each sentence below. Check your answers in the back of the book.

acquisitions          consolidate          fluency          laborious          monetary
authoritarian          deprivation          graphic          methodical          nonpartisan

1. Loan companies that _____ your debts into one often charge high rates of interest.

2. A good automobile mechanic will approach a difficult car problem in a _____ manner, ruling out one possibility at a time.

3. The League of Women Voters publishes _____ information so that the public can examine all sides of an issue.

4. The well-liked Prince Rainier III of Monaco is head of an _____ government.

5. There is a trend in television programs to show crimes in _____ detail in an effort to be "realistic."

6. Before Gutenberg's invention of the printing press in 1455, reproducing a book was a _____ task that had to be done by hand.

7. The Yap Islanders of the South Pacific use 18-foot-high stone rings for _____ purposes. Obviously, they don't have wallets.

8. _____ in oral English is usually not required to take college classes, but the ability to write English well may be necessary.

9. One of the New York City Police Department's recent _____ was a bullet-proof clipboard, capable of stopping a bullet from four yards away.

10. Military research has proven that sleep _____ results in irritability, hallucinations and loss of ability to concentrate.

**apprehensive** (ap′rə hen′siv) *adj.*    anxious; uneasy

**designate** (dez′ig nāt′) *v.*    1. to point out    2. to name    3. to appoint

**dignitary** (dig′nə ter′ē) *n.*    a person holding a high position

**fraudulent** (frô′jə lənt) *adj.*    based on or using deceit, trickery, or falsehood

**intimidate** (in tim′ə dāt′) *v.*    1. to make timid; make afraid    2. to force or prevent with threats or violence

**obligatory** (ə blig′ə tôr′ē, äb′lig ə tôr′ē) *adj.*    legally or morally binding; relating to obligation; required

**reliance** (ri lī′əns) *n.*    trust, dependence, or confidence

**reminiscent** (rem′ə nis′′nt) *adj.*    bringing to mind something from the past; suggestive [smells *reminiscent* of Christmas]

**sequential** (si kwen′shəl) *adj.*    having an order; following in time

**solitude** (säl′ə tōod′, säl′ə tyōod) *n.*    1. the state of being alone; isolation or remoteness    2. a lonely or isolated place

fat, ãpe, cär; ten, ēven; is, bīte; gō, hôrn, tōol, look; oil, out; up, fur; get; joy; yet; chin; she; thin, then; zh, leisure; ŋ, ring; ə for *a* in *ago, e* in *agent, i* in *sanity, o* in *comply, u* in *focus;* ′ as in *able* (ā′b′l)

Circle the letter before the word or phrase that best defines the italicized word in each sentence. Check your answers in the back of the book.

1. A person walking alone at night on dark streets in an unfamiliar city should be *apprehensive.*

   a. worried   b. confident   c. happy   d. relaxed

2. The only person *designated* as a Nobel Prize winner twice for an unshared prize was Linus Pauling. He won the Chemistry Prize in 1954 and the Peace Prize in 1962.

   a. dismissed   b. rejected   c. named   d. overlooked

3. The *dignitary* with the record for raising the most statues to himself is Generalissimo Trujillo, former president of the Dominican Republic. At the time of his assassination in 1961, there were more than 2,000.

   a. servant   b. follower   c. notable   d. nobody

4. A Bavarian cheesemaker was fined $166 for producing *fraudulent* Swiss cheese. He scooped the holes out mechanically when the ripening process failed to produce them naturally.

   a. rotten   b. misleading   c. real   d. aged

5. Some baseball pitchers try to *intimidate* batters by throwing balls at the person rather than over the plate.

   a. compliment   b. bribe   c. frighten   d. advise

6. In most states, it is *obligatory* to register a vehicle soon after purchase.

   a. optional   b. favorable   c. necessary   d. unnecessary

7. Teenagers sometimes resent their *reliance on* their parents but also fear total independence.

   a. dependence on   b. responsibility to   c. allowance from   d. flexibility towards

8. Often current fashions are *reminiscent of* earlier styles.

   a. rejecting of   b. stolen from   c. suggestive of   d. saved from

9. It would be very unlikely for a winning lottery ticket to consist of *sequential* numbers.

   a. random   b. ordered   c. backwards   d. illogical

10. The *solitude* of the bathroom is often the only place of escape for a mother of ten.

    a. crowdedness   b. activity   c. isolation   d. music

Place a *T* or an *F* in the space provided. Check your answers in the back of the book.

_____ 1. Fluency is usually a disadvantage.

_____ 2. A reminiscence involves memory.

_____ 3. A boss is a designated leader.

_____ 4. Reliance on someone else makes you more independent.

_____ 5. A nonpartisan vote would be divided along party lines.

## EXERCISE 9: ANALOGIES

In previous analogy exercises you looked for pairs of words that were synonyms or antonyms. This exercise contains a new type as well. In this kind of analogy the relationship of the pairs of words is CLASSIFICATION : EXAMPLE. The second word of each pair is an example of the first:

tree : oak :: obsolete : hoop skirts

Determine which of the three kinds is used in each group below. If the words are synonyms, put *S* in the blank. If they are antonyms, write *A*. If the relationship is a classification example, put *C*. Then fill in the blank to make the second pair agree with the first. Check your answers in the back of the book.

\_\_\_\_ 1. offensive : objectionable ::
acquisition : \_\_\_\_

    a. loss  b. sacrifice  c. theft
    d. possession

\_\_\_\_ 2. brutality : beating ::
dignitary : \_\_\_\_

    a. maid  b. president  c. clerk
    d. teller

\_\_\_\_ 3. ancestry : great-grandmother ::
monetary system : \_\_\_\_

    a. bank  b. government  c. coin
    d. bankrupt

\_\_\_\_ 4. frequency : rarity ::
deprivation : \_\_\_\_

    a. lacking  b. dieting  c. poverty
    d. plenty

\_\_\_\_ 5. temperament : nasty ::
graphic aid : \_\_\_\_

    a. map  b. art  c. music
    d. treasure

## EXERCISE 10: MATCHING MEANINGS

Write the letter of the word that means the opposite of the word in the first column. Check your answers in the back of the book.

_____ 1. consolidate          a. genuine

_____ 2. apprehensive          b. reassure

_____ 3. fraudulent          c. democratic

_____ 4. intimidate          d. confident

_____ 5. authoritarian          e. separate

## EXERCISE 11: WORD CONTRASTS

In each group below, circle the word that does not mean what the others mean. Check your answers in the back of the book.

1. methodical     orderly     careless     systematic
2. laborious     easy     effortless     relaxing
3. obligatory     compulsory     required     optional
4. sequential     random     following     ordered
5. solitude     loneliness     companionship     isolation

## EXERCISE 12: SENTENCE COMPLETION

Complete each sentence in your own words. Sample answers are provided in the back of the book.

1. John was happy with his new *acquisition* at first; afterward, _____

   _____.

2. Sylvia was able to *consolidate* her loans within _____

   _____.

3. Employees complain of *authoritarian* bosses like _____

   _____.

4. Sleep *deprivation* is quickly made up; as soon as _____

   _____.

5. *Fluency* in Spanish has many advantages whereas _____

   _____.

6.  Mnemonic devices are most effective when cues are very *graphic;* in fact, _____

    _____ .

7.  Bookkeeping can be *laborious;* moreover, _____

    _____ .

8.  It is best to take a *methodical* approach; if you don't, _____

    _____ .

9.  *Monetary* rewards are less _____

    _____ .

10. The bill had *nonpartisan* support; more important, _____

    _____ .

11. The leader was *designated* after _____

    _____ .

12. Visiting *dignitaries* usually _____

    _____ .

13. There have been several cases of *fraudulent* claims; accordingly, _____

    _____ .

14. Soldiers want to *intimidate* the enemy so that _____

    _____ .

15. Attendance is not *obligatory* even though _____

    _____ .

16. *Reliance* on stockbrokers is another _____

    _____ .

17. I enjoy *solitude* as long as _____

    _____ .

18. She had an *apprehensive* feeling; furthermore, _____

    _____ .

19. The teacher's manner was *reminiscent* of my father although _____

    _____ .

20. *Sequential* information is easy to remember, provided _____

    _____ .

# ADVANCED WORDS

**abortive** (ə bôrt′iv) *adj.*   unsuccessful; fruitless

**electorate** (ē lek′tər it) *n.*   all those qualified to vote in an election

**emphatic** (im fat′ik) *adj.*   1. felt or done with force of expression, action, etc.   2. using stress in speaking, etc.

**equitable** (ek′wit ə b′l) *adj.*   fair; just (said of actions, results of actions, etc.)

**erratic** (er rat′ik, e rat′ik, i rat′ik) *adj.*   1. irregular; random   2. strange

**fallible** (fal′ə b′l) *adj.*   1. liable to make a mistake   2. able to be fooled

**insightful** (in sīt′fəl) *adj.*   having the ability to see and understand clearly the inner nature of things, esp. by intuition

**liquidate** (lik′wə dāt′) *v.*   1. to pay (a debt)   2. to convert into cash   3. to get rid of, as by killing

**longevity** (län jev′ə tē) *n.*   long life

**reactionary** (rē ak′shə ner′ē) *adj.*   desiring to move back to a former or less advanced condition (especially in politics)—*n.*   someone favoring the return to former conditions

fat, āpe, cär; ten, ēven; is, bīte; gō, hôrn, to͞ol, look; oil, out; up, fʉr; get; joy; yet; chin; she; thin, then; zh, leisure; ŋ, ring; ə for *a* in *ago, e* in *agent, i* in *sanity, o* in *comply, u* in *focus;* ' as in *able* (ā′b′l)

**90**   *CHAPTER FIVE: SUFFIXES*

Fill in the correct word to complete each sentence below. Check your answers in the back of the book.

| abortive | emphatic | erratic | insightful | longevity |
|----------|----------|---------|------------|-----------|
| electorate | equitable | fallible | liquidate | reactionary |

1. In 1988, George Bush was _____ in stating that he would not raise income taxes; he often repeated, "Read my lips, no new taxes."

2. If anyone today proposed that all Americans go back to the use of kerosene lamps in place of electricity, almost everyone would call that person a _____.

3. Former President Jimmy Carter's _____ attempt to rescue the Iranian hostages probably cost him many votes in the 1984 presidential race.

4. The American judicial system is based on the theory that a group of jurors will arrive at an _____ decision.

5. Shigechiyo Izumi of Japan held the _____ record, having lived to the age 120 years 237 days.

6. A good teacher realizes that he or she is _____ and welcomes corrections by students.

7. The police may recognize that a driver is drunk by the _____ movements of his or her vehicle.

8. The largest mafia killing was in 1931, when enemies of top gangster Salvatore Maranzano managed to _____ him and 40 of his allies.

9. The 1824 U.S. Presidential election was won by John Adams, even though a larger portion of the _____ voted for Andrew Jackson. The electoral vote was so close that the decision went to the House of Representatives, which elected Adams.

10. We hope our Presidents are _____ as well as intelligent when dealing with other world leaders.

Fill in the puzzle below in pencil. The clues with an asterisk (*) refer to words in New Words lists in previous chapters. You can also check the word list on the inside front cover of this book. Check your answers in the back of the book.

**Across**

*1. Old-fashioned
5. T.V., newspapers, etc.
8. Antonym of *down*
10. Antonym of *amateur*
11. Abbr. for *id est*
12. Antonym of *off*
13. Abbr. for *touchdown*
*15. Facts
17. Abbr. for a subject in high school
*18. Type of art
19. Initials of actress Ruth Gordon
20. Sound of laughter
21. He, she, and _____
*22. Schemes
23. Donkey
24. "To _____ or not to _____, that is the question."
25. Initials of actor Carl Reiner
26. Abbr. for *northeast*
27. Antonym of *fail,* as on a test
28. Abbr. for *Alcoholics Anonymous*
29. Utilize
31. One news medium
32. Abbr. for *mountain*
33. Groups of words
35. Make fun of
37. Abbr. for *North Carolina*
39. Musical note (sound)
41. Antonym of *antonym*
46. Cantaloupe or honeydew
47. Antonym of *she*
*48. Out of use
49. To mail off

**Down**

*1. Equipment
2. Abbr. for *railroad*
*3. Thickness, e.g.
*4. Personal quality
5. Antonym of *you*
6. Abbr. for *dead on arrival*
*7. Complicated
9. Make happy
11. Hint or imply
14. Day of the month
*15. Hate
*16. Annoys
*17. Event
30. Antonym of *nonsense*
34. Catholic sisters
36. Bottom of a shoe
38. Past tense of sit
40. Finish
42. Antonym of *yes*
43. Abbr. for *obstetrician*
44. Spanish word for *I*
45. Abbreviation for *milliliter*

Choose from your outside reading ten words you would like to learn, and write them in the blanks below. When you look the words up in the dictionary, pay particular attention to the etymologies, including suffixes. Pronounce each word, put the definition in your own words, use the word in a sentence, make up a mnemonic, and put the word on a flash card for regular review.

1. _____

2. _____

3. _____

4. _____

5. _____

6. _____

7. _____

8. _____

9. _____

10. _____

# chapter 6

# PREFIXES

pre·scribe

4·23

B.C. by permission of Johnny Hart and Field Enterprises, Inc.

Whereas a suffix is added to the end of a word or a word base and has the primary function of changing its part of speech, a prefix goes in front of the base and changes its meaning. For example, the root *ject* (also spelled *jac* or *jet*) means *throw*. A jacket is something you throw over your shoulders, jacks are metal pieces thrown in a game, and planes move by jet propulsion, or throwing air out. In the list below, various prefixes have been added to this root. Notice how the meanings change.

| Prefix | Meaning | Word | Definition |
|--------|---------|------|------------|
| **ab** | from, down | abject | miserable (cast down) |
| **ad** | to | adjacent | next to (thrown to) |
| **con** | with, together | conjecture | guesswork (thrown together) |
| **de** | from, down | dejected | downcast |
| **e** | out | eject | throw out |
| **in** | into | inject | throw in |
| **inter** | between | interject | interrupt (throw between) |
| **ob** | against | object | oppose, disapprove (throw against) |
| **pro** | forward | projector | machine that throws an image forward |
| **re** | back | reject | throw back |
| **sub** | under | subject | to place under the control of another (throw under) |

Breaking words into recognizable parts is actually something you do automatically. The more word parts you know, the faster your vocabulary will develop. This is the reason that people who know a foreign language based on Latin (Spanish, French, Italian, Portuguese, and Romanian) have an advantage on vocabulary tests. More than half of our English words are derived either directly from Latin, or from Latin through Old French. Sometimes the new word conveys its meaning unchanged from the word parts, as in the word *eject,* which means *throw out.* At other times, the meaning of the word has changed over time so that the meanings of the separate parts no longer add up to the meaning of the word, although they do provide a clue, as in *conjecture.*

Sometimes a prefix will have more than one meaning. For example, *in* sometimes means *not,* as in *infrequent,* sometimes means *into,* as in *inside,* and sometimes means *very* (*inflammable* means *very flammable*). When you are unsure which meaning applies, you can use the context to figure it out or look up the derivation in the dictionary.

## Spelling Variations

Spellings of the word parts have also changed over the past 2000 years. For example, the prefix *con* means *with* or *together.* However, the prefix changes to *co* before a vowel (*cooperate*), *col* before *l* (*collect*), *com* before *p, b,* or *m* (*compromise*), and *cor* before *r* (*correct*). The main reason for these changes is that it's difficult for English speakers to pronounce words like *con*mitment or *con*rect. Several other prefixes follow this principle of changing their spellings to reflect pronunciation. Usually the last letter of the prefix changes to match the first letter of the base. The prefix *ob*, meaning *against*, changes to *oc* before *c* (*occupy*), *of* before *f* (*offense*), *op* before *p* (*oppose*), and *o* before *m* (*omit*).

# Types of Prefixes

Prefixes can be grouped according to their meanings. Learning them in groups helps you remember them.

### Negative Prefixes

The following prefixes have negative meanings.

| Prefix | Meaning | Examples |
|---|---|---|
| **anti,** *ant* | against | antisocial, antonym |
| **contra,** *contro,* *con* | against | contrary, controversial contrast |
| **ob,** *oc* (before *c*) *of* (before *f*) *op* (before *p*) *o* (before *m*) | against | obstruct, occupy offense oppose omit |
| **dis,** *dif* (before *f*) | not, apart | disbelief, different |
| **in,** *im* (before *p, b, m*) *il* (before *l*) *ir* (before *r*) | not | inability, immature illegal irregular |
| **non,** *n* | not | nonsense, never |
| **un** | not, reverse an action | unscrupulous, untie |
| **mis** | wrong | misspell, misinform |

### Placement Prefixes

Another group of prefixes concerns the placement or direction of things: whether they are down, behind, in front, between, etc.

| Prefix | Meaning | Examples |
|---|---|---|
| **ab,** *a* | away, down, from | abnormal, atypical |
| **de** | away, down, from | defrost, descend |
| **ad,** *ac* (before *c* or *q*) *af* (before *f*) *ag* (before *g*) *an* (before *n*) *ap* (before *p*) *ar* (before *r*) *as* (before *s*) *at* (before *t*) *a* (before *sc, sp, st*) | to | adjoining, accept afford aggravate annex appear arrive assembly attend ascend |

| con, com (before b, p, m) | with, together | conclusion, complete, |
| *co* (before a vowel) | | coauthor |
| *col* (before *l*) | | collect |
| *cor* (before *r*) | | correct |
| ex, *e* (before b, d, g, l, m, n, v) | out, former | exile, ex-president, emerge |
| *ec* (before *c* or *s*) | | eccentric |
| *ef* (before *f*) | | effect |
| in, *en* | into, very | invaluable, entrust |
| *em, im* (before b, p, m) | | embrace, impress |
| *intro, intra* | | introduce, intravenous |
| inter | between | intermission |
| per | through, by, thorough | persist, perfume, perfect |
| pro, *pur* | forward, before, for | proceed, pursue |
| re, *retro* | back | return, retroactive |
| sub, *suc* (before *c*) | under, below | subnormal, succeed |
| *suf* (before *f*) | | suffer |
| *sup* (before *p*) | | suppose |
| *sus* (before c, p, t) | | suspect |
| super, *sur* | above, beyond | supervise, surface |
| trans | across | translate |

## Time Prefixes

Another group of prefixes deals with the location of things in time: whether they are before, after, and so on.

| Prefix | Meaning | Examples |
| --- | --- | --- |
| post | after | postpone, postgraduate |
| pre | before | premature, preliminary |
| re | again | replica, rediscover |

To check on your understanding of the common prefixes discussed in this chapter, complete the following exercise by providing your own example (one not given in the preceding list) for each prefix. Try to pick a word that will help you remember what the prefix means. For example, a good mnemonic for *ab* might be *absent* because it means *away*. Check in a dictionary that provides word origins to be sure your word is based on the right prefix.

| Prefix | Definition | Example |
|---|---|---|
| a, ab | away, down, from | _____ |
| ad, ac, af, ag, an, ap, ar, as, at, a | to | _____ |
| ant, anti | against | _____ |
| con, com, co, col, cor | with, together | _____ |
| contra, contro, con | against | _____ |
| de | away, down, from | _____ |
| dis, dif | not, apart | _____ |
| ex, e, ec, ef | out, former | _____ |
| en, in, em, im, intra, intro | not, into, very, within | _____ |
| in, im, il, ir | not | _____ |
| inter | between | _____ |
| mis | wrong | _____ |
| n, non | not | _____ |
| ob, oc, of, op, o | against | _____ |
| per | through, by, thorough | _____ |
| post | after | _____ |
| pre | before | _____ |
| pro, pur | forward, before, for | _____ |
| re | again | _____ |
| re, retro | back | _____ |
| sub, suc, suf, sup, sus | under, below | _____ |
| super, sur | above, beyond | _____ |
| trans | across | _____ |
| un | not, reverse an action | _____ |

Before you look at the definitions for the Review Words on the next page, use the prefixes in this chapter to fill in the blanks below. Check your answers on the next page.

**Review Word**

1. _____ normal
2. _____ mature
3. _____ versial
4. _____ existent
5. _____ mortal
6. _____ ile
7. _____ claim
8. _____ trieve
9. _____ struct
10. _____ dote

**Definition**

*away* from (not) normal

*before* the proper or usual time

subject to argument (*against* each other)

*not* real; imaginary

living or lasting forever (*not* mortal)

force *out* of one's country

announce publicly (cry *forth*)

to get *back*

block or hinder (build *against*)

something to counteract poison or evil (*against* poison)

# REVIEW WORDS

**abnormal** (ab nôr′m'l) *adj.*    not normal, average, or typical; irregular

**antidote** (an′tə dōt′) *n.*    1. a remedy to counteract a poison    2. anything that works against an evil

**controversial** (kän′trə vʉr′shəl) *adj.*    causing much argument or disagreement; debatable

**exile** (eks′īl, eg′zīl) *n.*    a prolonged living away from one's country, usually enforced

**immortal** (im mort′'l) *adj.*    1. living forever    2. having lasting fame

**nonexistent** (nōn′eg zist′ənt) *n.*    1. not real    2. not living    3. not occurring

**obstruct** (əb strukt′) *v.*    1. to block or stop up (a passage)    2. to stop or slow down (progress, etc.)    3. to cut off from view

**premature** (prē′mə choor′, prē′mə tyoor′) *adj.*    happening, done, arriving, etc. before the proper or usual time; too early

**proclaim** (prō klām′) *v.*    to announce officially; announce to be

**retrieve** (ri trēv′) *v.*    1. to get back; recover    2. to restore    3. to make good (a loss, error, etc.)    4. to recover (information) from data stored in a computer    5. to find and bring back

fat, āpe, cär; ten, ēven; is, bīte; gō, hôrn, tōol, look; oil, out; up, fʉr; get; joy; yet; chin; she; thin, *th*en; zh, leisure; ŋ, ring; ə for *a* in *ago*, *e* in *agent*, *i* in *sanity*, *o* in *comply*, *u* in *focus*; ' as in *able* (ā′b'l)

Read the following list of Review Words. Then in each space below write the word that best completes that sentence.

| | | | | |
|---|---|---|---|---|
| abnormal | controversial | immortal | obstruct | proclaim |
| antidote | exile | nonexistent | premature | retrieve |

1. Sometimes the _____ for loneliness is doing things for others.

2. "Blue babies" have an _____ opening between the chambers of their hearts.

3. In ancient Rome, political enemies were often forced into _____ by the ruling powers.

4. The proverb, "Don't count your chickens before they hatch," means don't make _____ judgements.

5. While most dogs today only _____ the newspaper, some are still used to bring back wild game.

6. Mermaids are historically _____, but they have been part of mythology at least since the days of ancient Greece.

7. Birth announcements are the modern way to _____ the birth of a child.

8. The role of women in the military is _____, especially their role in combat.

9. Cholesterol is dangerous because of its ability to _____ the flow of blood to the heart.

10. The _____ ballet, "The Nutcracker Suite," is widely performed every Christmas.

**acclimate** (ak′lə māt′, ə klī′mət) *v.*    to accustom or become accustomed to a new climate or environment

**atypical** (ā tip′ə k′l) *adj.*    not typical or regular; abnormal

**coincide** (kō′in sīd′) *v.*    1. to occur at the same time or place    2. to be in agreement; to be similar or identical [our interests *coincide*]

**collaborate** (kə lab′ə rāt′) *v.*    1. to work together, esp. in literary or scientific work    2. to cooperate with the enemy

**intervene** (in′tər vēn′) *v.*    to come between

**irrelevant** (i rel′ə vənt) *adj.*    not to the point; not relating to the subject

**misconstrue** (mis′kən strōō′) *v.*    to misunderstand; misinterpret

**posterity** (päs ter′ə tē) *n.*    future generations

**subdue** (səb dōō′, səb dyōō′) *v.*    1. to conquer    2. to control    3. to make less intense; reduce; soften    4. to repress (emotions)

**unbiased** (un bī′əst) *adj.*    fair; without prejudice

fat, āpe, cär; ten, ēven; is, bīte; gō, hôrn, tōōl, look; oil, out; up, fur; get; joy; yet; chin; she; thin, *th*en; zh, leisure; ŋ, ring; ə for *a* in *ago, e* in *agent, i* in *sanity, o* in *comply, u* in *focus;* ' as in *able* (ā′b'l)

# EXERCISE 4: FILL-IN

Write in the proper word to complete each sentence below. Check your answers in the back of the book.

| | | | | |
|---|---|---|---|---|
| acclimate | coincide | intervention | misconstrues | subdued |
| atypical | collaborated | irrelevant | posterity | unbiased |

1. Even though television news programs are supposed to be _____ , a critical thinker may discover that only a particular point of view is expressed.

2. Multiple births are _____ in human beings; most human mothers give birth to only one child at a time.

3. A marriage is often made stronger when at least some of the interests of the spouses _____ .

4. Some people splash water on themselves to _____ their bodies to the temperature of the water before jumping or diving into a swimming pool.

5. President Theodore Roosevelt became the first American to win the Nobel Peace Prize as a result of his _____ to help settle the Russo-Japanese war.

6. When writing a term paper, try not to include _____ information.

7. We should take care of our environment, not only for ourselves, but also for our _____ .

8. Decorators tend to use _____ colors for a bedroom so that the room will have a calming effect.

9. It can be very embarrassing when a friend of the opposite sex _____ your feelings and believes that you are sexually attracted to him or her.

10. Although Gilbert and Sullivan _____ on many successful light operas, the two hated each other so much that they only communicated through their agent.

# NEW WORDS II

**adjacent** (ə jā′sənt) *adj.*   next to

**depreciate** (di prē′shē āt′) *v.*   1. to reduce in value or price; to make seem less important

**disreputable** (dis rep′yoo tə b'l) *adj.*   1. not respectable; having a bad reputation   2. dirty or shabby

**enlighten** (in līt′'n) *v.*   1. to free from ignorance, prejudice, etc.   2. to inform

**entice** (in tīs′) *v.*   to tempt with hope of reward or pleasure; to try to involve by offering rewards

**excerpt** (ek surpt′) *v.*   to select or quote (passages from a book, etc.); extract—*n.*   (ek′surpt′) a passage selected or quoted; an extract

**irrational** (i rash′ən'l) *adj.*   unreasonable; senseless; absurd

**succumb** (sə kum′) *v.*   1. to give in to [to *succumb* to persuasion]   2. to give up   3. to die [to *succumb* to a plague]

**superfluous** (se pur′floo əs, soo pur′floo əs) *adj.*   more than needed; extra; unnecessary [a *superfluous* remark]

**surpass** (sər pas′) *v.*   to do better than [riches *surpassing* belief]

fat, āpe, cär; ten, ēven; is, bīte; gō, hôrn, tool, look; oil, out; up, fur; get; joy; yet; chin; she; thin, *th*en; zh, leisure; ŋ, ring; ə for *a* in *ago, e* in *agent, i* in *sanity, o* in *comply, u* in *focus;* ′ as in *able* (ā′b'l)

Circle the letter before the word or phrase that best defines the italicized word in each sentence. Check your answers in the back of the book.

1. When your children are too big to sleep in your hotel room, you probably will want them to stay in the *adjacent* room.

   a. prettier  b. next  c. most expensive  d. smallest

2. If the value of a house *depreciates,* you might have to sell it for less than you paid.

   a. decreases  b. increases  c. stabilizes  d. is destroyed

3. It was considered so *disreputable* to show one's legs in the Victorian era that even piano legs had covers.

   a. honest  b. unusual  c. fun loving  d. offensive

4. Contrary to popular belief, most educated people during the time of Columbus were *enlightened* enough to realize that the world was not flat.

   a. educated  b. stupid  c. confused  d. friendly

5. Stripper Gypsy Rose Lee *enticed* her audience but never removed all of her clothing.

   a. tempted  b. cheated  c. begged  d. fooled

6. When orchestras give concerts, they often play *excerpts* from several different symphonies.

   a. music  b. selections  c. instruments  d. original works

7. It is *irrational* to think that you can solve all of your friend's problems.

   a. bright  b. cruel  c. unreasonable  d. evil

8. In the James Bond movies, all the females eventually *succumbed* to the charms of the hero.

   a. expected  b. surrendered  c. adjusted  d. escaped

9. Even dual income families feel that they never have *superfluous* money.

   a. enough  b. extra  c. any  d. plenty of

10. Because Hank Aaron went to bat 2,890 more times than Babe Ruth did, it is questionable whether he really *surpassed* the home run record set by Ruth.

    a. succumbed to  b. accepted  c. exceeded  d. equalled

## EXERCISE 6: TRUE-FALSE

Place a *T* or an *F* in the space provided. Check your answers in the back of the book.

_____ 1. Two people can collaborate when writing a movie script.

_____ 2. You enlighten someone by carefully avoiding telling him or her certain facts.

_____ 3. If the times of two sports events coincide, you can attend both.

_____ 4. An excerpt from a book must be shorter than the book.

_____ 5. When someone intervenes in your affairs, she minds her own business.

## EXERCISE 7: ANALOGIES

The analogies below are of the three types you have already done. First, decide if the words in the first pair are synonyms, if they are antonyms, or if the second word is an example of the first. If they are synonyms, write *S* in the blank. If they are antonyms, write *A*. If they are classification : example, write *C*. Then choose the word that best completes the analogy. Check your answers in the back of the book.

_____ 1. abnormal : unusual ::
  surpass : _____

  a. explain  b. outdo  c. talk about
  d. fail

_____ 2. premature : baby ::
  adjacent : _____

  a. adjoining  b. room  c. ocean
  d. separate

_____ 3. immortal : human ::
  misconstrue : _____

  a. feelings  b. misrepresent
  c. understand  d. mischief

_____ 4. exile : banish ::
  acclimate : _____

  a. adjust  b. suffer  c. reject  d. climb

_____ 5. retrieve : recover ::
  irrational : _____

  a. ideas  b. logical  c. crazy  d. simple

Write the letter of the word that means the opposite of the word in the first column.
Check your answers in the back of the book.

| | | | |
|---|---|---|---|
| _____ | 1. entice | a. | lacking |
| _____ | 2. irrelevant | b. | ancestry |
| _____ | 3. irrational | c. | crucial |
| _____ | 4. superfluous | d. | sane |
| _____ | 5. posterity | e. | drive away |

## EXERCISE 9: WORD CONTRASTS

In each group below, circle the word that does not mean what the others mean.
Check your answers in the back of the book.

1. atypical     unique     characteristic   abnormal
2. unbiased     unfair     partial     opinionated
3. disreputable     unscrupulous     dishonorable     distinguished
4. depreciate     discredit     increase     cheapen
5. succumb     oppose     defy     withstand

## EXERCISE 10: SENTENCE COMPLETION

Complete each sentence in your own words. Sample answers are provided in the
back of the book.

1. If you do not become *acclimated* to the thin air in most mountain resorts, _____
_____.

2. The two houses were on *adjacent* lots; moreover, _____
_____.

3. A snowstorm in Southern California is *atypical*, yet _____
_____.

4. In case an earthquake and a power blackout *coincide*, _____
_____.

5. When two people *collaborate* on a business deal, _____
_____.

6. If the value of the dollar *depreciates*, _____ _____.

7. As long as some car repair shops are *disreputable*, _____ _____.

8. A general education is supposed to *enlighten* college students; however, _____ _____.

9. Some people find food so *enticing* that _____ _____.

10. After reading an *excerpt* from the latest best selling book, _____ _____.

11. It is not wise to try to *intervene* when two dogs are fighting; in fact, _____ _____.

12. *Irrational* behavior is often exhibited when _____ _____.

13. During an argument, it is *irrelevant* to _____ _____.

14. A teacher can *misconstrue* a situation; for example, _____ _____.

15. After a person's death, that individual may live in *posterity* if _____ _____.

16. It is difficult to *subdue* people when _____ _____.

17. During a heat wave, some people *succumb* to the heat, which means _____ _____.

18. One way to lose *superfluous* weight is to diet; another _____ _____.

19. Whenever you try to *surpass* the accomplishments of people like your friends and family, _____ _____.

20. A jury should be *unbiased* because _____ _____.

# ADVANCED WORDS

**agnostic** (ag näs′tik) *n.*   a person who does not know whether God exists

**dissident** (dis′ə dənt) *adj.*   not agreeing; dissenting—*n.*   a dissenter

**elude** (i lōōd′) *v.*   1. to avoid or escape from   2. to escape notice or understanding [his name *eludes* me]

**inanimate** (in an′ə mit) *adj.*   not moving; lifeless

**inexplicable** (in eks pli′kə b'l) *adj.*   that which cannot be explained

**obscure** (əb skyoor′) *adj.*   1. dim; dark [the *obscure* light]   2. not easily seen; faint [an *obscure* figure]   3. vague; ambiguous [an *obscure* explanation]   4. hidden [an *obscure* village] 5. not well known [an *obscure* scientist]—*v.*   1. to hide or make less visible [a success that *obscured* earlier failures]   2. to make less intelligible; to confuse [testimony that *obscures* the issues]

**permeate** (pur′mē āt) *v.*   to pass into or through and affect every part of [ink *permeates* blotting paper]

**posthumous** (päs′choo məs) *adj.*   1. published after the author's death   2. arising or continuing after one's death

**remuneration** (ri myoo′nə rā′shən) *n.*   payment for [work, a loss, etc.]

**transcend** (tran send′) *v.*   1. go beyond the limits of; exceed   2. surpass; excel

fat, āpe, cär; ten, ēven; is, bīte; gō, hôrn, tōōl, look; oil, out; up, fur; get; joy; yet; chin; she; thin, *then*; zh, leisure; ŋ, ring; ə for *a* in *ago*, *e* in *agent*, *i* in *sanity*, *o* in *comply*, *u* in *focus*; ′ as in *able* (ā′b'l)

Use the Advanced Words to fill in the blanks in the sentences that follow. Check your answers in the back of the book.

| | | | | |
|---|---|---|---|---|
| agnostic | elude | inexplicable | permeate | remuneration |
| dissidents | inanimate | obscure | posthumous | transcends |

1. An _____ believes that it is impossible to know whether God exists.

2. Thomas Edison took a series of photographs and invented a machine that made the _____ characters appear to move. Thus, he created the first "motion pictures."

3. Leonard T. Fristoe is the prisoner who holds the record for the longest prison escape. He was able to _____ police for 46 years before his recapture in 1969.

4. The Grand Canyon is so spectacular, it _____ any written description.

5. Shirley Temple's almost two million dollars _____ from movie roles by the age of 10 was more than any other star made in a similar period of time.

6. Wherever you find the President speaking, you usually find _____ protesting outside.

7. Vincent Van Gogh, though he was an _____ artist in his lifetime, is now highly regarded.

8. At a military funeral, the next of kin is given an American flag as a _____ honor to the dead person.

9. There are now medical patches for seasickness and cigarette addiction that work by slowly releasing medication which can _____ the skin and enter the bloodstream.

10. The Air Force Operation Blue Book was an attempt to explain all UFO sightings. However, more than a dozen of the sightings were _____ .

Fill in the puzzle in pencil so you can change your mind if necessary. Remember that the clues with an asterisk (*) refer to words from the New Words list in previous chapters. You can also check the word list on the inside front cover of this book. Check your answers in the back of the book.

### Across

*1. Bringing something of the past to mind
9. Antonym for *front*
13. Antonym for *odd*
14. Measurement in electricity
16. Kind of grain used for bread
17. Allow
*18. The ability to speak smoothly
19. Suffix meaning *like*, as in child_____, fool_____
20. Capital of Peru
*23. Having to do with money
29. Abbr. for *Norway*
*30. An important person
32. Part of the face
33. An unmarried girl
*35. Vivid
39. Abbr. for *amount*
*40. Information
42. Chemical sign for nickel
43. A person from one Arabian country
*44. Isolation
46. Where Adam and Eve lived
49. Abbr. for *Old Latin*
50. Colloquial for energy
51. Conveys
55. A small crawling insect
56. Everybody or everything
57. Suffix meaning *a person who does something* as in visit _____; profess_____
59. Dictionary abbreviation for *that is*
60. Abbr. for *touchdown*
61. Abbr. for *postscript*
*62. Unite

### Down

*1. Trust or confidence
2. Nights like the one before Christmas
*3. Orderly or systematic
4. Antonym of *out*
5. Nickname for Sally
6. The singular of 2 down
7. Not controlled by one political party
8. Abbr. for *tender loving care*
10. Suffix meaning *a person who does something* as in bank _____, or danc_____
11. Archaic word for *yes*
12. Antonym of *punishments*
15. Baseball player Cobb's first name
*21. To make afraid
22. Abbr. for *month*
23. Chemical sign for *magnesium*
24. Antonym of *off*
25. Same as 42 across
26. Abbr. for *extraterrestrial*
27. Abbr. for *teaching assistant*
28. Robert Young's monogram
31. Antonym of *out*
33. Constructed
34. Abbr. for *street*
35. Opening in a fence
36. Conjunction meaning *also*
37. Round baked desserts
38. Abbr. for *California*
40. Child's toys
41. Point of a pencil
44. Used for bathing
45. On
47. Antonym of *beginning*
48. Abbr. for *New Testament*
52. Snakelike sea creature
53. Past tense of *do*
54. Large body of water
58. Rod Serling's monogram

# EXERCISE 13: OWN WORDS

Choose ten words from your outside reading that you would like to learn, and write them in the spaces below. When you look the words up in the dictionary, pay particular attention to the etymologies, including prefixes. Pronounce each word, put the definition in your own words, use the word in a sentence, make up a mnemonic, and put the word on a flash card for regular review.

1. _____

2. _____

3. _____

4. _____

5. _____

6. _____

7. _____

8. _____

9. _____

10. _____

# MIDTERM REVIEW

## Review Words: Chapters 2–6

### I. Fill-in

Use the context to fill in the blanks in the following mystery story with words from the review list below. Then solve the mystery.

absurd
contemplating
conveyed

deduction
deliberate
elaborate

minute
nonexistent
ordeal

priceless
proclaiming
solemnly

### The Case of the Priceless Painting

Inspector Keane listed _____ as Mrs. Skeemer
                                    1
rapidly _____ her recent _____. Her
                2                                  3
_____ Picasso painting in its _____ frame had
          4                                          5
been stolen. She said that after taking a hot shower, she had opened the bathroom

door. At the same time, she had glanced out of the closed bathroom window and had

seen a man running across the lawn with the painting.

After glancing at the small bathroom, Inspector Keane spent only a

_____   _____ the facts. He didn't
            6                        7
_____ long before _____ the crime
            8                              9
_____.
      10
How did Inspector Keane arrive so quickly at his _____ that
                                                              11
Mrs. Skeemer's story was _____?
                                12

### Solution

If she had just stepped out of a hot shower in a closed room, the bathroom

window would have been steamed over and she couldn't have seen anyone through it!

## II. Sentence Completions

Circle the word that best completes each sentence.

1. _____ lines never meet. (Parallel, Immortal)

2. A _____ parent leaves poisons where children can reach them. (negligent, preliminary)

3. Because he was curious about where he came from, Alex Haley, the author of *Roots,* traced his _____ to his African origins. (temperament, ancestry)

4. The government _____ funds to various agencies. (exiles, appropriates)

5. It is difficult to _____ many problems at the same time. (retrieve, cope with)

6. If a matter is important, you make it a _____. (priority, frequency)

7. Miss America is supposed to _____ the best in America's young women. (exemplify, imply)

8. Each clan in Scotland has a(n) _____ tartan because traditionally each family group was identified by its clothes. (decisive, unique)

9. If the TV game show contestant gives a(n) _____ answer to a question, a duck quacks. (invalid, contemporary)

10. A landslide on a highway will _____ traffic. (obstruct, maneuver)

## III. True-False

If the sentence is true, write *T* in the blank. If it is false, write *F* in the blank.

_____ 1. Random brutality is offensive to most people.

_____ 2. Extreme neurotic behavior is abnormal.

_____ 3. Careful scientists try to avoid premature analysis of research findings.

_____ 4. The news media should be precise in reporting controversial events.

_____ 5. To negotiate a contract is never a complex task.

_____ 6. Police should try to stabilize a hostile situation before violence breaks out.

_____ 7. It is a calamity if a child drinks a poison for which there is no antidote.

_____ 8. An acute illness is never terminal.

Check your answers to the *Midterm Review: Review Words* in the back of the book.

## New Words: Chapters 2–6

### I. Sentence Completions

Circle the word that best completes each sentence.

1. A comet is an interesting _____. (phenomenon, fallacy)

2. _____ tests are easier for teachers to grade than essay tests. (Objective, Reminiscent)

3. Capital punishment is a _____ form of punishment. (monetary, drastic)

4. Arabia has a(n) _____ climate. (arid, frigid)

5. A _____ is a copy. (replica, posterity)

6. An _____ can be mechanical. (excerpt, apparatus)

7. Every military commander wants to _____ the enemy. (intrigue, subdue)

8. A dictionary gives the _____ of words. (attributes, derivations)

9. A _____ example is vivid. (graphic, sequential)

10. In times of war, military service is usually _____. (compulsory, irrelevant)

11. When two people enjoy the same things, their interests _____. (coincide, intervene)

12. Paying a traffic fine is _____. (obligatory, archaic)

13. It takes time to _____ to a new country. (consolidate, acclimate)

14. Geniuses are _____. (fraudulent, atypical)

15. Pablo Picasso's *Les Demoiselles d'Avignon,* painted in 1907, is considered the most significant work in the development toward modern _____ painting. (abstract, nonpartisan)

16. Being alone in a dark alley is liable to make you feel _____. (apprehensive, durable)

17. The houses of next-door neighbors are _____. (intricate, adjacent)

18. All lovers are _____. (intimate, implicit)

19. A memorial _____ a person or event. (commemorates, enlightens)

20. "She's a great gal" is a _____ expression. (colloquial, notorious)

## II. True-False

If the sentence is true, write *T* in the blank. If it is false write *F* in the blank.

_____ 1. To assess achievement, data are needed.

_____ 2. Under conditions of extreme deprivation, most people succumb to illness.

_____ 3. People who crave solitude like to collaborate.

_____ 4. A disreputable person is likely to default on a loan.

_____ 5. Bland food tends to have a mushy consistency.

_____ 6. Getting an unbiased opinion can be invaluable before making an important decision.

_____ 7. A shrewd person is irrational.

_____ 8. Naive people can misconstrue the intentions of others.

_____ 9. A difficult plight can aggravate an ulcer.

_____ 10. A world's record is easier to surpass than to attain.

_____ 11. A thesis statement is superfluous in a term paper.

_____ 12. A liberal detests change.

_____ 13. Criminals try to evade capture and foil the police.

_____ 14. Dignitaries can be intimidating.

_____ 15. The Irish ethnic group is known for its fluency.

_____ 16. When inflation escalates, the dollar depreciates.

_____ 17. Abridging a book makes it more concise.

_____ 18. One attribute of a hoax is deception.

_____ 19. "Patent pending" means that the patent is expected at a subsequent date.

_____ 20. Reliance on ambiguous information can lead you to unwanted problems.

## III. Fill-in

Using the words below, fill in the blanks in the story. Each word is used only once.

aptitude
authoritarian
chronic
compensate
criterion

designated
dilemma
endeavor
entice

exempt
exert
integrity
laborious

methodical
obsolete
pondered
shrewdness

skeptical
spontaneously
unscrupulous
venture

### The Doggie Jogger
by Peggy Jacobowitz

Before my husband and I bought our two Saint Bernards we made a solemn promise to take the dogs jogging morning and night, a(n) _____ 1 that we hoped would also reduce our waistlines. However, after the dogs arrived, we both felt _____ 2 about getting up at 6:00 A.M. and exercising the beasts. In fact, it came to seem like a horrible ordeal. Being people of high _____ 3, we tried to arrive at a fair solution to our _____ 4 based on who had the greater _____ 5 for the task. I thought this was my husband, since he was more muscular than I. I suggested that the _____ 6 also be the size of our waistlines, since his was clearly larger. However, my _____ 7 husband, not wishing to _____ 8 himself at that early hour, countered my suggestion with the argument that he should be _____ 9 because his _____ 10 back ailment prevented him from keeping both dogs from running should they spot a stray cat. Unconvinced by these weak arguments, I reluctantly assumed the duty.

As it turned out, being _____ 11 official doggie jogger was not only _____ 12 but also risky as well. A more _____ 13 person would have _____ 14 the dangers rather than _____ 15 setting out that first morning. Only one block from home, I found myself in a ridiculous situation. One dog spotted the milkman while the other spied a neighbor's dog. I quickly discovered that neither kind words nor _____ 16 commands could _____ 17 two large dogs to remain in one place. My _____ 18 could not _____ 19 for their strength. It was absurd to think I could resist. I let both leashes go, yelled "Last one home doesn't get breakfast!" and ran as fast as I could. The dogs, probably thinking I had seen something more interesting than they did, followed me. My

maneuver worked. Arriving home in one piece, I immediately decided that doggie jogging was a(n) _____ profession. Now the dogs never
                                               20

_____ beyond the back yard. They get less exercise, but then con-
                     21

sider: How much exercise would I get from a hospital bed with two dislocated shoulders and a broken leg?

Check your answers to the *Midterm Review: New Words* in the back of the book.

## Advanced Words: Chapters 2–6

### I. Sentence Completions

Circle the word that best completes each sentence.

1. The group that selects leaders is known as the _____. (collateral, electorate)

2. People who make mistakes are _____. (fallible, inanimate)

3. A salary is a form of _____. (guise, remuneration)

4. A logical argument is _____. (dubious, coherent)

5. Her name _____ me at the moment. (transcends, eludes)

6. Some people are _____ fans of ballet. (perennial, abortive)

7. The latest fashion is the _____. (juncture, mode)

8. An abandoned wreck is a _____. (derelict, hypocrite)

9. A corpse is _____. (erratic, defunct)

10. Obedience in the military is _____. (negligible, imperative)

11. An _____ stamp collector will be thrilled to find a printing error on a postage stamp. (obscure, avid)

### II. Synonyms and Antonyms

If the words in each pair are synonyms, write *S* in the blank. If they are antonyms, write *A* in the blank.

_____ 1. irate             belligerent

_____ 2. precipitate     perpetrate

_____ 3. feasible        futile

_____ 4. procrastinate   defer

## III. True-False

If the sentence is true, write *T* in the blank. If the sentence is false, write *F* in the blank.

_____ 1. Tangible assets can be liquidated.

_____ 2. Lethal substances increase longevity.

_____ 3. Late at night, desolate areas can appear ominous.

_____ 4. Agnostics don't usually belong to any denomination.

_____ 5. Reactionary people tend to be adamant in their beliefs.

_____ 6. Arbitrary decisions can appear inexplicable.

_____ 7. After a deluge, the ground is permeated with water.

_____ 8. An insightful judge makes equitable decisions.

_____ 9. Martyrs are usually cited posthumously.

_____ 10. Political dissidents are often so emphatic in their beliefs that the ruling powers want to imprison them.

Check your answers to the *Midterm Review: Advanced Words* in the back of the book.

# chapter 7

# ROOTS I

120

The roots of the English language come from two main sources: Anglo-Saxon and Latin.

## Anglo-Saxon Roots

The Anglo-Saxons, tribes who spoke Germanic dialects, invaded England around the fifth century A.D., and their language became known as Old English. Most of the small, common words in modern English came from Anglo-Saxon; *water, tree,* and *barn* are examples.

## Latin Roots

Most of the larger, more difficult English words, such as the ones presented in this book, come from Latin or from Greek through Latin. They came into English from four main sources.

The first source was the Roman occupation of England. Julius Caesar conquered England in 55 B.C., and his Latin-speaking troops remained there for nearly 500 years. The second source was the church. During the time of Anglo-Saxon rule, Christianity arrived in England with its Latin ceremonies and Latin-speaking priests. Words like *martyr, monk,* and *altar* came into use. The third source was the Norman conquest in A.D. 1066. William the Conqueror spoke Norman-French. Although Anglo-Saxon remained the language of the majority of English, many Old French words came into everyday use. Old French derived directly from Vulgar Latin, the everyday form of Latin spoken by the Romans. This combination of Anglo-Saxon, Norman-French, and Latin, which was spoken from about 1100 to 1500, is known as Middle English. You can see Middle English if you read the untranslated version of the *Canterbury Tales,* or any other work by Chaucer.

The fourth source of Latin (and Greek) in English was the revival of classical Latin and Greek culture in the beginning fifteenth century. During this period, which was known as the Renaissance, all educated Europeans used Latin or Greek for formal communication. Therefore, words were coming into English directly from Latin. Many of these were the same words that had already come in indirectly through Old French. English, therefore, has a number of word pairs in which one word is from Latin and the other is from Latin through Old French. For example, the words *retract* and *retreat* both mean *pull or draw back* and they come from the same prefix and root. However, notice the differences in their derivations.[1]

**re-tract** (ri trakt′) *vt., vi.* [ME. *retracten;* in sense 1 < L. *retractus,* pp. of *retrahere,* to draw back < *re-,* back + *trahere,* to DRAW; in sense 2 < MFr. *retracter* < L. *retractare,* to draw back, withdraw < *re-,* back + *tractare,* to pull, draw, freq. of *trahere*]

**re-treat** (ri trēt′) *n.* [ME. *retret* < OFr. *retraite* < pp. of *retraire,* to draw back < L. *retrahere:* see RETRACT]

*Retract* comes fairly directly into Middle English from Latin, but *retreat* comes indirectly through Old French.

---

[1]From *Webster's New World Dictionary, Third College Edition* (Victoria Neufeldt, Editor-in-Chief) (New York: Simon & Schuster, 1988). Copyright © 1988 by Simon & Schuster, Inc.

## Word Analysis

A **root** is a group of letters that has a particular meaning. The meaning and part of speech can be changed by adding prefixes and suffixes. You use your knowledge of roots in the same way you use your knowledge of base words. For example, if you have never seen the word *circumspect* before, you still probably have some idea that it has to do with sight. This is because you think of other words like *spectacles* and *spectator*, which contain the same root. If you didn't know the definition of the prefix *circum*, you would still most likely think of other words that begin the same way, such as *circum-navigate* (*circum = around + navigate = sail*). Therefore, you could make an educated guess that *circumspect* has to do with looking around. In fact, *circumspect* now means *cautious or careful* and describes someone who looks before leaping into anything.

People who can make these kinds of mental associations between familiar words and new words increase their vocabularies rapidly. For example, the combination of prefixes and suffixes added to the root *jet, jac, ject*, as listed in Chapter 6, unlocks dozens of words. To assist you in learning to make these associations more quickly, the next three chapters will present some of the most common roots used in English. Once you get a feel for identifying roots, you should try to do it on your own when you read. Words coming from the same root can be thought of as coming from the same family, and remembering one family is easier than remembering the several dozen separate words of similar derivation. Therefore, learning roots not only helps you recognize unfamiliar words, it also works as a mnemonic device. Get in the habit of looking at the derivations of words when you use your dictionary.

## Remembering Roots

One way to remember a word part is to relate it to a word you already know. For example, you could think of a game of jacks to remember the root *jac* (to throw). Another mnemonic device is visualization. For example, to remember *spec, spect, spic, spis* (*to see* or *look*), you could picture an inspector inspecting *spec* words.

On the next page are several of the words derived from the root *spec*, which is taught in this chapter. The words on the left are common words that you can use as mnemonics to remember the meaning of the root. The words on the right are New Words and Advanced Words in this chapter.

# New Roots

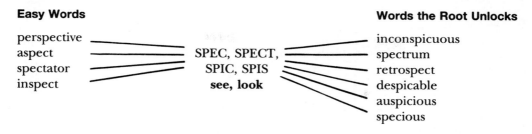

**Easy Words**

perspective
aspect
spectator
inspect

SPEC, SPECT,
SPIC, SPIS
**see, look**

**Words the Root Unlocks**

inconspicuous
spectrum
retrospect
despicable
auspicious
specious

Another root is *dic, dict, dit: say* or *speak*

**Easy Words**

contradict
verdict
dictation
dictator

DIC, DICT,
DIT
**say, speak**

**Words the Root Unlocks**

syndicate
abdicate
jurisdiction
indicative
edict
vindicate

As a mnemonic for *dic,* you might picture a *dict*ionary *speak*ing into a *Dict*aphone or taking *dict*ation from a *dict*ator.

A third root is *voc, vok: call*

**Easy Words**

vocation
provoke
vocal
vocalist

VOK, VOC
**call**

**Words the Root Unlocks**

irrevocable
provocative
advocate
evoke
avocation
equivocate

Picture a singer *voc*alizing while making a phone *call.*

A fourth root is *vers, vert, verg: turn*

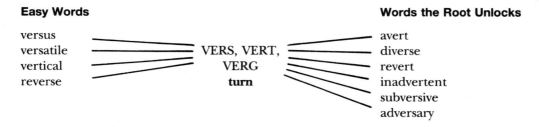

**Easy Words**

versus
versatile
vertical
reverse

VERS, VERT,
VERG
**turn**

**Words the Root Unlocks**

avert
diverse
revert
inadvertent
subversive
adversary

Picture a car going in re*vers*e while *turn*ing a corner while onlookers *turn* their heads to see what's going on.

A fifth root is *gen, gin: birth, origin, race*

**Easy Words**                                                    **Words the Root Unlocks**

genetic                                                           degenerate
generalize         GEN, GIN                                       generic
generation         **birth, origin,**                             ingenious
genuine            **race**                                       regenerate
                                                                  indigenous
                                                                  engender

Picture a new*born* baby who is a *gen*ius buying an ori*gin*al painting by Picasso.

## EXERCISE 1: ROOTS FILL-IN

To check on your understanding of the five common roots discussed in this chapter, complete the following exercise by providing your own example (one not given in the preceding list) for each root. Try to pick a word that will help you remember what the root means. Check in a dictionary that provides word origins to be sure your word is based on the right root.

| Root | Definition | Example |
|------|-----------|---------|
| dic, dict, dit | say, speak | _____ |
| gen, gin | birth, race, origin | _____ |
| spec, spect, spic, spis | see, look | _____ |
| vers, vert, verg | turn | _____ |
| voc, vok | call, voice | _____ |

Before you look at the definitions for the Review Words on the next page, use the roots in this chapter to fill in the blanks below. Check your answers on the next page.

1. — — — eralize       to draw a conclusion based on examples or sources (origins)

2. per — — — — — ive       point of view; the way things look

3. — — — — us       against or in contrast with (turned against)

4. ver — — — —       decision of the jury (true saying)

5. pro — — — e       to call forth

6. — — — — atile       many sided; able to turn easily from one subject or occupation to another

7. — — — etic       inherited from the parents before birth

8. a — — — — —       looks, appearance

9. contra — — — —       disagree with (say against)

10. — — — ation       job or calling

# REVIEW WORDS

**aspect** (as′pekt) *n.*   1. the way one appears   2. the appearance of a person, thing or idea from a specific viewpoint

**contradict** (kän′trə dikt′) *v.*   1. to assert the opposite of or deny (a statement)   2. to be contrary to

**generalize** (jen′ər ə līz′) *v.*   1. to state in terms of a general law   2. to infer or derive (a general law) from (particular instances)   3. to form an opinion after considering a small number of facts   4. to speak only in broad terms

**genetic** (jə net′ik) *adj.*   explained by the branch of biology dealing with heredity and variation in animal and plant species

**perspective** (pər spek′tiv) *n.*   1. the art of picturing objects as to show relative distance or depth   2. the appearance of objects as determined by their relative distance and positions; point of view   3. sense of proportion

**provoke** (prō vōk′) *v.*   1. to anger or irritate   2. to call forth or produce some action or feeling

**verdict** (vur′dikt) *n.*   1. the formal finding of a jury   2. any decision or judgment

**versatile** (vur′sə t′l) *adj.*   competent in many things

**versus** (vur′səs) *prep.*   1. against   2. in contrast with

**vocation** (vō kā′shən) *n.*   1. the career to which one feels he is called   2. any occupation

---

fat, āpe, cär; ten, ēven; is, bīte; gō, hôrn, to͞ol, look; oil, out; up, fur; get; joy; yet; chin; she; thin, *then*; zh, leisure; ŋ, ring; ə for *a* in *ago, e* in *agent, i* in *sanity, o* in *comply, u* in *focus;* ′ as in *able* (ā′b′l)

Read the following list of Review Words. Then in each space below write the word that best completes that sentence. Check your answers in the back of the book.

| aspect | generalize | perspective | versatile | versus |
|--------|-----------|-------------|-----------|--------|
| contradict | genetic | provoke | verdict | vocation |

1. It is not enough to _____ in a term paper; you must give specific examples.

2. If you don't keep a financial problem in proper _____, it may seem much larger than it really is.

3. The 1954 Supreme Court ruling in the case of *Brown* _____ *the Board of Education* stated that separate but equal schools were not constitutional.

4. In the United States, the _____ is the formal finding of a judge or jury at a trial.

5. If you pull a dog's tail, you may _____ it to bite you.

6. Plastic is a _____ material that is not only used for packaging, but also for furniture and automobile parts.

7. Hemophilia is a _____ blood disease that is often passed to sons by a mother who doesn't have the anticlotting problem.

8. You have only considered one _____ of the problem, but there are many.

9. It is difficult to _____ someone politely.

10. Teaching is more than a way of earning a living; it is a _____.

**abdicate** (ab′də kāt′) *v.*   1. to give up formally (a high office, throne, authority, etc.)   2. to surrender (a right, responsibility, etc.)

**advocate** (ad′və kit) *n.*   1. a person who pleads another's cause, specifically a lawyer   2. a person who speaks or writes in support of something [an *advocate* of lower taxes]—*v.* (ad′və kāt′)   1. to speak or write in support of   2. to be in favor of

**avocation** (av′ə kā′shən) *n.*   something one does in addition to his or her regular work; a hobby

**evoke** (ē vōk′, i vōk′) *v.*   1. call forth or summon, conjure up [*evoke* a demon]   2. draw forth or call up [*evoke* a reaction, *evoke* a mental image]

**generic** (jə ner′ik) *adj.*   1. of, applied to, or referring to a whole class or group [*generic* name]   2. not referring to a trademark

**inconspicuous** (in′kən spik′yōō wəs) *adj.*   1. hard to see   2. attracting little attention

**irrevocable** (i rev′ə kə b′l) *adj.*   unable to be recalled or redone

**provocative** (prə väk′ə tiv) *adj.*   causing or tending to arouse thoughts, feelings, desires, etc.

**spectrum** (spek′trəm) *n.*   1. the series of colored bands of light in a rainbow or prism   2. a continuous range or entire extent [a wide *spectrum* of opinion]

**syndicate** (sin′də kit) *n.*   1. an association of individuals or corporations formed to carry out some financial project; any group organized to further some undertaking: specif., an association of criminals set up to control prostitution, gambling, etc.; a group of similar organizations, as of newspapers, owned as a chain   2. an organization that sells special articles or features for publication by many newspapers or magazines—*v.* (sin′də kāt′)   1. to form a group to further an undertaking   2. to sell (an article, feature, etc.) through an organization for publication in many newspapers or magazines

fat, āpe, cär; ten, ēven; is, bīte; gō, hôrn, tōol, look; oil, out; up, fʉr; get; joy; yet; chin; she; thin, *th*en; zh, leisure; ŋ, ring; ə for *a* in *ago, e* in *agent, i* in *sanity, o* in *comply, u* in *focus;* ′ as in *able* (ā′b′l)

Fill in the word that best completes each sentence. Check your answers in the back of the book.

| abdicated | avocation | generic | irrevocable | spectrum |
| advocate | evoke | inconspicuous | provocative | syndicate |

1. A mnemonic device for the colors of the _____ is the name Roy G. Biv, which stands for the first letter of each color.

SPECTRUM

2. Many creators of comic strips _____ their columns to reach audiences across the country.

3. In the 1960s Ralph Nader became a strong _____ of automobile safety.

4. Although Albert Einstein's career was in physics, his _____ was playing the violin.

5. Edward VIII _____ the throne of England in 1936 because Parliament refused to change the law that prohibited his marrying an American divorcée.

6. It is fortunate that most decisions are not _____ because people frequently change their minds.

7. The President made a _____ speech about taxes that resulted in many arguments.

8. Because he thought it important to be _____ in a crowd, fictional detective Sherlock Holmes became a master of disguise.

9. Aspirin is a _____ drug; therefore, no company can patent the name.

10. The smell of tobacco smoke may _____ memories of one's grandfather.

# NEW WORDS II

**avert** (ə vʉrt′) *v.*   1. to turn away   2. to keep from happening; prevent

**degenerate** (di jen′ər it) *adj.*   1. having sunk below a former or normal condition, character, etc.   2. morally corrupt—*n.*   a person who is morally corrupt, especially in reference to sexual activity—*v.*   (di jen′ə rāt′)   1. to lose former, normal, or higher qualities   2. to decline or become morally or culturally corrupt

**despicable** (des′pik ə b'l, di spik′ə b'l) *adj.*   deserving to be hated, disliked, or scorned [a *despicable* character]

**diverse** (di vʉrs′) *adj.*   1. different   2. varied

**inadvertent** (in′əd vʉr′tənt) *adj.*   1. not attentive or observant   2. due to an oversight; unintentional

**indicative** (in dik′ə tiv) *adj.*   giving an indication, suggesting, showing, signifying [a look *indicative* of joy]

**ingenious** (in jēn′yəs) *adj.*   1. clever, resourceful, etc.   2. made or done in a clever or original way

**jurisdiction** (joor′is dik′shən) *n.*   1. the administering of justice; authority or power to hear and decide cases   2. authority or power in general   3. the range or territory in which authority can be legally exercised   4. a law court or system of law courts

**retrospect** (ret′rə spekt′) *n.*   a review or contemplation of things in the past

**revert** (ri vʉrt′) *v.*   to go back or return

---

fat, āpe, cär; ten, ēven; is, bīte; gō, hôrn, tōōl, look; oil, out; up, fʉr; get; joy; yet; **ch**in; **sh**e; **th**in, **th**en; **zh**, leisure; ŋ, ring; ə for *a* in *ago, e* in *agent, i* in *sanity, o* in *comply, u* in *focus;* ′ as in *able* (ā′b'l)

Circle the letter before the word or phrase that best defines the italicized word in each sentence. Check your answers in the back of the book.

1. In some cultures, it is seen as a sign of respect to *avert* your eyes when meeting someone. In others, it is interpreted as a sign of rudeness or suspicion.

   a. close  b. turn away  c. open  d. blink

2. Because everyone's reaction time *degenerates* with age, people over 65 should be tested to make sure they are still capable of driving safely.

   a. increases  b. expands  c. declines  d. clarifies

3. The robbing of an elderly woman by a group of thugs is a *despicable* act.

   a. friendly  b. hateful  c. praiseworthy  d. common

4. Native American cultures in what is now the United States were very *diverse* in their methods of supporting themselves. Southwestern tribes relied on agriculture, California tribes gathered wild plants and hunted, and tribes in the Pacific Northwest fished for a living.

   a. successful  b. interesting  c. similar  d. different

5. It's no excuse to tell a police officer that you *inadvertently* ran a red light after he or she stops you to issue a ticket.

   a. accidentally  b. quickly  c. purposefully  d. stupidly

6. Teachers try to create final exams that will be *indicative* of their students' knowledge; otherwise, the test will be useless.

   a. atypical  b. free  c. characteristic  d. uncharacteristic

7. The Roman aqueducts were *an ingenious* solution to the problem of transporting water from the river to the city of Rome.

   a. a boring  b. a clever  c. a crazy  d. a dull-witted

8. Whether an 18 year-old can be served at a bar depends upon which state has *jurisdiction over* the place of business.

   a. authority over  b. a right to  c. a judgment on  d. emphasis on

9. Peru was conquered for Inca gold, but in *retrospect,* Incan food plants were even more valuable. The potato, the pumpkin, and the pineapple came from South America, as did coca and cinchona, the sources of cocaine and quinine.

   a. foresight  b. hindsight  c. popular opinion  d. science

10. Young children sometimes *revert* to wearing diapers when a new baby joins the family.

   a. progress  b. advance  c. go on  d. return

Place a *T* or an *F* in the space provided. Check your answers in the back of the book.

_____ 1. The light spectrum is the same as the colors of the rainbow.

_____ 2. Generic products are usually more expensive than brand names.

_____ 3. Regular criminal courts do not have jurisdiction over minors; therefore, they cannot put juveniles on trial.

_____ 4. Memories can evoke emotions.

_____ 5. Grades are generally indicative of the amount of course material learned.

## EXERCISE 7: ANALOGIES

In previous exercises of this type, you learned how to find pairs of words that were synonyms, were antonyms, or had the relationship of classification : example. This exercise contains those types of analogies plus a new type. In this kind of analogy, the relationship of the pairs of words is CAUSE : EFFECT. The first word describes something that not only precedes the second in time but also causes it.

rain : wet ground :: inadvertent mistake : wrong total

Determine which of the four types is used in each group below. In the blank before each analogy, write *S* for synonym, *A* for antonym, *C* for classification :: example, and *C/E* for cause : effect. Then fill in the blank to make the second pair agree with the first. Check your answers in the back of the book.

_____ 1. versus  :  against  ::         a.  masterly  b.  easy  c.  foolish  d.  slow
ingenious  :  _____

_____ 2. contradictory opinions  :  fights  ::   a.  crime  b.  partnership  c.  wealth
syndication  :  _____                            d.  tax loss

_____ 3. versatile  :  one-sided  ::   a.  accidental  b.  unnecessary
inadvertent  :  _____                  c.  adventurous  d.  purposeful

_____ 4. verdict  :  guilty  ::       a.  golf  b.  work  c.  slavery
avocation  :  _____                   d.  employment

_____ 5. vocation  :  work  ::        a.  varied  b.  same  c.  alike  d.  uniform
diverse  :  _____

Write the letter of the word that means the opposite of the word in the first column. Check your answers in the back of the book.

———— 1. degenerate            a. take

———— 2. irrevocable           b. likable

———— 3. abdicate              c. negotiable

———— 4. provocative           d. repair

———— 5. despicable            e. boring

## EXERCISE 9: WORD CONTRASTS

In each group below, circle the word that does not mean what the others mean. Check your answers in the back of the book.

1. avert        cause        hinder        prevent

2. revert        progress        advance        proceed

3. retrospect        forecast        reflection        review

4. advocate        favor        oppose        plead

5. inconspicuous        obvious        visible        undisguised

## EXERCISE 10: SENTENCE COMPLETION

Complete each sentence in your own words. Sample answers are provided in the back of the book.

1. Gus kept trying to *abdicate* his responsibility as department chair; what is more, ————
   ————————————————————————————.

2. Joan was a strong *advocate* of such renters' rights as ————————————
   ————————————————————————————.

3. Betty pursues her *avocation* of playing chess wherever ————————————
   ————————————————————————————.

4. Zebras are *inconspicuous* unless ————————————————————
   ————————————————————————————.

5. *Generic* medicines are cheaper because ————————————————
   ————————————————————————————.

6. A word or gesture can *evoke* complex feelings; for instance, _____
_____.

7. Some decisions are *irrevocable;* hence, _____
_____.

8. *Provocative* behavior can get results; however, _____
_____.

9. It covered the entire political *spectrum* from _____
_____.

10. Real estate *syndicates* can provide excellent investments so long as _____
_____.

11. Stanley is *despicable;* in contrast, _____
_____.

12. Alzheimer's disease causes brain cells to *degenerate;* as a result, _____
_____.

13. People from *diverse* backgrounds sometimes _____
_____.

14. The invention was *ingenious,* but _____
_____.

15. In spite of Gloria's efforts to *avert* the disaster, _____
_____.

16. The mistake was *inadvertent;* still, _____
_____.

17. The matter was under the *jurisdiction* of Judge Brown because _____
_____.

18. Her expression was *indicative* of joy, and _____
_____.

19. Things seem different in *retrospect;* besides, _____
_____.

20. Under stress, people will *revert* to such childish behavior as _____
_____.

# ADVANCED WORDS

**adversary** (ad′və ser′ē) *n.*   enemy; opponent

**auspicious** (ôs pish′əs) *adj.*   1. of good omen   2. favorable   3. favored by fortune; successful

**circumspect** (sʉr′kəm spekt′) *adj.*   cautious

**edict** (ē′dikt) *n.*   an official public proclamation or order issued by authority; a decree

**engender** (en jen′dər, in jen′dər) *v.*   to bring into being; to cause; to produce

**equivocate** (ē kwiv′ə kāt′, i kwiv′ə kāt) *v.*   to use terms that can be interpreted more than one way in a deliberate attempt to mislead or hedge; to be deliberately ambiguous

**indigenous** (in dij′ə nəs) *adj.*   1. existing, growing, or produced naturally in a region or country [*indigenous* plants]   2. inborn   3. original [*indigenous* people]

**specious** (spē′shəs) *adj.*   seeming to be good, sound, correct, etc., without really being so

**subversive** (səb vʉr′siv) *adj.*   tending or seeking to overthrow or destroy [*subversive* acts against a government or belief]—*n.*   a person regarded as wishing to overthrow

**vindicate** (vin′də kāt′) *v.*   1. clear from criticism, blame, guilt, suspicion [*vindicate* of a crime] 2. serve as justification for [a success that *vindicated* their belief in him]

fat, āpe, cär; ten, ēven; is, bīte; gō, hôrn, to͞ol, look; oil, out; up, fʉr; get; joy; yet; chin; she; thin, then; zh, leisure; ŋ, ring; ə for *a* in *ago, e* in *agent, i* in *sanity, o* in *comply, u* in *focus;* ′ as in *able* (ā′b'l)

## EXERCISE 11: ADVANCED WORDS IN CONTEXT

Use the Advanced Words to fill in the blanks in the sentences that follow. Check your answers in the back of the book.

| | | | | |
|---|---|---|---|---|
| adversary | circumspect | engender | indigenous | subversive |
| auspicious | edict | equivocate | specious | vindicated |

1. One of the United States scientists working on the highly secretive task of developing the first atomic bomb was a _____ who smuggled all of the plans to the Soviets.

2. In 1992, an official _____ dissolved the Soviet Union.

3. Corn was not _____ to Europe; Spanish and British explorers to the New World brought it home with them.

4. In the American legal system, the prosecuting attorney is the _____ of the defense attorney.

5. The purpose of *Aesop's Fables* is to _____ moral behavior in children. For example, in "The Tortoise and the Hare" the moral is that "slow and steady wins the race."

6. Bernard Jackson was arrested and sent to prison for rape, but five years later was _____ and released when another man confessed to the crime.

7. The signing of an actor's first major contract is an _____ occasion; everyone hopes many more contracts will follow.

8. A _____ argument is one which appears true, but isn't.

9. Police are taught to be _____ when approaching a vehicle stopped on the side of the road because they do not know the intentions of the occupants.

10. A judge should not _____ in giving his decision; it should be clear to all parties.

The clues with an asterisk (*) have an answer that is one of the words from the New Words list in previous chapters. You can also check the word list on the inside front cover of this book. Remember to fill in the puzzle with a pencil, so you can erase. Check your answers in the back of the book.

### Across

*1. Yield
*5. False idea
9. Abbr. for *New Hampshire*
10. Past tense of *lead*
12. Past tense of *eat*
15. A Scottish cap
17. Adolescent
*20. Devaluation
23. Robert Wagner's initials
24. Abbr. for *right*
25. Grayish powder from burnt tobacco
*26. Next to
30. Long-handled spoon for serving soup
33. Alternative spelling of prefix meaning *to*, as in _____tempt
34. Prefix meaning *down*, as in _____preciate
35. Past tense of *eat*
36. _____ Ranger
38. Never dying
*44. Exceed
*48. To occur at the same time
49. Antonym of *day*
50. Abbr. for a large U.S. city
51. Opposite of *well done*, as in meat
52. Alternate spelling of prefix meaning *with*, as in _____author; _____incident
53. Same as 18 down
54. The colloq. for elevated railway
55. Same as 32 down
57. Four-year college degree
58. Antonym of *off*
59. Facial feature
*60. Political reformer
61. Abbr. for *foot*

### Down

*1. Clever
2. Same as 52 across
3. Abbr. for *milliliter*
4. Second letter of the Greek alphabet
6. Two-year college degree
7. Abbr. for *lieutenant*
8. Antonym for *forbid*
*11. Facts
*13. Senseless
14. Alternate spelling of prefix meaning *to*, as in _____cident, _____cept
*16. Misunderstand
18. Spanish for *the*, as in _____ Cid
19. Not real
*20. Harsh or severe
21. Abbr. for *and so forth*
22. Exclamation of surprise
27. Initials of second U.S. president
28. Abbr. for *North Dakota*
29. Bank clerk
30. Abbr. for *Louisiana*
*31. Unusual
32. Same as 34 across
37. Abbr. for Europe
39. Abbr. for *Missouri*
40. One who runs 5280 ft.
41. Brand of cola drink
42. Past tense of *tie*
43. Prefix meaning *to*, as in _____mire; _____mit
45. Abbr. for *registered nurse*
46. Gone by; long _____
47. Sound for "be quiet"
53. Abbr. for *physical education*
54. Symbol for chemical radium
56. Spanish for *the*
57. Same as 57 across
58. Prefix meaning *against*, as in _____fensive; _____ficer

Choose from your outside reading ten words that you would like to learn and write them in the spaces below. When you look them up in the dictionary, pay particular attention to their etymologies, including roots. Pronounce each word, put its definition in your own words, use the word in a sentence, make up a mnemonic, and put the word on a flash card for regular review.

1. _____

2. _____

3. _____

4. _____

5. _____

6. _____

7. _____

8. _____

9. _____

10. _____

# chapter 8

# ROOTS II

## Meaning Variations

In the last chapter we discussed the usefulness of word parts in figuring out the meanings of unfamiliar words. For example the root *gen* comes from the Latin verb *generare* (*to produce or give birth to*) and the noun *genesis,* meaning *birth, race,* or *kind.* Many words are easy to understand through the definition of this root. Examples are *generate, generation,* and *genetic.* However, the meanings of words like *genius, gentleman,* and *generous* are harder to derive from *gen.* Their connection with the root is that the qualities of genius, gentlemanliness, and generosity were supposed to be in*born,* and *gen* has to do with birth. In this case, the way the word is currently used has come to be different from the etymological meaning, or exact meaning of the word parts. This difference is one reason you can't always "translate" word parts directly into English. Roots are used as *clues* to meaning, and the clues always have to be checked to see whether they fit the context of the sentence or paragraph you're reading.

Another reason that word parts sometimes don't translate is that the same combination of parts can add up to different words. For example, *divert* and *diverse* both come from the same word parts, but they have different meanings. *Divert* means *to turn aside,* and *diverse* means *different* or *varied.* You can use a mnemonic device to remember the difference. For example, you might associate *divert* with *turn* because both words contain the letter *t.* You could associate *diverse* with *several* as a clue both to meaning and to spelling.

## Spelling Variations

Another thing you have probably noticed about roots is that they are sometimes spelled in several different ways. For example, *spect* is also spelled *spic* and *spis.* One reason for spelling variations is that the parts of speech in Latin had different spellings. For example, the present infinitive *evadere* (to go) gave us *evade,* whereas the past participle *evasus* gave us *evasive. Submit* comes from *mittere,* and *submissive* comes from *missus,* different parts of speech of the same root. It is important to remember that the alternate spellings belong to the same root.

Another reason spelling varies is that many words came into English directly from Latin while others came in from the same Latin base through other languages. For example, the word *ditto* comes from the Latin root *dict,* but through Italian. *Dict* has also given us, through Old French, *ditty.* To get an idea how many words come directly from Latin versus indirectly through other languages, look at the derivations for words based on the root *tract,* shown in the illustration opposite.

You can see that the Latin spelling *tract* changed in Old French to *trace, treat,* and *trait,* among others.

# New Roots

Following are five new roots with some easy words and some difficult words **derived** from them.

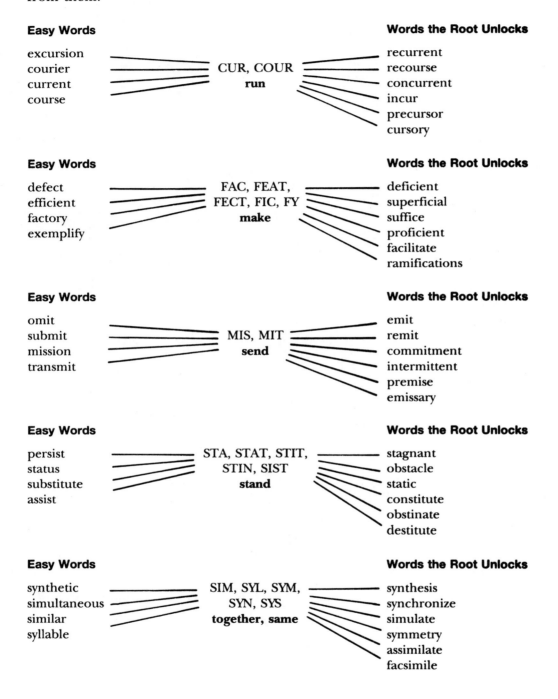

**Easy Words**

excursion
courier
current
course

CUR, COUR
**run**

**Words the Root Unlocks**

recurrent
recourse
concurrent
incur
precursor
cursory

**Easy Words**

defect
efficient
factory
exemplify

FAC, FEAT,
FECT, FIC, FY
**make**

**Words the Root Unlocks**

deficient
superficial
suffice
proficient
facilitate
ramifications

**Easy Words**

omit
submit
mission
transmit

MIS, MIT
**send**

**Words the Root Unlocks**

emit
remit
commitment
intermittent
premise
emissary

**Easy Words**

persist
status
substitute
assist

STA, STAT, STIT,
STIN, SIST
**stand**

**Words the Root Unlocks**

stagnant
obstacle
static
constitute
obstinate
destitute

**Easy Words**

synthetic
simultaneous
similar
syllable

SIM, SYL, SYM,
SYN, SYS
**together, same**

**Words the Root Unlocks**

synthesis
synchronize
simulate
symmetry
assimilate
facsimile

For each of the roots below, fill in an example not previously provided in this chapter. Check the examples in your dictionary to be sure they are from the correct roots.

| Root | Meaning | Example |
| --- | --- | --- |
| cur, cour | run, flow | _____ |
| fac, feat, fect, fic, fy | do, make | _____ |
| mis, mit | send | _____ |
| sta, stat, stit, stin, sist | stand | _____ |
| sim, syl, sym, syn, sys | together | _____ |

## EXERCISE 2: REVIEW WORDS

Before you look at the definitions for the Review Words on the next page, use the roots in this chapter to fill in the blanks below. Check your answers on the next page and in the back of the book.

1. per __ __ __ __            stand by your ideas; not give up
2. ef __ __ __ ient           effective; working well (do out)
3. __ __ __ thetic            not real; artificial (put together)
4. sub __ __ __               yield or give in (send under)
5. ex __ __ __ sion           short trip (run out)
6. __ __ __ tus               position or standing
7. __ __ __ __ ier            messenger (runner)
8. o __ __ __                 leave out (send against)
9. __ __ __ ultaneous         at the same time
10. de __ __ __ __            flaw, shortcoming (made from)

# REVIEW WORDS

**courier** (kur′ē ər) *n.*    a messenger

**defect** (dē′fekt′) *n.*    1. a lack of something necessary for completeness    2. an imperfection; fault—*v.*    (de fekt′) to abandon a (political) party, cause, etc., esp. so as to join the opposition

**efficient** (ə fish′ənt) *adj.*    producing the desired result with a minimum of effort, expense, or waste

**excursion** (eks kur′zhən) *n.*    1. a short trip, as for pleasure    2. a round trip at reduced rates    3. a turning aside, esp. from the main subject in talking or writing

**omit** (ō mit′) *v.*    1. to leave out; fail to include    2. to neglect; fail to do

**persist** (pər sist′) *v.*    1. to refuse to give up, esp. when faced with opposition    2. to continue insistently    3. to endure; remain

**simultaneous** (sī m′l tā′nē əs) *adj.*    occurring, done, etc. at the same time

**status** (stat′əs, stāt′əs) *n.*    1. legal condition    2. position; rank    3. state, as of affairs

**submit** (səb mit′) *v.*    1. to present to others for consideration    2. to yield to the power or control of another    3. to offer as an opinion    4. to yield; give in

**synthetic** (sin′thet′ik) *adj.*    1. of or involving the combining of parts or elements so as to form a whole compound, etc.    2. produced by chemical synthesis rather than of natural origin    3. not real; artificial—*n.*    something not real; artificial

fat, āpe, cär; ten, ēven; is, bīte; gō, hôrn, tool, look; oil, out; up, fur; get; joy; yet; chin; she; thin, *th*en; zh, leisure; ŋ, ring; ə for *a* in *ago, e* in *agent, i* in *sanity, o* in *comply, u* in *focus;* ′ as in *able* (ā′b'l)

# EXERCISE 3: REVIEW WORDS IN CONTEXT

Read the following list of Review Words. Then in the space below write the word that best completes that sentence.

courier          efficient          omit          simultaneous          submit
defect           excursion          persist       status                synthetic

1. The use of computer word processing made typing more _____ because secretaries could have programs to check grammar and spelling.

2. An average of two toys per week must be recalled by toy manufacturers because of a _____ which makes them dangerous for children.

3. A weekend _____ out of town can significantly reduce stress, according to leading doctors.

4. Whether it is legal for an employer to require you to _____ to drug testing is debatable.

5. You cannot _____ the source from which you copied your quotations in a term paper.

6. Frequently an automobile, such as a Mercedes-Benz, is purchased as a _____ symbol as well as for its practical value.

7. Winter in the southern hemisphere and summer in the northern hemisphere are _____ occurrences.

8. If you _____ in breaking the law, you will eventually go to jail.

9. Women's stockings were made of silk until the _____ nylon was developed.

10. You expect a _____ to deliver mail by the fastest possible method.

**constitute** (kän′stə tōōt′, kän′stə tyōōt′) *v.*   1. to set up (a law, government, institution, etc.); establish   2. to make up; be the components of elements of; to form; to compose [twelve people *constitute* a jury]   3. to be actually as designated [such action *constitutes* a felony]

**obstacle** (äb′sti k′l) *n.*   anything that stands in the way; an obstruction

**proficient** (prə fish′ənt) *adj.*   highly competent; skilled

**recourse** (rē′kôrs, ri kôrs′) *n.*   1. a turning or seeking for aid, safety, etc. [to have *recourse* to the law]   2. that to which one turns seeking aid, safety, etc. [one's last *recourse*]

**recurrent** (ri kur′ənt) *adj.*   appearing or occurring again or periodically

**stagnant** (stag′nənt) *adj.*   1. without motion or current; not flowing or moving   2. lacking in activity, interest, etc.; sluggish [a *stagnant* mind]

**static** (stat′ik) *adj.*   1. at rest; inactive   2. (of electricity) not flowing in a current—*n.* atmospheric electrical discharges causing noise on a radio or TV

**superficial** (sōō′pər fish′əl) *adj.*   1. of, or being on, the surface [a *superficial* burn]   2. concerned with and understanding only the easily apparent and obvious; shallow   3. quick and shallow [a *superficial* reading]   4. seeming such only at first glance; merely apparent [a *superficial* resemblance]

**symmetry** (sim′ə trē) *n.*   1. correspondence of opposite parts in size, shape, and position   2. (the pleasing effect resulting from) the exact likeness between the opposite sides of something

**synchronize** (siŋ′krə nīz′) *v.*   1. to move or occur at the same time or rate   2. to set (clocks and watches) to show the same time

---

fat, āpe, cär; ten, ēven; is, bīte; gō, hôrn, tōōl, look; oil, out; up, fur; get; joy; yet; chin; she; thin, *th*en; zh, leisure; ŋ, ring; ə for *a* in *ago, e* in *agent, i* in *sanity, o* in *comply, u* in *focus;* ′ as in *able* (ā′b′l)

Write the word that correctly completes each sentence below. Check your answers in the back of the book.

| constitute | proficient | recurrent | static | symmetry |
| obstacles | recourse | stagnant | superficial | synchronize |

1. A _____ knee problem can force an athlete, whether a football star or an ice skater, to retire.

2. During periods of great inflation, prices do not remain _____. One day you may pay one price; the next day, more.

3. It is important for the New York City Rockettes to _____ their movements even though their heights vary.

4. Until World War II morphine, which doctors knew was addictive, was the best painkiller widely available. Today, we have _____ to a variety of painkillers which are non-narcotic.

5. Bleeding from a _____ cut can be stopped by applying direct pressure over the wound for several minutes.

6. Residential burglaries _____ 65 percent of the total of 2 million burglaries that occur each year; many could have been prevented if the owners had been more careful.

7. There are two schools of thought in flower arranging: one emphasizes _____ and order; the other, variation in color, shape, and texture.

8. Horses in a steeplechase must clear _____ like ditches, hedges and walls.

9. Using a computer for word processing is easier if you already are a _____ typist.

10. When the economy is _____, the Federal Reserve sometimes lowers interest rates in an attempt to increase business activity.

# NEW WORDS II

**commitment** (kə mit′mənt) *n.*   1. a pledge or promise to do something   2. an official sending by court order of a person to prison, to a mental hospital, etc.

**concurrent** (kən kur′ənt) *adj.*   occurring at the same time; existing together

**deficient** (di fish′ənt) *adj.*   lacking; inadequate; defective; not sufficient

**emit** (ē mit′, i mit′) *v.*   1. to send out; give forth [geysers *emit* water]   2. to utter (sounds, etc.)   3. to transmit (a signal) as by radio waves   4. to give off (electrons) under the influence of heat, radiation, etc.

**incur** (in kur′) *v.*   1. to come into or acquire, esp. something undesirable [to *incur* a debt]   2. to bring upon oneself [to *incur* someone's anger]

**intermittent** (in′tər mit′′nt) *adj.*   stopping and starting again at intervals; pausing from time to time; periodic

**remit** (ri mit′) *v.*   1. to send money in payment   2. to decrease [without *remitting* one's efforts]

**simulate** (sim′yoo lāt′) *v.*   1. to give a false indication or appearance of; pretend [to *simulate* an interest]   2. to have or take on the appearance of; look or act like [an insect *simulating* a twig]

**suffice** (sə fīs′) *v.*   to be enough; be sufficient or adequate

**synthesis** (sin′thə sis) *n.*   putting together parts to form a whole

fat, āpe, cär; ten, ēven; is, bīte; gō, hôrn, tool, look; oil, out; up, fur; get; joy; yet; chin; she; thin, *th*en; zh, leisure; ŋ, ring; ə for *a* in *ago, e* in *agent, i* in *sanity, o* in *comply, u* in *focus;* ' as in *able* (ā′b'l)

# EXERCISE 5: MULTIPLE CHOICE

Circle the letter before the word or phrase that best defines the italicized word in each sentence. Check your answers in the back of the book.

1. The *commitment* of a person to a mental institution requires a doctor's signature.

   a. transfer   b. sudden   c. official sending   d. leading

2. Because the sound of the bang and the bullet leaving the gun occur *concurrently,* it is too late to duck when you hear the shot.

   a. one after another   b. at the same time   c. in any order   d. in no certain order

3. Milk is almost a perfect food for infants; it is, however, *deficient* in iron.

   a. excessive   b. lacking   c. costly   d. cheap

4. The people of the Canary Islands *emit* sounds in a whistle language, called Silbo, that can communicate messages five miles across a valley.

   a. leave off   b. take in   c. invent   d. send out

5. Children usually try hard not to *incur* their parents' disapproval right before Christmas.

   a. create in others   b. bring upon themselves   c. specifically avoid   d. completely change

6. The *intermittent* rains at Mt. Waialeale, Hawaii, add up to an average of 460 inches a year, making it the wettest spot in the world.

   a. seasonal   b. temporary   c. periodic   d. infrequent

7. If you do not *remit* payment for a parking ticket within the given time, your fine will increase.

   a. incur   b. collect   c. send   d. pledge

8. With interactive video, you can *simulate* skiing without ever going near a slope.

   a. excel at   b. avoid   c. begin   d. imitate

9. English is a *synthesis* of words from over twenty languages.

   a. combination   b. sequence   c. lot   d. sample

10. It is desirable to earn an income that will *suffice* for your needs.

    a. be enough   b. be deficient   c. be too low   d. be incorrect

Place a *T* or an *F* in the space provided. Check your answers in the back of the book.

_____ 1. When you are sneaking up on someone, you must be careful to emit sounds.

_____ 2. When you have no recourse, you have nowhere to turn.

_____ 3. Recurrent events happen more than once.

_____ 4. If you wish to synthesize your ideas, you must combine things from several different sources.

_____ 5. Fifty individual states constitute the United States of America.

## EXERCISE 7: ANALOGIES

The analogies below are either synonyms, antonyms, classification : example, or cause : effect. First, decide which type of comparison is used in the first pair of words. Second, indicate the type by writing the appropriate letter before each analogy: *S* for synonyms, *A* for antonym, *C* for classification : example, and *C/E* for cause : effect. Third, find a word from the choices that will make the second pair of words have the same relationship. Check your answers in the back of the book.

_____ 1. courier : messenger ::     a. watches   b. following   c. coordinate
synchronize : _____      d. similarity

_____ 2. defect : bridge's collapse ::   a. thirst   b. draught   c. abundance
food deficiency : _____    d. hunger

_____ 3. synthetic : nylon ::    a. order   b. lie   c. marriage   d. burden
commitment : _____

_____ 4. simultaneous : same time ::   a. landslide   b. solution   c. advantage
obstacle : _____      d. difficulty

_____ 5. omit : include ::    a. stationary   b. electricity   c. mobile
static : _____      d. noisy

## EXERCISE 8: MATCHING MEANINGS

Write the letter of the word that means the opposite of the word in the first column.
Check your answers in the back of the book.

_____ 1. remit            a. continuous

_____ 2. suffice          b. refuse

_____ 3. proficient       c. owe

_____ 4. incur            d. incompetent

_____ 5. intermittent     e. lack

## EXERCISE 9: WORD CONTRASTS

Circle the word below that does not mean what the others mean. Check your
answers in the back of the book.

1. superficial     shallow     significant     surface
2. stagnant     moving     still     standing
3. symmetry     imbalance     proportion     harmony
4. simulate     imitate     invent     mimic
5. concurrently     simultaneously     randomly     together

## EXERCISE 10: SENTENCE COMPLETION

Complete each sentence in your own words. Sample answers are provided in the
back of the book.

1. When two people make a *commitment* to each other, _____
_____.

2. If two events are *concurrent*, _____
_____.

3. Although getting a D in a class might *constitute* a passing grade in some courses, _____
_____.

4. Unless you are *deficient* in writing, _____
_____.

5. Whenever their baby *emits* a sound, some new parents _____
_____.

6. After you *incur* a large debt, _____
_____.

7. If rain is *intermittent* all night, _____
_____.

8. An *obstacle* to success in college might be _____
_____.

9. Until you are *proficient* in doing a task, you should not _____
_____.

10. One *recourse* when you have been cheated would be to _____
_____.

11. *Recurrent* asthma attacks can exhaust you by _____
_____.

12. You should *remit* payments on loans as soon as they are due because _____
_____.

13. During a *simulated* flight, future pilots _____
_____.

14. *Stagnant* water is dangerous because _____
_____.

15. When your telephone line has a lot of *static*, _____
_____.

16. If your food supply will not *suffice* on a camping trip, _____
_____.

17. After you get a *superficial* cut, _____
_____.

18. In the movies soldiers *synchronize* their watches just before _____
_____.

19. Although we are comfortable seeing things that have *symmetry*, _____
_____.

20. After you *synthesize* your thoughts about a career, _____
_____.

# ADVANCED WORDS

**assimilate** (ə sim′ə lāt′)  *v.*   1. to change (food) into a form that can be taken up by and made part of the body tissues; to absorb into the body   2. to absorb and incorporate into one's thinking   3. to absorb (groups of different cultures) into the main cultural body

**cursory** (kʉr′sər ē)  *adj.*   hastily, often superficially, done; performed rapidly with little attention to detail

**destitute** (des′tə tōōt′)  *adj.*   1. not having; being without (*destitute* of trees)   2. lacking the necessities of life; living in complete poverty

**emissary** (em′ə ser′ē)  *n.*   a person or agent sent on a specific mission

**facilitate** (fə sil′ə tāt′)  *v.*   to make easy or easier

**facsimile** (fak sim′ə lē)  *n.*   an exact reproduction or copy

**obstinate** (äb′stə nit)  *adj.*   stubborn

**precursor** (pri kʉr′sər)  *n.*   a person or thing that goes before; forerunner

**premise** (prem′is)  *n.*   a previous statement or assertion that serves as the basis for an argument

**ramification** (ram′ə fi kā′shən)  *n.*   1. a branch or offshoot   2. a derived effect, consequence, or result [the *ramification* of an act]

fat, āpe, cär; ten, ēven; is, bīte; gō, hôrn, tōōl, look; oil, out; **up, fʉr; get; joy; yet; chin; she; thin, *th*en; zh,** leisure; **ŋ,** ring; ə for *a* in *ago, e* in *agent, i* in *sanity, o* in *comply, u* in *focus;* ' as in *able* (ā′b'l)

Use the Advanced Words to fill in the blanks in the sentences that follow. Check your answers in the back of the book.

assimilate      destitute      facilitate      obstinate      premise
cursory         emissary       facsimile       precursor      ramification

1. A diabetic cannot _____ sugar well because he or she lacks the ability to produce insulin.

2. With the introduction of fax machines, police could send a _____ of the likeness of a wanted person all over the world within seconds.

3. Learning American Sign Language will _____ communication with the hearing impaired.

4. One _____ of the use of asbestos for insulation in houses and schools was lung damage to some people who breathed in its particles.

5. Operating on the _____ that the secretary was the only person to have a motive for killing the millionaire, the detective began to check into his alibi.

6. You should not sign a contract after only a _____ examination. What is written in the fine print may cause disastrous consequences.

7. Marco Polo, a Venetian trader in China, became Kublai Khan's

   _____. He traveled throughout the Eastern world and Europe transacting the emperor's business.

8. Betrand Russell, the famous philosopher, used a series of synonyms for humorous effect

   when he said, "I am firm; you are _____; and he is a pig-headed fool."

9. After the stock market crash of 1929, many formerly wealthy people found themselves

   _____.

10. The _____ of the U.S. Constitution was the Articles of Confederation.

Fill in the puzzle below. Remember that the words with an asterisk (*) come from the New Words list in previous chapters. You can also check the word list on the inside front cover of this book. Check your answers in the back of the book.

### Across

*1. Hard to see
11. Antonym of *yes*
*12. Avoids
13. Abbr. for the place where you get your driver's license
*15. Spoke or wrote in support of
18. Largest city in Brazil
19. Abbr. for *electrical engineer*
21. To endeavor
23. Abbr. for *veteran*
*25. Not referring to a trademark
30. Abbr. for *electron-volt*
*31. Unable to be recalled or redone
*34. To go back or return
36. Small pellet fired from an air gun
37. Abbr. for *Louisiana*
38. President Theodore Roosevelt's monogram
39. Actress Gina Lollobrigida's monogram
40. I am; he _____
41. Perfect
42. Used for vision
45. Used instead of Miss or Mrs.
47. Alt. spelling of prefix meaning *not*, as in _____regular
48. Alt. spelling of prefix meaning *to*, as in _____tendance
*50. The series of colors in the rainbow
55. Cassette or video are samples
*56. Giving an indication
58. To decorate something like a Christmas tree
61. What you get from the sun
*62. Different; varied
*63. To put forth energetically; to try hard

### Down

*1. Unintentional
2. To move the head up and down in approval
3. Reed instrument
4. Animal kept as a companion
5. The contraction for *I have*
6. Abbr. for *computer-aided design*
7. Abbr. for *unilateral declaration*
8. Abbr. for *Old English*
9. Abbr. for *United States*
*10. Call forth
13. Arid
14. Abbr. for *mile*
16. Same as 23 across
*17. To turn away; prevent
20. Actions of an uncontrollable mob
22. Thief
24. Each
25. Antonym of *boy*
26. Nancy Reagan's monogram
27. Snakelike sea creatures
28. Abbr. for *recreational vehicle*
29. Abbr. for *cubic centimeter*
*32. To surrender an office
33. Female name as for singer _____ Fitzgerald
35. Dictionary abbreviation for *for example*
43. Sixth sense
44. Abbr. for *alternating current*
45. Wet earth
46. Grin
49. "Trick or _____"
51. Nickname for Peter
52. What you look at your watch to see
53. Abbr. for *registered nurse*
54. Type of evergreen tree
57. Payment to the government
59. Abbr. for *railroad*
60. I am; he _____

Choose from your outside reading ten words that you would like to learn and write them in the spaces below. When you look the words up in the dictionary, pay particular attention to the etymologies, including roots. Pronounce each word, put the definition in your own words, use the word in a sentence, make up a mnemonic, and put the word on a flash card for regular review.

1. _____

2. _____

3. _____

4. _____

5. _____

6. _____

7. _____

8. _____

9. _____

10. _____

# chapter 9
# ROOTS III

"I'M A DEVIL ... HE'S A DEVIL'S ADVOCATE !"

Chronicle Features, 1979.

# Continuing Study of Roots

Because of the tremendous frequency of root words in college textbooks, it is to your advantage to continue your study of roots beyond the 15 you are learning in this book. We suggest that you start putting roots on flash cards. Put the root on the front. On the back write (1) the meaning of the root and (2) a word that you can use as a mnemonic for the meaning of the root. For example, if you have discovered the root *min* in re*min*isce, you might use the word *remind* as a way of remembering that *min* means *memory*. Think of as many other words as possible that contain the same root. Whenever you come across an unfamiliar word containing the root, write it on the back of the card under your mnemonic word. Use the etymology in your dictionary to check whether the word comes from the same root. Note any alternative spellings you may discover, such as *mem* (*memorandum*, *memento*) and *mn* (*amnesia*, *mnemonic*). See the sample flash card.

---

*min, mem, men, mn*

---

*memory (remind)*

| | | |
|---|---|---|
| *mentality* | *reminiscent* | *remembrance* |
| *demented* | *memorial* | *memoriam* |
| *mnemonic* | *commemorate* | *immemorial* |
| *amnesia* | *memento* | *memorable* |
| *amendment* | *memoirs* | *memorandum* |
| *monumental* | *memorabilia* | *amnesty* |

---

Using flash cards for roots will serve two purposes. First, you will have many of the unfamiliar words grouped by families, so they will be easier to remember than if you had one word on each card. Second, the fact that you are learning the roots themselves will help you understand still more unfamiliar words. You will be taking a shortcut to a good college vocabulary.

# New Roots

Following are the five new roots for this chapter, each presented with several familiar words and several words that you will learn.

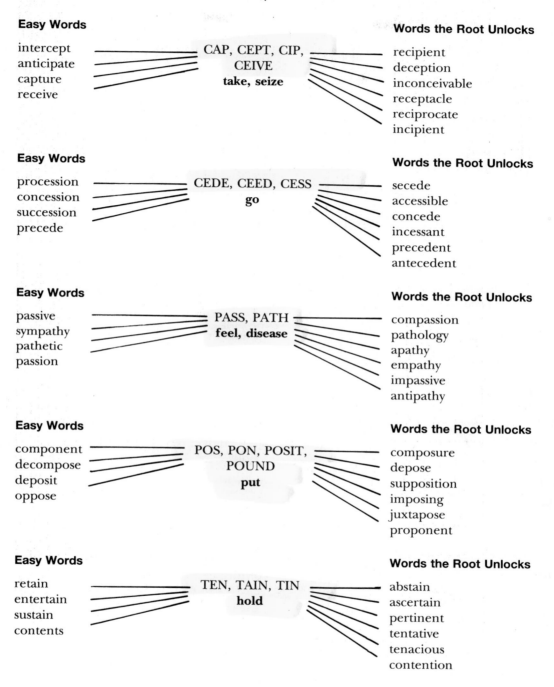

**Easy Words**

intercept
anticipate
capture
receive

CAP, CEPT, CIP, CEIVE
**take, seize**

**Words the Root Unlocks**

recipient
deception
inconceivable
receptacle
reciprocate
incipient

**Easy Words**

procession
concession
succession
precede

CEDE, CEED, CESS
**go**

**Words the Root Unlocks**

secede
accessible
concede
incessant
precedent
antecedent

**Easy Words**

passive
sympathy
pathetic
passion

PASS, PATH
**feel, disease**

**Words the Root Unlocks**

compassion
pathology
apathy
empathy
impassive
antipathy

**Easy Words**

component
decompose
deposit
oppose

POS, PON, POSIT, POUND
**put**

**Words the Root Unlocks**

composure
depose
supposition
imposing
juxtapose
proponent

**Easy Words**

retain
entertain
sustain
contents

TEN, TAIN, TIN
**hold**

**Words the Root Unlocks**

abstain
ascertain
pertinent
tentative
tenacious
contention

## EXERCISE 1: ROOTS FILL-IN

For each of the roots below, fill in an example not previously provided in this chapter. Check the examples in your dictionary to be sure they are from the correct roots.

| Root | Meaning | Example |
|------|---------|---------|
| cap, cept, cip, ceive | take, seize | _____ |
| cede, ceed, cess | go | _____ |
| pass, path | feel, disease | _____ |
| pos, pon, posit, pound | put | _____ |
| ten, tain, tin | hold | _____ |

## EXERCISE 2: REVIEW WORDS

Before you look at the definitions for the Review Words on the next page, use the roots in this chapter to fill in the blanks below. Check your answers on the next page.

1. anti __ __ __ ate      to expect (take in advance)

2. inter __ __ __ __      to seize on the way, before arrival

3. sus __ __ __ __      to provide for the support of (hold up from below)

4. sym __ __ __ __ y      feeling for another (feel together)

5. com __ __ __ ent      a part that can be put with other parts to make a whole

6. pro __ __ __ __ ion      parade (go forward)

7. decom __ __ __ e      to rot (put the parts from)

8. __ __ __ __ ive      yielding, inactive (feeling in silence)

9. re __ __ __ __      keep (hold back)

10. suc __ __ __ __ ion      coming after another (to go under)

# REVIEW WORDS

**anticipate** (an tis′ə pāt′) *v.*   1. to look forward to; to await   2. to take care of, in advance   3. to be ahead of in doing

**component** (kəm pō′nənt) *adj.*   serving as one of the parts of a whole—*n.*   a part, element, or ingredient

**decompose** (dē′kəm pōz′) *v.*   1. to break up into basic parts   2. to rot; to decay

**intercept** (in′tər sept′) *v.*   1. to stop or seize in its course   2. (math) to cut off or mark off between two points, lines, etc.

**passive** (pas′iv) *adj.*   1. inactive, but acted upon   2. offering no resistance; submissive   3. (grammar) denoting the voice of a verb whose subject receives the action

**procession** (prō sesh′ən) *n.*   a number of persons or things moving forward, a parade

**retain** (ri tān′) *v.*   1. to keep in possession, use, etc.; to avoid losing   2. to hold in   3. to keep in mind   4. to hire by paying a retainer (fee)

**succession** (sək shesh′ən) *n.*   1. (a) the act of succeeding another, as to an office (b) the right to do this   2. a number of persons or things coming one after another; a series

**sustain** (sə stān′) *v.*   1. to keep in existence; maintain or prolong   2. to provide sustenance for   3. to carry the weight of; support   4. to endure; withstand   5. to suffer (an injury, loss, etc.)   6. to uphold the validity of   7. to confirm; corroborate

**sympathy** (sim′pə thē) *n.*   1. sameness of feeling   2. agreement in qualities   3. mutual liking or understanding   4. ability to share another's ideas, emotions, etc., esp. pity or compassion

fat, āpe, cär; ten, ēven; is, bīte; gō, hôrn, to͞ol, look; oil, out; up, fʉr; get; joy; yet; chin; she; thin, *th*en; zh, leisure; ŋ, ring; ə for *a* in *ago, e* in *agent, i* in *sanity, o* in *comply, u* in *focus;* ' as in *able* (ā′b'l)

# EXERCISE 3: REVIEW WORDS IN CONTEXT

Read the following list of Review Words. Then in each space below write the word that best completes the sentence. Check your answers in the back of the book.

| anticipate | decompose | passive | retain | sustain |
|---|---|---|---|---|
| components | intercept | procession | succession | sympathy |

1. If you _____ rain, you should take an umbrella with you.

2. Perpendicular lines _____ each other at a 90° angle.

3. Some gardeners let their garbage and grass cuttings _____ into fertilizer.

4. Even after immigrating to another country, some people will work hard to _____ their first language and customs.

5. During the Revolutionary War, the fact that British troops always marched in _____ on main roads allowed the inexperienced colonists to attack the soldiers easily from behind trees along the roadside.

6. Baseball players who _____ serious injuries are placed on a disabled list.

7. On television, Murphy Brown has had a _____ of secretaries who leave after one day.

8. It takes many different _____ to make up a computer.

9. Mahatma Gandhi opposed violence in his country, India, and supported _____ resistance.

10. It is customary to send a _____ card to a friend who has suffered the loss of a loved one; in fact, there are even cards to send when someone loses a pet.

# NEW WORDS I

**abstain** (əb stān′, ab stān′) *v.*  to hold oneself back; voluntarily do without [to *abstain* from smoking]; refrain (from something) or forego

**concede** (kən sēd′) *v.*  1. to admit as true or valid; acknowledge [to *concede* a point in argument]  2. to admit as certain or proper [to *concede* a victory to an opponent]  3. to grant as a right or privilege

**deception** (di sep′shən) *n.*  1. the act or practice of misleading or deceiving  2. the fact or condition of being misled or deceived  3. something that deceives, as an illusion, or is meant to deceive, as a fraud or imposture

**depose** (di pōz′) *v.*  to remove from office; dethrone

**imposing** (im pō′ziŋ) *adj.*  making a strong impression because of great size, strength, dignity; impressive

**pathology** (pə thäl′ə jē) *n.*  1. any abnormal variation from a sound condition  2. the branch of medicine that deals with the nature of disease

**pertinent** (pʉr′t′n ənt) *adj.*  having some connection with the matter at hand; relevant; to the point

**precedent** (pres′ə dənt) *n.*  1. an act, statement, legal decision, case, etc. that may serve as an example, reason, or justification for a later one  2. existing practice resulting from earlier actions

**recipient** (ri sip′ē ənt) *n.*  a person or thing that receives

**supposition** (sup′ə zish′ən) *n.*  1. a supposing, an assumption  2. something supposed

fat, ăpe, cär; ten, ēven; is, bīte; gō, hôrn, tōōl, look; oil, out; up, fʉr; get; joy; yet; chin; she; thin, *th*en; zh, leisure; ŋ, ring; ə for *a* in *ago*, *e* in *agent*, *i* in *sanity*, *o* in *comply*, *u* in *focus*; ′ as in *able* (ā′b′l)

Write the correct word below that completes each sentence. Check your answers
in the back of the book.

abstain          deception          imposing          pertinent          recipient
conceded         deposed            pathology         precedent          supposition

1. If Woodrow Wilson had _____ when his manager told him that he
   had no chance of winning the Democratic nomination, he would never have become the
   28th President.

2. A _____ of the Nobel Prize also receives a grant for continued
   research.

3. Any member of Alcoholics Anonymous will tell you how difficult it is for an alcoholic to
   _____ from that first drink.

4. Several members of the audience asked _____ questions after the
   lecturer on Middle Eastern affairs had finished speaking.

5. If you let the children stay up late tonight, you will set a _____ and
   they'll expect to stay up late again.

6. The Cuban revolution, led by Fidel Castro and Che Guevara, _____
   President Batista in 1959.

7. Some people think it is a harmful _____ to tell children that there is
   a Santa Claus, while others think it is just healthy make-believe.

8. Charles de Gaulle was an _____ individual because of his height,
   bearing and the clarity of his thought.

9. His illogical statements and fixed stare contributed to the conclusion that he suffered
   from mental _____.

10. Her belief that having a child will improve her marriage is pure
    _____.

**accessible** (ak ses′ə b'l) *adj.*   1. that which can be approached or entered   2. easy to approach or enter   3. that which can be gotten; obtainable   4. open to the influence of [he is not *accessible* to pity]

**apathy** (ap′ə thē) *n.*   1. lack of emotion or feeling   2. indifference; listlessness

**ascertain** (as′ər tān′) *v.*   to find out with certainty; determine

**compassion** (kəm pash′ən) *n.*   deep sympathy; pity

**composure** (kəm pō′zhər) *n.*   calmness of mind or manner; tranquillity; self-possession

**empathy** (em′pə thē) *n.*   understanding so intimate that the feelings, thoughts, and motives of one are readily understood by another

**inconceivable** (in′kən sē′və b'l) *adj.*   that which cannot be conceived; that which cannot be thought of, understood, imagined, or believed; unthinkable

**receptacle** (ri sep′tə k'l) *n.*   a container

**secede** (si sēd′) *v.*   to withdraw formally from membership in or association with a group, federation, or organization, etc., esp. a political or religious group

**tentative** (ten′tə tiv) *adj.*   1. made or done, etc., as a test or experiment   2. uncertain

fat, āpe, cär; ten, ēven; is, bīte; gō, hôrn, tōōl, look; oil, out; up, fʉr; get; joy; yet; chin; she; thin, *th*en; zh, leisure; ŋ, ring; ə for *a* in *ago, e* in *agent, i* in *sanity, o* in *comply, u* in *focus;* ′ as in *able* (ā′b'l)

# EXERCISE 5: MULTIPLE CHOICE

Circle the letter before the word or phrase that best defines the italicized word in each sentence. Check your answer in the back of the book.

1. Tulips were first grown in Persia and were not *accessible to* Europeans until 1601, when the Flemish botanist Clusius brought some to the Netherlands.

   a.  wanted by   b.  purchased by   c.  known to   d.  available to

2. Hate is not the opposite of love; *apathy* is.

   a.  hatred   b.  dishonesty   c.  indifference   d.  disease

3. King Alfonso of Spain, who reigned from 1886 to 1931, was so tone deaf that he could not recognize the Spanish national anthem. He hired an Anthem Man whose only duty was to *ascertain* when the anthem was being played and tell the king to stand up.

   a.  sing   b.  find out   c.  play   d.  signal

4. Followers of Jainism, a religion practiced in India by about two million people, believe in *compassion* toward all living things, even insects. They do not wear shoes because they believe shoes will kill more insects than bare feet.

   a.  anger   b.  envy   c.  pity   d.  sorrow

5. It is easy to lose your *composure* if, when giving a speech, you are heckled by persons in the audience.

   a.  flexibility   b.  calmness   c.  hostility   d.  hesitancy

6. Psychotherapy is often more successful if the therapist feels *empathy for* the person he or she is trying to help.

   a.  faith in   b.  indifference towards   c.  hope for   d.  understanding of

7. All the time it seemed *inconceivable* that the planners of Brazil's capital city, Brasilia, would decide to build this modern masterpiece in the middle of the jungle.

   a.  unimaginable   b.  stupid   c.  an error   d.  impractical

8. A true student must be more than a *receptacle* of knowledge; he or she must seek wisdom.

   a.  city   b.  container   c.  transmitter   d.  sender

9. The scientific method of problem solving involves thinking up a *tentative* solution and then testing to see whether it works.

   a.  find   b.  practice   c.  silly   d.  preliminary

10. Seven southern states made the decision to *secede from* the Union to form the Confederate States of America.

    a.  unite with   b.  argue with   c.  withdraw from   d.  destroy

## EXERCISE 6: TRUE-FALSE

Place a *T* or an *F* in the space provided. Check your answers in the back of the book.

_____ 1.  A person with empathy will have few friends.

_____ 2.  A supposition is an assumption.

_____ 3.  When you concede a point you give in.

_____ 4.  Everyone thinks of inconceivable ideas.

_____ 5.  When you don't want to take sides in a vote, you can abstain.

## EXERCISE 7: ANALOGIES

In the previous exercises of this type you learned how to find pairs of words that were synonyms, antonyms, classification : example, and cause : effect. This exercise contains one of each of those types, plus one new type, in which the relationship of the pairs of words is PART : WHOLE. The first word describes something that is only part of the second thing or idea.

leaf : tree :: chapter : book

Decide which of the five kinds of analogies is used in each group below. Fill in the type of analogy in the first blank. Use *S* for synonym, *A* for antonym, *C* for classification, *C/E* for cause : effect, and *P* for part : whole. Then fill in the blank to make the second pair agree with the first. Check your answers in the back of the book.

_____ 1.  anticipation  :  excitement  ::        a.  coldness  b.  kindness  c.  resentment
           compassion  :  _____                  d.  mother

_____ 2.  sustain  :  release  ::               a.  passion  b.  boredom  c.  indifference
           apathy  :  _____                      d.  passivity

_____ 3.  decomposing  :  corpses  ::           a.  sky  b.  air  c.  water  d.  box
           receptacle  :  _____

_____ 4.  succession  :  sequence  ::           a.  success  b.  forerunner  c.  judge
           precedent  :  _____                   d.  sequence

_____ 5.  component  :  stereo  ::              a.  botany  b.  book
           pathology  :  _____                   c.  invention  d.  medical science

# EXERCISE 8: MATCHING MEANINGS

Write the letter of the word that means the opposite of the word in the first column.
Check your answers in the back of the book.

_____ 1. recipient       a. elect

_____ 2. pertinent       b. forget

_____ 3. composure       c. donor

_____ 4. ascertain       d. unrelated

_____ 5. depose       e. nervousness

# EXERCISE 9: WORD CONTRASTS

In each group below, circle the word that does not mean what the others mean.
Check your answers in the back of the book.

1. tentative     preliminary     definite     temporary

2. imposing     ordinary     dignified     stately

3. secede     resign     join     withdraw

4. deception     treachery     deceit     honesty

5. accessible     unapproachable     guarded     restricted

# EXERCISE 10: SENTENCE COMPLETION

Complete each sentence in your own words. Sample answers are provided in the
back of the book.

1. Some people find it hard to *abstain* from smoking, whereas _____
   _____.

2. I am willing to *concede* the election whenever _____
   _____.

3. *Deception* leads to distrust; therefore, _____
   _____.

4. The dictator was *deposed* after _____
   _____.

5. Chester's imposing manner *impressed* his friends, awed his enemies, and won the respect of
   strangers; in summary, _____.

6.  Her *supposition* was wrong; nevertheless, _____

_____.

7.  All were happy for the *recipient* of the award although _____

_____.

8.  The case set a legal *precedent* until _____

_____.

9.  The *pertinent* data were not available due to _____

_____.

10.  He was closely monitored for signs of *pathology* in case _____

_____.

11.  The conclusion is still *tentative*, yet _____

_____.

12.  Feelings of *apathy* can be a sign of illness, or _____

_____.

13.  Inside the *receptacle* _____

_____.

14.  Her reaction seemed *inconceivable* at first; later, _____

_____.

15.  I was surprised to find the vault so *accessible* because _____

_____.

16.  She usually shows *compassion*, except _____

_____.

17.  *Empathy* is a virtue; indeed, _____

_____.

18.  There were good reasons to *secede*; most important, _____

_____.

19.  Gabrielle was known for her *composure*; in general, _____

_____.

20.  The motive was difficult to *ascertain*; in fact, _____

_____.

# ADVANCED WORDS

**antecedent** (an'tə sēd''nt) *n.*   1. anything prior to another   2. one's ancestry, past life, etc. —*adj.*   going or coming before

**antipathy** (an tip'ə thē) *n.*   1. a strong or deep-rooted dislike   2. the object of such dislike

**contention** (kən ten'shən) *n.*   argument; strife; controversy

**impassive** (im pas'iv) *adj.*   not feeling or showing emotion; calm

**incessant** (in ses''nt) *adj.*   never ceasing; continuing or being repeated without stopping or in a way that seems endless; constant

**incipient** (in sip'ē ənt) *adj.*   in the first stage of existence; just beginning to exist or to come to notice [an *incipient* illness]

**juxtapose** (juk'stə pōz') *v.*   to put side by side or close together

**proponent** (prə pō'nənt) *n.*   1. a person who supports a cause   2. a person who makes a proposal or proposition

**reciprocate** (ri sip'rə kāt) *v.*   1. to interchange; to give and get or feel mutually [*reciprocated* feelings]   2. to give, do, feel, etc., in return; return in kind or degree [*reciprocate* a favor]

**tenacious** (tə nā'shəs) *adj.*   1. holding firmly [a *tenacious* grip]   2. that which retains well; retentive [a *tenacious* memory]   3. that which holds together strongly; tough [a *tenacious* wood]   4. that which clings; adhesive; sticky   5. persistent; stubborn [*tenacious* courage]

fat, āpe, cär; ten, ēven; is, bīte; gō, hôrn, tōōl, look; oil, out; up, fur; get; joy; yet; chin; she; thin, *th*en; zh, leisure; ŋ, ring; ə for *a* in *ago, e* in *agent, i* in *sanity, o* in *comply, u* in *focus;* ' as in *able* (ā'b'l)

Use the Advanced Words to fill in the blanks in the sentences that follow. Check your answers in the back of the book.

| | | | | |
|---|---|---|---|---|
| antecedent | contention | incessant | juxtapose | reciprocate |
| antipathy | impassive | incipient | proponent | tenacious |

1. It is a mistake to _____ feuding relatives at a banquet table.

2. In some cultures if someone gives you a gift you are required to _____ .

3. Many parents feel a great _____ to their children's choice of music.

4. One species of shark is particularly _____ in its bite. It can exert a pressure of 22 tons per inch.

5. Native Americans are usually pictured in art and movies as extremely _____ except when fighting. They are almost never seen laughing, crying, or being angry.

6. Martin Luther King was a _____ of civil rights.

7. The _____ noise of jets landing at the nearby airport may cause many residents in an area to move away.

8. Among the symptoms of _____ diabetes are weight loss and thirst.

9. The first mechanical road vehicle, _____ to the automobile, was a steam powered tractor designed in 1769 for pulling cannon. Its inventor drove it into a wall, earning a jail sentence as the first traffic violator.

10. In 1854, to support his _____ that he invented the first elevator that would not crash, C. G. Otis rode an elevator to a great height and had the cable cut completely through. He descended slowly and safely.

This crossword puzzle reviews the New Words from previous chapters. Clues referring to New Words have an asterisk (*). You can also check the word list on the inside front cover of this book. Check your answers in the back of the book.

### Across

*1. On the surface
11. Signal
14. Join together
*15. Obligation
18. Abbr. for *12 inches*
19. Antonym of *stop*
21. A color
22. Abbr. of *for instance*
*24. False belief
27. Latin abbr. for *id est*
28. Abbr. for *United Artists*
30. One meaning of the root *fic*
31. Yiddish exclamation
32. A color
35. Monogram of Edison
36. Abbr. for a western Canadian province
37. Alt. spelling of prefix meaning "in," as in _____*brace*
*38. To bring upon oneself
41. Abbr. for *Chicago's elevated train*
43. A group formed to carry out a financial project
*48. Paper required for a master's degree at some colleges
52. Transmitter of inherited characteristics
53. Chemical symbol for *aluminum*
*54. Lacking
56. Antonym of *off*
57. Alt. spelling of prefix meaning *not*, as in _____*mature*
59. Antonym of *nor*
61. Abbr. for *Los Angeles*
*62. To remain motionless
67. Antonym of *pa*
*68. Position or rank
69. Root meaning birth, race
70. Abbr. for *South America*

### Down

*1. To be adequate
2. Reverse of *tie*
3. Greek letter represented by π
4. Abbr. for *extraterrestrial*
5. Abbr. for *regiment*
6. Alt. spelling of suffix that forms adjectives, as in *magnet*_____
7. Alt. spelling of prefix meaning *with*, as in _____*author*
8. Alt. spelling for prefix meaning *not*, as in _____*mobile*
9. First person sing. of verb *to be*
10. Chem. symbol for *lithium*
11. Root meaning *yield* or *go*, as in se _____
12. Prefix meaning *not*, as in _____*necessary*
*13. Having to do with various races
16. Endeavor
17. Antonym of *you*
20. Alt. spelling of prefix meaning *against*, as in _____*fend*
23. Where you take a bath
25. Fruit drink, as in lemon_____
26. Abbr. of *company*
29. Boxer's last name
*31. Hindrances
33. Prefix used in 2 down
34. Alt. spelling of prefix meaning *out*, as in _____*centric*
35. Endeavor
39. Them or _____
40. Lowest or highest card
41. Abbr. for *extra high frequency*
42. Hawaiian neck wreath
44. Abbr. for *New Guinea*
45. Prefix meaning *down*, as in _____*cline*
46. Taxable earnings
47. Same as 41 across
48. Camping shelter
49. Smell of flowers
50. Roman numeral for 2
51. Abbr. for *southeast*
54. Portion of medicine
55. Seventh note on the musical scale
58. Antonym of *your*
60. Past tense of *run*
63. Gertrude Stein's monogram
64. Abbr. for *Alcoholics Anonymous*
65. Monogram of Tina Turner
66. Abbr. for Europe

Choose ten words that you would like to learn from those you have studied thus far in this book and enter them in the blanks below. You should choose words that you have had difficulty remembering. Look them up in the dictionary, paying particular attention to the etymologies, including roots. Pronounce each word, put the definition in your own words, use the word in a sentence, make up a mnemonic, and put the word on a flash card for regular review.

1. _____

2. _____

3. _____

4. _____

5. _____

6. _____

7. _____

8. _____

9. _____

10. _____

# chapter 10
# WORD HISTORIES

## The Family Circus

"It's not a 'Victrola,' Grandma. It's
a stereo."

Nobody knows how or where language began, since there were no records before the invention of writing. However, it's a good bet that the first words probably **sounded** like the things they were meant to represent. The word *roar* sounds like the noise a lion makes, and *chirp* and *squawk* sound like different kinds of birds. Brooks make a *babbling* sound, and when things hit against each other, they *crash*. Words still come into our language this way.

Another source of new words is **foreign languages.** In Chapter 7 we discussed the Anglo-Saxon, Latin, and Greek roots of English. Words based on Latin and Greek are still coming into our language today. For example, one word that was invented in the past five years is *bioethics,* the study of the ethical problems arising from scientific advances in biology and medicine (such as creating new forms of life, cloning, and making babies in test tubes). The word comes from the Greek roots *bio,* which means *life,* and *ēthikē,* which means *morality.* Hundreds of other European and non-European languages have also contributed to English. *Boondocks* comes from Tagalog (the chief language of the Philippine Islands); *chili, avocado, tomato,* and *chocolate* come from Nahuatl (the language of the Aztecs); *tattoo* is Tahitian; *tycoon* is Japanese; and *harem, hashish,* and *mattress* are from Arabic. Foreign languages continue to contribute new words.

Another source of new words is the **names** of people, places, and events. For example, the word *diesel* comes from Rudolf Diesel (1858–1913), the German engineer who invented the diesel engine. Joseph Hooker was a general in the American Civil War whose troops were stationed in Washington, D.C.; there were so many prostitutes hanging around his army that they became known as "Hooker's extra division," or *hookers,* and thus we gained another word.

**Ancient myths** also contributed words. The Greek god Tantalus, after being caught spying, was plunged into water up to his chin under trees that dangled fresh fruit just above his head. The punishment was that, when he tried to drink the water or eat the fruit, they moved just enough so he could not reach them. From this story, we get the word *tantalize,* which means to tease or disappoint by promising or showing something desirable and then withholding it. The name of the *Olympic* Games comes from the name of Mt. Olympus, the mythical home of the gods. Some of the months of the year and most of the planets come from the names of the Roman gods. *January* is from the god *Janus; March* is from *Mars,* the god of war, who also gave his name to the planet; *Neptune* was the god of the sea; *Mercury* was the messenger of the gods; *Pluto* was the god of the underworld; *Venus* was the goddess of love and beauty; *Saturn* was the god of agriculture; and *Uranus* was the god who represented the heavens. *Jupiter* was the Roman name for Zeus, the ruler of all the gods. In fact the only planet whose name does not come from Roman mythology is *Earth.* The name of our planet is based on an Old English word, *eorthe,* which means ground.

Other examples of how names became words in our language are **brand names** that have come to stand for a whole category of products. For example, *Kleenex* is often used to refer to any brand of paper tissue used as a handkerchief. *Kleenex* is a made-up word coming from *clean + ex.*

Another type of made-up word is an **acronym.** An acronym is a word formed from the first (or first few) letters of a series of words. *Radar* is an acronym coming from *ra*dio *d*etecting *a*nd *r*anging. The *zip* in *zip code* stands for *Z*one *I*mprovement *P*lan.

When something new is invented or discovered, a new word is often created to describe it. Think of *workaholic, glitz* and *paramedic.*

Learning the etymologies of words can help you in two ways: it can help you understand the words more thoroughly, and it can help you remember the words better. For example, knowing the origin of the word *tantalize* or the Latin words parts from which *retract* is made helps you understand why each word means what it means. Knowing the stories behind the words or knowing the prefixes and roots also makes the words more vivid and serves as a mnemonic device.

Languages continually change. Some day, people of the future will regard the vocabulary of today as archaic in much the same way that we think of the language of Shakespeare as belonging to the past.

**colossal** (kə läs′′l) *adj.*   1. like a colossus in size; huge   2. extraordinary

**harass** (hə ras′, her′as) *v.*   1. to worry or torment   2. to trouble by constant raids or attacks

**hazard** (haz′ərd) *n.*   1. risk; danger   2. an obstacle on a golf course

**jest** (jest) *n.*   1. a mocking remark   2. a joke   3. fun; joking   4. a thing to be laughed at
     —*v.*   1. to mock   2. to joke

**lunatic** (lo͞o′nə tik) *adj.*   1. insane or for the insane   2. utterly foolish—*n.*   an insane person

**prestige** (pres tēzh′) *n.*   1. the power to impress or influence   2. reputation based on high
     achievement, character, etc.

**sabotage** (sab′ə täzh′) *n.*   deliberate destruction of machines, etc. by employees in labor
     disputes or railroads, bridges, etc. by enemy agents or by underground resistance
     —*v.*   to commit sabotage on

**subtle** (sut′′l) *adj.*   1. thin; not dense   2. mentally keen   3. delicately skillful   4. crafty
     5. not obvious

**trivial** (triv′ē əl) *adj.*   unimportant; insignificant

**vandal** (van′d′l) *n.*   one who purposely destroys works of art or property

fat, āpe, cär; ten, ēven; is, bīte; gō, hôrn, to͞ol, look; oil, out; up, fʉr; get; joy; yet; chin; she; thin, *th*en; zh, leisure; ŋ, ring; ə for *a* in *ago, e* in *agent, i* in *sanity, o* in *comply, u* in *focus;* ′ as in *able* (ā′b′l)

Read the following list of Review Words. In each space below write the word that best completes that sentence. Check your answers in the back of the book.

| | | | | |
|---|---|---|---|---|
| colossal | hazard | lunatic | sabotage | trivial |
| harass | jest | prestige | subtle | vandal |

1.  The _____ Superdome in New Orleans, Louisiana, has a diameter of 680 feet.

2.  Some politicians try to _____ their competitors' campaigns by planting false rumors in the press.

3.  If, as an employer, you _____ an employee, you may be sued.

4.  Many a truth is told in _____.

5.  For many reasons, smoking is a _____ to your health.

6.  Try not to get upset over _____ matters.

7.  A _____ used a key, knife, or other sharp object to scratch the paint on my brand new car.

8.  Some people consider bungee-jumping fun; others consider it _____ behavior.

9.  It is difficult for people acquiring English as a second language to understand the _____ difference between "going to see John" and "going to the john."

10. Harvard is a university which has great _____.

Paperback dictionaries usually abbreviate the etymology of a word to save space. Using the short etymologies in your dictionary as clues, match the ten Review Words with the more extended etymologies presented below. Place the letter of the correct answer in the blank. Check your answers in the back of the book.

———  1. hazard

———  2. vandal

———  3. harass

———  4. lunatic

———  5. jest

———  6. prestige

———  7. subtle

———  8. colossal

———  9. trivial

——— 10. sabotage

a. Borrowed from a French word meaning magic, juggling tricks, or illusions (prestidigitation)

b. Named for an uncivilized Germanic tribe who sacked ancient Rome, destroying the property of others

c. Originally meant brave or famous deed (*geste*) in French

d. From the Arabic word for a dice game

e. Delicately woven; from the Latin word *subtilis*, meaning finespun

f. Originated when French peasants, angered by poor working conditions, threw their wooden shoes (*sabots*) into the factory machinery to destroy it

g. A crossroad where people would meet to gossip. Literally it means *three* roads.

h. From the Old French *harer*, which means to *set the dogs on*, from which we also get harum-scarum

i. One made insane by the Roman goddess of the moon

j. From a Latin word referring to a 100-foot statue, the Colossus of Rhodes, built 2,000 years ago

# NEW WORDS I

**abhor** (əb hôr′, ab hôr′) *v.*   to shrink away from in fear, disgust, or hatred; detest

**bizarre** (bi zär′) *adj.*   1. odd in manner, appearance, etc.; grotesque; queer   2. marked by extreme contrasts of color, design, or style   3. unexpected and unbelievable; fantastic [a *bizarre* sequence of events]

**chaos** (kā′äs) *n.*   1. the disorder of formless matter and infinite space supposed to have existed before the ordered universe   2. extreme confusion or disorder

**cliché** (klē shā′) *n.*   an expression or idea that has become overused; something trite; something worn out by constant use

**culprit** (kul′prit) *n.*   1. a person accused of a crime or offense, as in court; prisoner at the bar   2. a person guilty of a crime or offense; offender

**cynical** (sin′i k'l) *adj.*   1. believing that people are motivated in all their actions only by selfishness; denying the sincerity of people's motives and actions, or the value of living   2. sarcastic, sneering, etc.

**dismal** (diz′m'l) *adj.*   1. causing gloom or misery; depressing   2. dark and gloomy; bleak; dreary   3. depressed; miserable

**fanatic** (fən at′ik) *adj.*   unreasonably enthusiastic—*n.*   a person whose enthusiasm is excessive

**harangue** (hə raŋ′) *n.*   a long, noisy speech—*v.*   to attack or try to persuade with a long, often loud and scolding speech

**jeopardy** (jep′ər dē) *n.*   great danger; peril [to have one's life in *jeopardy*]

fat, āpe, cär; ten, ēven; is, bīte; gō, hôrn, tōōl, look; oil, out; up, fʉr; get; joy; yet; chin; she; thin, *then*; zh, leisure; ŋ, ring; ə for *a* in *ago, e* in *agent, i* in *sanity, o* in *comply, u* in *focus;* ' as in *able* (ā′b'l)

Match the correct etymology with the word from your New Word list below. Use your dictionary if you need help. Check your answers in the back of the book.

_____ 1. abhor

_____ 2. bizarre

_____ 3. chaos

_____ 4. cliché

_____ 5. culprit

_____ 6. cynical

_____ 7. dismal

_____ 8. fanatic

_____ 9. harangue

_____ 10. jeopardy

a. An even or equally divided game, from the Old French *ieu parti*

b. An Anglo-French contraction of the Latin legal phrase "*culpable: prest d'averre nostre bille*" or "He is guilty and I am ready to prove our charge." The phrase was shortened to *cul. prit.*

c. An area to assemble for speeches or have horse races. It comes from the Gothic word *hrings* = circle.

d. From the Latin *ab* = away and *horreo* = bristle or stand on end. It was thought that when something is horrible your hair stands on end.

e. Stereotype (originally a uniform printing plate made of clay). It comes from the German word for clay, *klitseh.*

f. Gas; in Greek also means an endless pit or emptiness

g. From the Spanish word *bizarro,* meaning bold or knightly; probably came from the Basque word *bizar,* meaning *beard*

h. Set of 24 days (2 each month) that were identified as unlucky on the French calendar (*dis mal*). It is thought they originally came from Egyptian superstition.

i. A school of Greek philosophers scorned luxury and thought that a love of virtue was the highest good. The followers distorted the teachings into self-righteous criticism of everyone else, so the other Greeks nicknamed them *cynics,* meaning "like a dog."

j. From the Latin *fanum* or *temple;* originally meant inspired by divinity. It is the etymology of our word *fan.*

## EXERCISE 4: FILL-IN

Choose the word that correctly completes each sentence and write it in the blank.
Check your answers in the back of the book.

| abhorred | chaotic | culprit | dismal | harangue |
|----------|---------|---------|--------|----------|
| bizarre | cliché | cynical | fanatics | jeopardy |

1. Hitler is still _____ for killing six million Jews in World War II.

2. Charles Dickens' Ebenezer Scrooge was at first _____ but later became a believer in the spirit of Christmas.

3. In the nineteenth century, Aaron Burr was involved in a _____ plot to separate the western U.S. states and territories from the Union.

4. Joan of Arc is one of the few _____ who is admired by most people.

5. Driving while drunk places your life in _____ .

6. When the illustrator drew a composite picture of the man who robbed the Bank of America, the police had a clue to the identity of the _____ .

7. A _____ by a member of the U.S. Senate to defeat a bill is called a filibuster.

8. The beautiful young woman was tired of hearing the _____ "You're as pretty as a picture" every time she visited her family.

9. Registration day on college campuses is frequently _____ .

10. _____ weather can significantly change some people's behavior. For example, many psychologists now believe that the lack of sunlight for long periods of time causes a chemical change that can lead to depression in some light-sensitive individuals.

**jovial** (jō′vē əl) *adj.*   full of hearty, playful good humor; gay; joyful

**martial** (mär′shəl) *adj.*   1. of or suitable for war   2. warlike   3. military

**nonchalant** (nän′shə länt′) *adj.*   1. without warmth or enthusiasm; not showing interest   2. showing cool lack of concern; casually indifferent

**ostracize** (äs′trə sīz′) *v.*   to exile, bar, exclude, etc., by general consent, as from a group or from acceptance by society

**preposterous** (pri päs′tər əs) *adj.*   so contrary to nature, reason, or common sense as to be laughable; absurd; ridiculous

**robust** (rō bust′, rō′bust) *adj.*   1. strong and healthy; hardy   2. full-flavored

**sinister** (sin′is tər) *adj.*   1. threatening harm, evil, or misfortune; ominous [*sinister*-looking clouds]   2. wicked, evil, or dishonest, esp. in some dark mysterious way [a *sinister* plot]   3. most unfavorable or unfortunate; disastrous [met a *sinister* fate]

**stereotype** (ster′ē ə tīp′) *n.*   a fixed notion or concept of a person or group held by a number of people—*v.*   to form a fixed notion of a person or group; prejudge

**stigma** (stig′mə) *n.*   1. something that detracts from the character or reputation of a person, group, etc.   2. a mark or sign, etc., indicating that something is not considered normal or standard

**taboo** (ta boo′, tə boo′) *n.*   1. any social prohibition or restriction that results from convention or tradition   2. among some Polynesian peoples, a sacred prohibition put upon certain people, things, or acts that makes them untouchable, unmentionable, etc.   3. the highly developed system or practice of such prohibitions—*adj.*   sacred and prohibited; forbidden by tradition, convention, etc.

fat, āpe, cär; ten, ēven; is, bīte; gō, hôrn, tool, look; oil, out; up, fur; get; joy; yet; chin; she; thin, then; zh, leisure; ŋ, ring; ə for *a* in *ago, e* in *agent, i* in *sanity, o* in *comply, u* in *focus;* ′ as in *able* (ā′b'l)

Use your dictionary to find the etymologies of the words below. Fill in the appropriate word in each blank. Check your answers in the back of the book.

jovial          nonchalant          preposterous          sinister          stigma
martial         ostracize           robust                stereotype         taboo

_____  1.  Refers to Jove, another name for Jupiter, the ruler of the Roman gods, known for playing practical jokes

_____  2.  Greek, a prick with a pointed instrument (slave's mark)

_____  3.  Comes from the Latin words *prae* = before, and *posterus* = after. It suggests the absurd situation of the cart coming before the horse.

_____  4.  Means left-handed or unlucky in Latin

_____  5.  From the Latin *non* = not and *caleo* = warm; today it might be translated *lukewarm*

_____  6.  Borrowed from Tongan meaning *forbidden*

_____  7.  Latin, *meaning strong as an oak*

_____  8.  Comes from *Mars*, the name for the Roman god of War

_____  9.  From the Greek word meaning *tile* or *potsherd*. In Greece the citizens would assemble to make up their minds about public officials thought to be dangerous. They wrote the name of the undesirable man on the tile if they agreed that he should be exiled. The word is thought to have originally come from the word *shell* since colored shells were also used for such trials. We use the term *blackball* for the same practice.

_____  10.  From the Greek word *steros* = a hard, solid surface, and the Latin *typus* = a model, symbol; a one-piece printing plate cast in metal so the pattern would not vary

Circle the letter before the word or phrase that best defines the italicized word in each sentence. Check your answers in the back of the book.

1. Santa Claus is almost always portrayed as a *jovial* fellow. You seldom see him without a smile.

   a. surprised   b. happy   c. dishonest   d. stupid

2. When a military dictator takes over a country's government, he often imposes *martial* law.

   a. unusual   b. good   c. military   d. civil

3. He was *nonchalant* about being fired from his job.

   a. concerned   b. uninvolved   c. emotional   d. confused

4. A lion pride has only one mature male because other males are *ostracized* when they reach adulthood.

   a. driven out   b. welcomed   c. accepted   d. killed

5. Getting married while bungee-jumping is the most *preposterous* idea I have ever heard.

   a. brilliant   b. careless   c. impossible   d. ridiculous

6. Some small athletes, such as jockey Willie Shoemaker, don't appear *robust*, but are extremely strong.

   a. wealthy   b. capable   c. weak   d. strong

7. Darth Vader, the *sinister* character from *Star Wars,* was dressed completely in black to make him look more evil.

   a. famous   b. hated   c. evil   d. troublesome

8. Do not *stereotype* people from other cultures; try to judge each person as an individual.

   a. ignore   b. fear   c. invite   d. prejudge

9. Teenage boys consider it a *stigma* to be shorter than the girls in their class.

   a. positive sign   b. frightening experience   c. negative mark   d. surprising event

10. There are still some words which are *taboo* on television, especially ones dealing with sex.

    a. desirable   b. sacred   c. unwise   d. forbidden

## EXERCISE 7: TRUE-FALSE

Place a *T* or an *F* in the space provided. Check your answers in the back of the book.

_____  1.  Most middle-aged people are fanatics.

_____  2.  A cliché is a new way of saying something.

_____  3.  A stigma is a good thing to have.

_____  4.  Under martial law, the people vote for the government.

_____  5.  A harangue is meant to persuade.


## EXERCISE 8: ANALOGIES

The analogies below are either synonyms, antonyms, classification : example, cause : effect, or part : whole. First, decide which type of comparison is used in the first pair of words. Second, fill in the type of analogy in the first blank using *S* for synonym, *A* for antonym, *C* for classification, *C/E* for cause : effect, and *P* for part : whole. Third, find a word from the choices that will make the second pair of words have the same relationship. Check your answers in the back of the book.

_____  1.  jest  :  laughter  ::
            culprit  :  _____

a.  criminal   b.  crime   c.  reward
d.  innocence

_____  2.  trivial  :  essential  ::
            robust  :  _____

a.  strong   b.  weak   c.  unimportant
d.  sick

_____  3.  colossal  :  enormous  ::
            ostracize  :  _____

a.  exile   b.  welcome   c.  mistake
d.  forgive

_____  4.  prestige  :  executive position  ::
            taboos  :  _____

a.  restrictions   b.  marriage
c.  all cultures   d.  freedom

_____  5.  hazard  :  broken bottle  ::
            chaos  :  _____

a.  big sale   b.  confusion   c.  calm
d.  bank statement

## EXERCISE 9: MATCHING MEANINGS

Write the letter of the word that means the opposite of the word in the first column. Check your answers in the back of the book.

———— 1. sinister          a. mournful

———— 2. bizarre          b. involved

———— 3. jeopardy         c. angelic

———— 4. jovial           d. commonplace

———— 5. nonchalant       e. safety

## EXERCISE 10: WORD CONTRASTS

In each group below, circle the word that does not mean what the others mean. Check your answers in the back of the book.

1. abhor     worship     adore     idolize

2. preposterous     logical     absurd     ridiculous

3. cynical     disillusioned     hopeful     scornful

4. harass     pester     torment     delight

5. dismal     somber     jovial     depressing

## EXERCISE 11: SENTENCE COMPLETION

Complete each sentence in your own words. Sample answers are provided in the back of the book.

1. I *abhor* it when _____

_____ .

2. A woman with green hair would be *bizarre* because _____

_____ .

3. When a storm causes *chaos* in a town, _____

_____ .

4. An example of a *cliché* I use is _____

_____ .

5. After you see a *culprit* steal something in a store, _____

_____ .

6. People in college aren't *cynical* about their futures because _____

_____.

7. I tend to think it is a *dismal* day if _____

_____.

8. People think you are *fanatic* when _____

_____.

9. The last time I received a long *harangue* was when _____

_____.

10. Unless you are in *jeopardy,* you shouldn't _____

_____.

11. Because a *jovial* person is nice to be around, _____

_____.

12. During the time a country is under *martial* law, _____

_____.

13. A *nonchalant* attitude toward your job will result in _____

_____.

14. Before a club *ostracizes* one of its members, _____

_____.

15. A *preposterous* statement is likely to _____

_____.

16. Because *robust* people tend to live longer, _____

_____.

17. Although a person may look *sinister,* _____

_____.

18. An example of a *stereotype* I have seen is when _____

_____.

19. Besides being embarrassing, a *stigma* _____

_____.

20. It is *taboo* in some states to _____

_____.

# ADVANCED WORDS

**anecdote** (an′ik dōt′) *n.*   a short, entertaining account of some happening, usually personal or biographical

**appease** (ə pēz′) *v.*   1. to pacify or quiet, esp. by giving in to the demands of   2. to relieve or satisfy [water *appeases* thirst]

**dexterous** (dek′strəs, dek′stər əs) *adj.*   1. having or showing skill in the use of the hands or body   2. having or showing mental skill (also spelled dextrous)

**pandemonium** (pan′də mō′nē əm) *n.*   1. any place or scene of wild disorder, noise, or confusion   2. wild disorder, noise, or confusion

**paraphernalia** (par′ə fər nāl′yə, par′ə fə nāl′yə) *n. pl.*   1. personal belongings   2. any collection of articles, usually things used in some activity; equipment; apparatus; trappings; gear

**precarious** (pri ker′ē əs) *adj.*   1. dependent upon circumstances; uncertain; insecure [a *precarious* living]   2. dependent upon chance; risky [a *precarious* foothold]   3. dependent upon mere assumption; unwarranted [a *precarious* assertion]

**scruples** (skrōō′p′lz) *n.*   1. feelings of hesitancy, doubt, or uneasiness arising from difficulty in deciding what is right, proper, or ethical; misgivings about something one thinks is wrong   2. very small quantities, amounts, or parts

**stoic** (stō′ik) *n.*   someone indifferent to the outside world and indifferent to passion or emotion—*adj.*   unemotional; strong and calm

**tantalize** (tan′tə līz′) *v.*   to tease or disappoint by promising or showing something desirable and then withholding it

**utopia** (yōō tō′pē ə) *n.*   1. any idealized place, state, or situation of perfection   2. any visionary scheme or system for an ideally perfect society

fat, āpe, cär; ten, ēven; is, bīte; gō, hôrn, tōōl, look; oil, out; up, fur; get; joy; yet; chin; she; thin, then; zh, leisure; ŋ, ring; ə for *a* in *ago, e* in *agent, i* in *sanity, o* in *comply, u* in *focus;* ′ as in *able* (ā′b′l)

Use the Advanced Words to fill in the blanks in the sentences that follow. Check your answers in the back of the book.

| | | | | |
|---|---|---|---|---|
| anecdote | dexterous | paraphernalia | scruples | tantalize |
| appease | pandemonium | precarious | stoic | utopia |

1. Scenes of pure _____, such as 20 people in a small compartment, were common in every Marx Brothers movie.

2. A _____ would be a world without war, government, bureaucracy, or taxes.

3. In the state of California, although it is still illegal to sell marijuana, it is legal to sell the _____ such as papers and roach clips.

4. There is a famous _____ about Babe Ruth's pointing to the center field fence just before hitting a World Series home run in 1932.

5. When his rope began to unravel, the mountain climber found himself in a very _____ position.

6. Some actors and actresses claim that to become a Hollywood star you cannot have any _____.

7. Few gymnasts are _____ enough to receive a perfect score of 10 in an event.

8. In the 1930s, England's Prime Minister tried to _____ Hitler by giving in to his demands. The plan backfired, and soon Great Britain was defending itself against "der Fuhrer."

9. Japanese food is purposely varied in color and texture to _____ the diner.

10. After Franklin D. Roosevelt was stricken with polio in 1921, he became widely admired for his broad smile and excellent sense of humor, which reflected his _____ attitude toward his illness.

Use your dictionary to find the etymologies of the ten Advanced Words. They may be found either in brackets after the part of speech or they may be listed as the first definition of the word. The first one is done for you. Check your answers in the back of the book.

1. anecdote _Gr: not given out; unpublished_

2. appease _____

3. dexterous _____

4. pandemonium _____

5. paraphernalia _____

6. precarious _____

7. scruples _____

8. stoic _____

9. tantalize _____

10. utopia _____

# EXERCISE 14: CROSSWORD PUZZLE

This crossword puzzle reviews the New Words from previous chapters. The clues with an asterisk (*) have an answer that is from a New Words list in a previous chapter. Remember to use a pencil to complete the puzzle so that you can change your mind. Check your answers in the back of the book.

## Across

- *1. Unbelievable
- 10. Antonym of *far*
- 11. Flesh of animals
- *14. Relevant
- 17. Where satellites stay
- 18. Latin for *eggs*
- 19. Football player Ernie Stautner's monogram
- *21. To formally withdraw from
- 22. Satisfied
- 25. Alt. spelling of verb suffix *ize*
- 26. Abbr. for *district attorney*
- *28. Lack of feeling
- *29. Fraud
- 31. Archaic for *you*
- 32. Abbr. for *Georgia*
- 34. Beginning of a letter: _____ Sir,
- 35. Abbr. for *South Dakota*
- 37. "I _____," said the bride
- 39. Alt. spelling of prefix meaning *to*, as in _____mire
- 40. Abbr. for *audiovisual*
- *41. Finds out with certainty
- 48. Abbr. for direction *south-southeast*
- 49. To strike lightly
- *50. Receivers
- 53. Abbr. for *North Atlantic Treaty Organization*
- 54. Alt. spelling of prefix meaning *to*, as in _____semble
- 55. Dictionary abbreviation meaning *for example*
- 56. Prefix meaning *having two*, as in _____cycle
- *57. Assumptions of truth
- 63. Alt. spelling of prefix meaning *to*, as in _____nounce
- 64. Antonym of *west*
- 65. Antonym of *off*
- 66. Hangs loosely

## Down

- *1. Awe-inspiring
- 2. Abbr. for *the tenth month*
- *3. Admitted as true or valid
- 4. Antonym of *outer*
- 5. Abbr. for *veterans*
- 6. Abbr. for *Alcoholics Anonymous*
- 7. Abbr. for *British*
- *8. Identification with another
- 9. Tic, _____, toe
- 12. Abbr. for *each*
- *13. Not definite or final
- 15. Nights before holidays like Christmas
- 16. Ran against others
- 20. Monies lent from the bank
- 22. Abbr. for *Chief Petty Officer*
- 23. Abbr. for *New Testament*
- 24. Organs for seeing
- 27. Large primate
- 28. What we breathe
- 30. Abbr. for *teaching assistant*
- *33. To hold oneself back
- 36. The day of the month
- *37. To remove from office
- 38. Antonym of *nor*
- *40. Evaluate
- 42. Abbr. for *computer-aided training*
- 43. Devices for catching animals
- 44. Albert Einstein's monogram
- 45. Suffix meaning *having to do with*, as in archa_____
- 46. Abbr. for Northern Ireland
- 47. Country whose capital is Madrid
- 48. Abbr. for *street*
- 51. Suffix meaning *one who*, as in violin_____
- 52. Abbr. for *National Council on Aging*
- 53. Abbr. for *National Basketball Association*
- 58. Abbr. for *United Artists*
- 59. Abbr. for *pint*
- 60. Abbr. for *south*
- 61. I am; he _____
- 62. Abbr. for *National Guard*

Choose from your outside reading ten words that you would like to learn and write them in the spaces below. When you look the words up in the dictionary, pay particular attention to their etymologies. Pronounce each word, put the definition in your own words, use the word in a sentence, make up a mnemonic, and put the word on a flash card for regular review.

1. _____
2. _____
3. _____
4. _____
5. _____

6. _____
7. _____
8. _____
9. _____
10. _____

# chapter 11

# THESAURUS

Bill Proctor and Jules Lenier

Take exactly one minute (time yourself) and write as many synonyms as you can think of for the word *money:*

| | | |
|---|---|---|
| _____ | _____ | _____ |
| _____ | _____ | _____ |
| _____ | _____ | _____ |
| _____ | _____ | _____ |
| _____ | _____ | _____ |

The average person thinks of about eight synonyms in a minute. Compare this number with the number of synonyms contained in the thesaurus sample on the next page. Did you think of most of them?

Because it is so difficult to think of all the synonyms for a word, the thesaurus is a useful tool for all college students. It is used constantly by professional writers and speakers. You can use it for writing papers and making oral reports, as well as for vocabulary improvement. For example, suppose you are writing a paper about the rich. Instead of repeating the words *rich* and *money* over and over, you could look in the thesaurus under *money* to locate words like *wealth, capital, assets, prosperity,* and *affluence.*

The purpose of a thesaurus is to suggest words you need but haven't been able to think of. A thesaurus cannot replace a dictionary. It usually does not give definitions, pronunciations, or etymologies. Some words, such as *ethnic,* have no natural synonyms; they do not appear in the thesaurus at all. But a thesaurus can give you more words to describe the same concept than you could find in any dictionary. The word *thesaurus* comes from Greek and Latin words meaning *treasury,* and a good thesaurus really is a treasury of related words.

## Thesaurus Structure

Although there are several different thesauruses, one of the most commonly used by college students is *The New American Roget's College Thesaurus in Dictionary Form.*[1] The paperback edition is about the size of a pocket dictionary. Here is a sample page showing the key features.

[1]Unless otherwise noted, the thesaurus quotations within this chapter are from *The New American Roget's College Thesaurus in Dictionary Form* by Philip D. Morehead and Andrew T. Morehead. Copyright © 1985. Revised edition prepared by Philip D. Morehead. Copyright © 1958, 1962 by Albert H. Morehead. Copyright © 1978 by Andrew T. Morehead and Philip D. Morehead. Reprinted by arrangement with The New American Library, Inc., New York, N.Y.

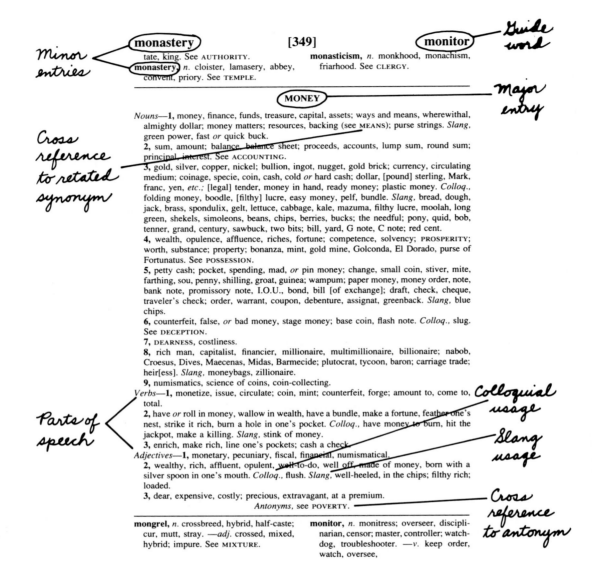

*minor entries*

**monastery**
tate, king. See AUTHORITY.
**monastery**, *n.* cloister, lamasery, abbey, convent, priory. See TEMPLE.

[349]

**monitor** — *Guide word*

monasticism, *n.* monkhood, monachism, friarhood. See CLERGY.

**MONEY** — *Major entry*

*Nouns*—**1,** money, finance, funds, treasure, capital, assets; ways and means, wherewithal, almighty dollar; money matters; resources, backing (see MEANS); purse strings. *Slang,* green power, fast *or* quick buck.

**2,** sum, amount; balance, balance sheet; proceeds, accounts, lump sum, round sum; principal, interest. See ACCOUNTING.

**3,** gold, silver, copper, nickel; bullion, ingot, nugget, gold brick; currency, circulating medium; coinage, specie, coin, cash, cold *or* hard cash; dollar, [pound] sterling, Mark, franc, yen, *etc.;* [legal] tender, money in hand, ready money; plastic money. *Colloq.,* folding money, boodle, [filthy] lucre, easy money, pelf, bundle. *Slang,* bread, dough, jack, brass, spondulix, gelt, lettuce, cabbage, kale, mazuma, filthy lucre, moolah, long green, shekels, simoleons, beans, chips, berries, bucks; the needful; pony, quid, bob, tenner, grand, century, sawbuck, two bits; bill, yard, G note, C note; red cent.

**4,** wealth, opulence, affluence, riches, fortune; competence, solvency; PROSPERITY; worth, substance; property; bonanza, mint, gold mine, Golconda, El Dorado, purse of Fortunatus. See POSSESSION.

**5,** petty cash; pocket, spending, mad, *or* pin money; change, small coin, stiver, mite, farthing, sou, penny, shilling, groat, guinea; wampum; paper money, money order, note, bank note, promissory note, I.O.U., bond, bill [of exchange]; draft, check, cheque, traveler's check; order, warrant, coupon, debenture, assignat, greenback. *Slang,* blue chips.

**6,** counterfeit, false, *or* bad money, stage money; base coin, flash note. *Colloq.,* slug. See DECEPTION.

**7,** DEARNESS, costliness.

**8,** rich man, capitalist, financier, millionaire, multimillionaire, billionaire; nabob, Croesus, Dives, Maecenas, Midas, Barmecide; plutocrat, tycoon, baron; carriage trade; heir[ess]. *Slang,* moneybags, zillionaire.

**9,** numismatics, science of coins, coin-collecting.

*Verbs*—**1,** monetize, issue, circulate; coin, mint; counterfeit, forge; amount to, come to, total.

**2,** have *or* roll in money, wallow in wealth, have a bundle, make a fortune, feather one's nest, strike it rich, burn a hole in one's pocket. *Colloq.,* have money to burn, hit the jackpot, make a killing. *Slang,* stink of money.

**3,** enrich, make rich, line one's pockets; cash a check.

*Adjectives*—**1,** monetary, pecuniary, fiscal, financial, numismatical.

**2,** wealthy, rich, affluent, opulent, well-to-do, well off, made of money, born with a silver spoon in one's mouth. *Colloq.,* flush. *Slang,* well-heeled, in the chips; filthy rich; loaded.

**3,** dear, expensive, costly; precious, extravagant, at a premium.

*Antonyms,* see POVERTY.

mongrel, *n.* crossbreed, hybrid, half-caste; cur, mutt, stray. —*adj.* crossed, mixed, hybrid; impure. See MIXTURE.

monitor, *n.* monitress; overseer, disciplinarian, censor; master, controller; watchdog, troubleshooter. —*v.* keep order, watch, oversee,

*Cross reference to related synonym*

*Parts of speech*

*Colloquial usage*

*Slang usage*

*Cross reference to antonym*

## Guide Words

Like a dictionary, the thesaurus has a guide word or words on each page.

## Major Entry

Our sample has major entries and minor entries. The major entry, *money,* is in capital letters. Major entries are always the noun form of the word. Listed underneath are synonyms, classified by part of speech. Under each part of speech is a group of synonyms for a different meaning of the word. In our sample, *money* has nine different classifications of meanings as a noun.

### Minor Entry

Minor entries, which are not in capital letters, are alphabetized. They can be any part of speech.

**monastery**                                                                   **monitor**

monastery, *n.* cloister, lamasery, abbey, convent, priory. See TEMPLE.

monasticism, *n.* monkhood, monachism, friarhood. See CLERGY.

### Cross-references

Synonyms that have their own major entries are printed in SMALL CAPITAL letters. Examples are TEMPLE and CLERGY under **monastery** and **monasticism** in the previous sample. Cross-references are worth looking up, since each of them will contain synonyms not appearing under the original entry. Cross-references are also used to refer you to antonyms, if the word has any.

### Usage

To help you use a word, the thesaurus gives you the part of speech and tells you whether the word is colloquial, slang, or dialect.

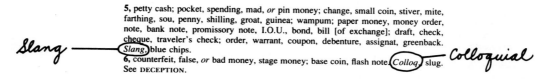

**5,** petty cash; pocket, spending, mad, *or* pin money; change, small coin, stiver, mite, farthing, sou, penny, shilling, groat, guinea; wampum; paper money, money order, note, bank note, promissory note, I.O.U., bond, bill [of exchange]; draft, check, cheque, traveler's check; order, warrant, coupon, debenture, assignat, greenback. *Slang,* blue chips.
**6,** counterfeit, false, *or* bad money, stage money; base coin, flash note, *Colloq.,* slug. See DECEPTION.

*Slang* ———                                                      ——— *Colloquial*

### Additional Material

Like a dictionary, the back of the thesaurus often contains additional material, such as a list of foreign phrases with definitions and cross-references to related words included in the thesaurus. It's always wise to be aware of any additional material contained in the thesaurus you own.

### Different Types of Thesauruses

Another type of thesaurus, also in dictionary form, is the *Merriam-Webster Thesaurus.* (See next page.) This type of thesaurus, unlike *The New American Roget's College Thesaurus in Dictionary Form,* provides a brief definition of all major entries and usually includes a phrase using the word in context. If the word has more than one meaning, or if it is used as other parts of speech, this thesaurus lists a separate entry with a definition and example. The words following the entry are grouped into exact synonyms, related words, contrasted words, and antonyms. If there are any relevant idioms, they are listed after the antonyms. The classification system and the use of the word in context means there is less need to use a dictionary than with *The New American Roget's College Thesaurus.* This type of thesaurus has many more cross-references than *The New American Roget's College Thesaurus.* The following is a page from the *Merriam-Webster Thesaurus* that contains the entries for *money.* You can compare it with the sample from *The New American Roget's College Thesaurus in Dictionary Form* found at the beginning of this chapter.

*syn* bait, heckle, persecute, torment

*rel* annoy, badger, bother, irk, pester; pother, tease; bedevil, beset, devil, trouble; harass, harry, vex

**moll** *n syn see* PROSTITUTE

**mollify** *vb* **1** *syn see* PACIFY

*rel* lighten; temper; abate, decrease, lessen, reduce

*ant* exasperate

**2** *syn see* RELIEVE 1

‖**molly** *n syn see* WEAKLING

**mollycoddle** *n syn see* WEAKLING

*rel* ‖mollycot

**mollycoddle** *vb syn see* BABY

*ant* neglect; abuse

**molt** *vb syn see* SHED 2

**mom** *n syn see* MOTHER 1

‖**momble** *vb syn see* CONFUSE 2

**moment** *n* **1** *syn see* INSTANT 1

*ant* eternity

**2** *syn see* POINT 7

**3** *syn see* OCCASION 5

**4** *syn see* IMPORTANCE

*rel* advantage, avail, profit, use

**momentaneous** *adj syn see* TRANSIENT

**momentary** *adj syn see* TRANSIENT

*rel* brief, quick, short; impulsive

*ant* agelong

**momentous** *adj* **1** *syn see* IMPORTANT 1

*ant* trivial

**2** *syn see* EPOCHAL

**momentousness** *n syn see* IMPORTANCE

*ant* triviality

**mommy** *n syn see* MOTHER 1

**momus** *n syn see* CRITIC

**monarchal** *adj syn see* KINGLY

**monarchial** *adj syn see* KINGLY

**monarchical** *adj syn see* KINGLY

**mondaine** *adj syn see* SOPHISTICATED 2

**monetary** *adj syn see* FINANCIAL

*rel* numismatic

**money** *n* something (as pieces of stamped metal or paper certificates) customarily and legally used as a medium of exchange 〈the only thing that he liked about his job was the *money*〉

*syn* ‖blunt, ‖brass, ‖bread, ‖cabbage, cash, ‖chink, ‖chips, ‖coin, currency, ‖dibs, ‖dinero, ‖do-re-mi, dough, filthy lucre, ‖gelt, ‖greenbacks, ‖jack, ‖kale, legal tender, ‖lettuce, ‖long green, loot, lucre, ‖mazuma, ‖moolah, ‖mopus, needful, ‖ooftish, pelf, rhino, rocks, ‖scratch, ‖shekels, ‖smash, stuff, ‖stumpy, ‖sugar, swag, ‖wampum

*rel* bankroll, capital, coinage, finances, funds, mammon, resources, riches, treasure, wealth, wherewithal; boodle, hay; ‖stiff

**moneyed** *adj syn see* RICH 1

*ant* penniless, unmoneyed

**moneygrubber** *n syn see* MISER

**moneymaking** *adj syn see* ADVANTAGEOUS 1

**monger** *n syn see* PEDDLER

**monger** *vb syn see* PEDDLE 2

**mongerer** *n syn see* PEDDLER

**mongrel** *n syn see* HYBRID

‖**moniker** *n* **1** *syn see* NAME 1

**2** *syn see* NICKNAME

**monish** *vb syn see* REPROVE

**monition** *n syn see* WARNING

**monitorial** *adj syn see* MONITORY

**monitory** *adj* giving a warning 〈the parents wrote their son a *monitory* letter〉

*syn* admonishing, admonitory, cautionary, cautioning, monitorial, warning

*rel* advisory, counseling; critical, expostulatory, remonstratory; exhortatory, hortatory; moralistic, moralizing, preachy

**monkey** *n* **1** *syn see* FOOL 3

**2** *syn see* URCHIN

**monkey** *adj syn see* SMALL 1

**monkey** (with) *vb syn see* MEDDLE

**monkeyshine** *n usu* monkeyshines *pl*

*syn see* PRANK

**monocratic** *adj syn see* ABSOLUTE 4

*con* democratic

**monogram** *n* a sign of identity usually formed of the combined initials of a name 〈everything he owned had his *monogram* on it〉

*syn* cipher

*rel* device, initials; John Hancock, signature

**monograph** *n syn see* DISCOURSE 2

**monography** *n syn see* DISCOURSE 2

**monopolize** *vb* to take up completely 〈he would attempt to *monopolize* every conversation〉

*syn* absorb, consume, engross, sew up

*rel* corner, hog; devour; have, hold, own, possess; employ, use, utilize; control, manage

*con* contribute, participate, share

**monopolizing** *adj syn see* ENGROSSING

**monopoly** *n* exclusive possession 〈neither party has a *monopoly* on morality〉

*syn* corner

*rel* cartel, consortium, pool, syndicate, trust; copyright; ownership, possessorship, proprietorship

**monotone** *n syn see* MONOTONY

**monotone** *adj syn see* DULL 9

**monotonous** *adj syn see* DULL 9

*rel* samely, uniform, unvaried; repetitious; jog-trot, singsong

*con* changing, varying; fresh, new, novel; absorbing, engrossing, interesting

**monotonousness** *n syn see* MONOTONY

**monotony** *n* a tedious sameness or reiteration 〈the *monotony* of his job finally got to him〉

*syn* humdrum, monotone, monotonousness

*rel* boredom, ennui, tedium; dryness, flatness, uniformity

*con* variability, variation; diversification, diversity, multifariousness, variety

**monster** *n* **1** *syn see* FREAK 2

*rel* demon, devil, fiend, hellhound; bander snatch

**2** *syn see* GIANT

**monster** *adj syn see* HUGE

**monstrosity** *n* **1** *syn see* FREAK 2

**2** *syn see* EYESORE

**monstrous** *adj* **1** extremely impressive 〈the traditional burial ceremonies turned into a *monstrous* spectacle〉

*syn* cracking, fantastic, massive, monumental, mortal, prodigious, stupendous, towering, tremendous

*rel* grandiose, impressive, magnificent, showy, splendid, superb; colossal, enormous, huge, immense, mammoth, vast

# Using the Thesaurus

## Finding the Word

Let's say you want to find synonyms for the word *defunct*. The first thing you would do is look the word up in its alphabetical order. However, *Roget's* doesn't list this word (different thesauruses will contain different words). Because you know that *defunct* does have synonyms, your second step is to try to think of another word that has a similar meaning. One example might be *dead*. If you look under *dead*, you will find the following entry:

> **dead,** *adj.* deceased, perished, defunct; lifeless, inanimate; obsolete, extinct. See DEATH, NONEXISTENCE, INSENSIBILITY.

If you didn't find the synonyms you wanted under *dead*, you could look up the cross-references *death*, *nonexistence*, and *insensibility*, which will have their own entries with more synonyms.

Another possibility when you can't find a word in the thesaurus is to look under another part of speech. For example, if you were looking for *fortunately*, which is an adverb, you wouldn't find it in *Roget's*, but you would find the minor entry, *fortunate*, which is an adjective. A synonym listed under *fortunate* includes *lucky*. You could use it as a synonym for *fortunately* if you changed it to *luckily*.

## Using the Word

Sometimes you will find in the thesaurus synonyms that have meanings that are unfamiliar to you. For example, under *dead* are the words *inanimate* and *obsolete*. You know that *obsolete* is supposed to be a synonym for *dead*, but you don't know whether the two words have the same shade of meaning so that they can be used interchangeably. For example, you know that some of the words listed under *dead*, such as *perished* and *lifeless*, don't mean exactly the same thing. This is the time to go back to your dictionary. If you look up *obsolete*, you will find the following definition, which enables you to use the word correctly.

> **ob-so-lete** (äb′sə lēt′, äb′sə lēt′) *adj.* [< L. *obsoletus* < *ob-* (see OB-) + *exolescere*, to grow out of use] **1** no longer in use **2** out-of-date

A thesaurus should always be used in combination with a dictionary. You need the thesaurus to suggest words you haven't thought of, and you need the dictionary to tell you more about any words you aren't sure of.

# Practice

Below is a common English proverb inflated by three different students using the thesaurus.

1. An ornithological subject in one's possession transcends in value a plurality in the wilderness.
2. A singular feathered friend grasped in the extremity is valued as a duality in the thicket.
3. A fowl in the fist is estimated as a binary in the shrubbery.

What is the proverb? _____

Check your answer in the back of the book.

## EXERCISE 1: INFLATED PROVERBS

Use your thesaurus to find substitute words for those in the proverbs below. Your answers should resemble those for the practice above. Samples appear in the back of the book.

1. Haste makes waste.

   _____

2. Time heals all wounds.

   _____

3. That's a horse of a different color.

   _____

## EXERCISE 2: USING THE THESAURUS

Use the excerpt from *The New American Roget's College Thesaurus in Dictionary Form* on p. 196 of this book to complete the following exercise. Check your answers in the back of the book.

1. What parts of speech are given for the word for *mongrel?* _____

2. What is a slang term for *petty cash?* _____

3. Name a person mentioned in the **MONEY** entry who has become synonymous with being a rich man. _____

4. What three parts of speech are given for *money?* _____

5. What cross-reference is given for synonyms of *monastery?* _____

6. Under what entry would you find antonyms for *money?* _____

7. Would you expect *poverty* to have a major or a minor entry? _____

8. Does the guide word in the right-hand corner represent the first or the last word on page 349? _____

9. Name one vegetable that is slang for *money.* _____

10. What is the colloquial word for *counterfeit money?* _____

# REVIEW WORDS

**conspiracy** (kən spir′ə sē) *n.* 1. a plan made together secretly, esp. to commit a crime 2. an unlawful plot 3. a conspiring group

**corruption** (kə rupt′shən) *n.* 1. the act of being evil; the act of making morally bad 2. the act of taking bribes; the act of being dishonest

**eligible** (el′i jə b'l) *adj.* fit to be chosen; qualified

**enterprise** (en′tər prīz′) *n.* 1. an undertaking, esp. a big, bold, or difficult one 2. energy and initiative

**excessive** (ek ses′iv) *adj.* too much; immoderate

**peril** (per′əl) *n.* 1. exposure to harm or injury 2. something that may cause harm; danger

**resist** (ri zist′, rē zist′) *v.* 1. to withstand 2. to oppose actively; fight against

**saturate** (sach′ə rāt′) *v.* 1. thoroughly soak 2. fill with the most it can absorb

**tactic** (tak′tik) *n.* any skillful method to gain an end; strategy

**treachery** (trech′ə rē) *n.* 1. betrayal of trust; disloyalty 2. treason

fat, āpe, cär; ten, ēven; is, bīte; gō, hôrn, tōol, look; oil, out; up, fʉr; get; joy; yet; chin; she; thin, *th*en; zh, leisure; ŋ, ring; ə for *a* in *ago, e* in *agent, i* in *sanity, o* in *comply, u* in *focus;* ' as in *able* (ā′b'l)

CHAPTER ELEVEN: THESAURUS   201

## EXERCISE 3: REVIEW WORDS IN CONTEXT

Read the following list of Review Words. Then in each space below write the word that best completes that sentence. Check your answers in the back of the book.

| | | | | |
|---|---|---|---|---|
| conspiracy | eligible | excessive | resist | tactic |
| corruption | enterprise | perils | saturated | treachery |

1. Police often advise people not to _____ if they are robbed at gunpoint.

2. _____ in the police departments of large cities was widespread in the 1920s.

3. Her _____ at work resulted in her promotion to junior vice-president.

4. It is generally considered an act of great _____ to have an affair with your best friend's spouse.

5. Many people still wonder if the death of President John F. Kennedy was the result of a _____.

6. No one wants to pay an _____ price for something purchased.

7. It is hard to get a job in the field of television today; the job market is quite _____.

8. According to the NCAA regulations, you can only be _____ to play collegiate football for four years.

9. James Bond was able to escape many _____ through cleverness.

10. He used a clever _____ to get the job; he read everything he could find about the company so that he could speak knowledgeably about its products during his interview.

## EXERCISE 4: REVIEW WORDS—1

Each italicized word below is a Review Word for this chapter. The choices are all New Words from previous chapters. Circle the letter of the best *synonym.* Check your answers in the back of the book.

1. During World War II the United States sent Great Britain the plans for the atomic bomb, but through *treachery* the Soviet Union acquired copies.

   a. heritage   b. deception   c. jurisdiction   d. integrity

2. The game Monopoly was invented in 1933 by Charles Darrow, who felt that young people living in the Depression should experience free *enterprise.*

   a. analysis   b. utopia   c. venture   d. turmoil

3. In 1914 children flocked to the movies for the latest adventure of "The *Perils* of Pauline" to see whether the heroine would escape the ferocious lion that was about to attack her, or free herself from the railroad track where she had been tied.

   a. corruption   b. attributes   c. stigma   d. jeopardies

4. One military *tactic* used in war is to leak information that troops will be landing in one location when, in fact, they are actually going to land hundreds of miles away.

   a. aptitude   b. maneuver   c. fallacy   d. ordeal

5. Although the Warren Commission concluded that Lee Harvey Oswald acted alone in the 1963 assassination of President John F. Kennedy, many people remain convinced that there was a *conspiracy.*

   a. default   b. endeavor   c. plight   d. intrigue

## EXERCISE 5: REVIEW WORDS—2

Each italicized word below is a Review Word for this chapter. The choices are all New Words from previous chapters. Circle the letter of the best *antonym.* Check your answers in the back of the book.

1. The French were not able to *resist* Hitler's attack in World War II, but the English were.

   a. speculate on   b. incur   c. succumb to   d. harass

2. The United States grows *excessive* amounts of wheat, which must be bought by the government to keep the market price stable.

   a. stagnant   b. deficient   c. immortal   d. random

3. After heavy rains, such as the ones that occurred in Southern California in 1993, the ground can be so *saturated* that houses slide down hills.

   a. arid   b. dismal   c. desolate   d. pliable

4. During the Vietnam War, many young men who would have normally taken jobs continued going to school so they would not be classified 1A or *eligible for* the draft.

   a. thrilled about   b. avid for   c. unqualified for   d. exempt from

5. Massive *corruption* in President Warren G. Harding's administration became public when Secretary of the Interior Albert Fall was found guilty of accepting bribes to grant oil leases permitting private individuals to use the naval oil reserves at Teapot Dome, Wyoming.

   a. integrity   b. consistency   c. longevity   d. fallacy

**credible** (kred′ə b'l) *adj.*   that can be believed; believable; reliable

**esteem** (ə stēm′) *v.*   1. to value highly; respect   2. to consider—*n.*   favorable opinion

**exasperate** (eg zas′pə rāt′, ig zas′pə rāt′) *v.*   to irritate or annoy very much; make angry

**flagrant** (flā′grənt) *adj.*   glaringly bad; notorious; outrageous

**insinuate** (in sin′yōō wāt′) *v.*   to hint or suggest indirectly; imply

**predicament** (pri dik′ə mənt) *n.*   a condition or situation that is difficult, unpleasant, embarrassing, or sometimes comical

**somber** (säm′bər) *adj.*   1. dark and gloomy or dull   2. mentally depressed or depressing; melancholy   3. earnest and solemn; grave

**tolerant** (täl′ər ənt) *adj.*   having or showing respect for others' beliefs or practices without sharing them; free from bigotry or prejudice

**torrid** (tôr′id) *adj.*   1. very hot; scorching   2. highly passionate; enthusiastic

**turmoil** (tʉr′moil) *n.*   commotion; uproar; confusion

fat, āpe, cär; ten, ēven; is, bīte; gō, hôrn, tōōl, look; oil, out; up, fʉr; get; joy; yet; chin; she; thin, *th*en; zh, leisure; ŋ, ring; ə for *a* in *ago, e* in *agent, i* in *sanity, o* in *comply, u* in *focus;* ′ as in *able* (ā′b'l)

Read the following list of words. Then in each space below write the word that best completes that sentence. Check your answers in the back of the book.

| | | | | |
|---|---|---|---|---|
| credible | exasperate | insinuated | somber | torrid |
| esteemed | flagrant | predicament | tolerance | turmoil |

1. Prehistoric people made cave paintings in France and Spain that are

   _____ today for their artistic as well as their historical value.

2. _____ weather because of its extreme heat can make even calm people irritable.

3. Some Americans view the burning of an American flag as a _____ unpatriotic act; others see it as an act of free speech.

4. After the birth of a baby, some women find themselves in a _____. Should they stay at home with the baby or return to the workplace?

5. The whole city was in _____ after the first snowfall in twenty years.

6. Many immigrant groups came to the United States seeking religious

   _____.

7. In the comics, Dennis the Menace is always doing something to

   _____ his parents or his neighbor, Mr. Wilson.

8. The *New York Times* is considered a _____ source of news; its journalists have won many awards for excellence.

9. When women first "broke the glass ceiling" and became executives in large male

   dominated business firms, they wore _____ suits, typically gray and very tailored, so that they would not stand out at meetings.

10. Because it was _____ but not proven that Leonardo da Vinci was performing dissections on living people, Pope Leo denied him permission to study anatomy in Rome.

**agitation** (aj′ə tā′shən) *n.*   1. violent motion or disturbance   2. emotional disturbance or excitement   3. discussion meant to stir up people and produce changes

**antiquated** (an′tə kuāt′id) *adj.*   1. no longer useful; obsolete, old-fashioned, out-of-date   2. aged

**crucial** (kr$\overline{oo}$′shəl) *adj.*   of supreme importance; decisive; critical

**curtail** (kər tāl′) *v.*   to cut short; reduce

**deteriorate** (dē tir′ē ə rāt′) *v.*   to make or become worse; to lower in quality or value

**dynamic** (dī nam′ik) *adj.*   1. of energy or physical force in motion   2. energetic; forceful; productive

**explicit** (eks plis′it, ik splis′it) *adj.*   1. clearly stated and leaving nothing implied; distinctly expressed; definite   2. saying what is meant, without reservation; outspoken   3. plain to see; readily observable

**mandatory** (man′də tôr′ē) *adj.*   required; obligatory

**relinquish** (ri liŋ′kwish) *v.*   1. to give up; abandon (a plan, policy, etc.)   2. to surrender (something owned, a right, etc.)   3. to let go (a grasp, hold, etc.)

**repudiate** (ri py$\overline{oo}$′dē āt′) *v.*   to refuse to have anything to do with; reject

---

fat, āpe, cär; ten, ēven; is, bīte; gō, hôrn, t$\overline{oo}$l, look; oil, out; up, fʉr; get; joy; yet; chin; she; thin, *th*en; zh, leisure; ŋ, ring; ə for *a* in *ago*, *e* in *agent*, *i* in *sanity*, *o* in *comply*, *u* in *focus*; ′ as in *able* (ā′b′l)

Circle the letter before the word or phrase that best defines the italicized word in each sentence. Check your answers in the back of the book.

1. The birth of Louise Brown, the first test-tube baby, on July 25, 1978, provoked a great deal of *agitation* about the ethics of artificial conception.

   a. sadness   b. pleasure   c. doubt   d. disturbance

2. When we look at photographs in family album, the clothing and hairstyles seem very *antiquated;* however, they were probably fashionable at the time the photographs were taken.

   a. outrageous   b. out of date   c. popular   d. unheard of

3. In the American and British invasion of Normandy, France, during World War II, surprise was an element *crucial* to victory.

   a. unimportant   b. critical   c. new   d. amazing

4. If President Clinton and Congress want to balance the federal budget, they must *curtail* government spending.

   a. pay for   b. reduce   c. increase   d. maintain

5. Constant exposure to loud music can cause hearing to *deteriorate,* and prolonged noise above 150 decibels will cause permanent deafness.

   a. worsen   b. improve   c. stop   d. sharpen

6. The Renaissance that occurred in Europe from the fourteenth to the middle of the seventeenth century was one of the most *dynamic* periods in human history. Some of the major figures of this period were Galileo, Shakespeare, Leonardo da Vinci, and Michelangelo.

   a. questionable   b. scenic   c. energetic   d. expensive

7. Parents need to supervise the television shows watched by their children because viewing a great deal of *explicit* violence may increase aggressive behavior.

   a. clear   b. extreme   c. vague   d. strange

8. In some colleges, attendance at every class meeting of a course is *mandatory* if one wants credit.

   a. spontaneous   b. absurd   c. tangible   d. required

9. A political candidate who withdraws from the presidential race *relinquishes* the right to Secret Service protection.

   a. takes   b. divides   c. avoids   d. surrenders

10. The astronomer Copernicus *repudiated* the theory that the earth was the center of the universe with the planets revolving around it.

    a. accepted   b. proved   c. supported   d. disproved

## EXERCISE 8: TRUE-FALSE

Place a *T* or an *F* in the space provided. Check your answers in the back of the book.

_____ 1. A skeptical person will find most things credible.

_____ 2. Antarctica has a torrid climate.

_____ 3. You will achieve your goals if you repudiate them.

_____ 4. Directions should be explicit.

_____ 5. A Model-T Ford is antiquated.

## EXERCISE 9: ANALOGIES

The analogies below are either synonyms, antonyms, classification : example, cause : effect, or part : whole. First, decide which type of comparison is used in the first pair of words. Second, fill in the blank for the type of analogy using *S* for synonym, *A* for antonym, *C* for classification, *C/E* for cause : effect, and *P* for part : whole. Third, find the word from the choices that will make the second pair of words have the same relationship. Check your answers in the back of the book.

_____ 1. excessive food : fat ::
turmoil : _____
a. happiness   b. calmness   c. confusion
d. anger

_____ 2. corruption : government ::
tolerance : _____
a. Golden Rule   b. arguments   c. hatred
d. bias

_____ 3. treachery : honor ::
crucial : _____
a. important   b. trivial   c. decisions
d. criticism

_____ 4. eligible : suitable ::
insinuate : _____
a. state   b. threaten   c. imply
d. promise

_____ 5. politician : Bill Clinton ::
somber event : _____
a. wedding   b. funeral   c. birthday
d. Christmas

## EXERCISE 10: MATCHING MEANINGS

Write the letter of the word that means the opposite of the word in the first column.
Check your answers in the back of the book.

_____ 1. relinquish        a. increase

_____ 2. deteriorate       b. subtle

_____ 3. mandatory       c. retrieve

_____ 4. flagrant        d. regenerate

_____ 5. curtail         e. optional

## EXERCISE 11: WORD CONTRASTS

In each group below, circle the word that does not mean what the others mean.
Check your answers in the back of the book.

1. agitation     excitement     calm     confusion

2. esteem     value     despise     respect

3. dynamic     static     fixed     unchanging

4. predicament     plight     dilemma     solution

5. exasperate     pacify     irritate     provoke

## EXERCISE 12: SYNONYMS

Each word in the first column is a New Word from this chapter. Match each with a
word in the second column, writing the letter of the word in the space provided.
Check your answers in the back of the book.

_____ 1. turmoil        a. abdicate

_____ 2. predicament     b. compulsory

_____ 3. tolerant        c. aggravate

_____ 4. deteriorate      d. abridge

_____ 5. antiquated      e. chaos

_____ 6. mandatory      f. unbiased

_____ 7. curtail         g. intimate

_____ 8. insinuate       h. dilemma

_____ 9. exasperate      i. obsolete

_____ 10. relinquish      j. degenerate

# EXERCISE 13: ANTONYMS

Each word in the first column is a New Word from this chapter. Match each word with a word in the second column that is an antonym. Write the letter of the word in the space provided. Check your answers in the back of the book.

| | | | |
|---|---|---|---|
| _____ | 1. torrid | a. | inconspicuous |
| _____ | 2. somber | b. | frigid |
| _____ | 3. flagrant | c. | superfluous |
| _____ | 4. credible | d. | advocate |
| _____ | 5. agitation | e. | static |
| _____ | 6. explicit | f. | inconceivable |
| _____ | 7. repudiate | g. | jovial |
| _____ | 8. esteem | h. | implicit |
| _____ | 9. crucial | i. | composure |
| _____ | 10. dynamic | j. | detest |

# EXERCISE 14: SENTENCE COMPLETION

Complete each sentence in your own words. Sample answers are provided in the back of the book.

1. A witness must appear _credible_ in order to _____
_____.

2. Otis won not only the _esteem_ of his colleagues, but also _____
_____.

3. Students can _exasperate_ instructors, especially _____
_____.

4. _Flagrant_ disregard of campus regulations will lead to _____
_____.

5. Hank _insinuated_ that Maria pilfered the petty cash even though _____
_____.

6. Her _predicament_ was both embarrassing and _____
_____.

7. An example of _somber_ clothing is _____
_____.

8. The boss was *tolerant* of tardiness provided that _____
_____.

9. The *torrid* affair was the most _____
_____.

10. Through all the *turmoil*, _____
_____.

11. The reason for the boy's *agitation* was _____
_____.

12. One *crucial* effect was _____
_____.

13. Willy did not *curtail* his gambling; on the contrary, _____
_____.

14. The building began to *deteriorate;* meanwhile, _____
_____.

15. Juliet was a *dynamic* speaker as a result of _____
_____.

16. *Explicit* instructions were provided so that _____
_____.

17. Attendance is *mandatory;* nevertheless, _____
_____.

18. Rather than *relinquish* his position, _____
_____.

19. The judge made *shrewd* decisions, such as _____
_____.

20. Now that he was rich and famous, Sam *repudiated* the friends he had grown up with,
primarily _____.

# ADVANCED WORDS

**affluence** (af′loo wəns) *n.*   1. an abundance of riches; wealth   2. great plenty; abundance   3. a flowing toward; influx

**arduous** (är′joo wəs) *adj.*   1. difficult to do; laborious   2. using much energy; strenuous   3. steep; hard to climb

**astute** (ə stoot′) *adj.*   having or showing a clever or shrewd mind; cunning; crafty; wily

**exuberant** (eg zoo′bər ənt, ig zoo′bər ənt) *adj.*   1. growing abundantly [*exuberant* vegetation]   2. characterized by good health and high spirits; full of life; uninhibited

**inept** (in ept′) *adj.*   1. not suitable to the purpose; unfit   2. wrong in a foolish and awkward way [*inept* praise]   3. clumsy or bungling; inefficient

**infamous** (in′fə məs) *adj.*   having a bad reputation; notorious

**integral** (in′tə grəl) *adj.*   necessary for completeness; essential [an *integral* part]

**loathe** (lō*th*) *v.*   to feel intense dislike, disgust, or hatred for; abhor; detest

**profound** (prə found′) *adj.*   1. very deep or low [a *profound* abyss, sigh, bow, sleep, etc.]   2. marked by intellectual depth [a *profound* discussion]   3. deeply or intensely felt [*profound* grief]   4. thoroughgoing [*profound* changes]   5. unbroken [a *profound* silence]

**renounce** (ri nouns′) *v.*   1. to give up (a claim, right, belief, etc.) usually by a formal public statement   2. to give up (a pursuit, practice, way of living or feeling, etc.)   3. to cast off or disown; refuse further association with; repudiate [to *renounce* a son]

---

**fat, āpe, cär; ten, ēven; is, bīte; gō, hôrn, tool, look; oil, out; up, fʉr; get; joy; yet; chin; she; thin, *th*en; zh, leisure; ŋ, ring; ə for *a* in *ago*, *e* in *agent*, *i* in *sanity*, *o* in *comply*, *u* in *focus*; ′ as in *able* (ā′b'l)**

Use the Advanced Words to fill in the blanks in the sentences that follow. Check your answers in the back of the book.

| affluence | astute | inept | integral | profound |
|-----------|--------|-------|----------|----------|
| arduous | exuberant | infamous | loathe | renounce |

1. Some people find pâté de foie gras, goose liver paste, a great luxury; others _____ liver in all its forms.

2. The _____ task of rebuilding Europe after the widespread destruction of World War II was made somewhat easier by the large amounts of economic aid provided by the United States under the Marshall Plan.

3. After World War II, the United States experienced a period of _____; for example, a large percentage of the population could afford automobiles for the first time.

4. Agatha Christie's Mrs. Marple was so _____ that she was able to solve mysteries and identify criminals when the police were completely baffled.

5. When Princess Margaret of England married commoner Anthony Armstrong Jones, she had to _____ all claims to the throne her sister held.

6. Her _____ manner made her a good choice for cheerleader of the football team.

7. Al Jolson's *Jazz Singer,* the first talking movie, had a _____ effect on film; it forced every major studio to convert to sound production within a year.

8. The housekeeper became an _____ part of the family; no holiday seemed complete in the home without her.

9. The _____ 1920s gangster Al Capone was never caught for his well-known involvement in murder, bootlegging, and prostitution. He was finally imprisoned for income tax evasion.

10. _____ police procedures in Habst, Austria, allowed Andreas Michanecz, a passenger involved in a car crash, to be placed in a holding cell at a local jail and starved for 17 days because officials forgot he was there.

In the first column are the ten Advanced Words from this chapter. In the second column are ten words that are either synonyms or antonyms for the words in the first column. First, find the synonym or antonym for each word in the first column. Write its letter in the space marked *Match.* In the column marked *Relationship,* write *A* if the two words are antonyms and *S* if the words are synonyms. Check your answers in the back of the book.

**Match**          **Relationship**

| Match | Relationship | | | | |
|-------|-------------|---|---|---|---|
| _____ | _____ | 1. | astute | a. | laborious |
| _____ | _____ | 2. | profound | b. | abdicate |
| _____ | _____ | 3. | arduous | c. | irrelevant |
| _____ | _____ | 4. | inept | d. | apathetic |
| _____ | _____ | 5. | exuberant | e. | deprivation |
| _____ | _____ | 6. | renounce | f. | detest |
| _____ | _____ | 7. | loathe | g. | shrewd |
| _____ | _____ | 8. | affluence | h. | superficial |
| _____ | _____ | 9. | infamous | i. | proficient |
| _____ | _____ | 10. | integral | j. | notorious |

Fill in the puzzle below in pencil. Remember that the clues with an asterisk (*) are for words from the New Words list in this or previous chapters. Check your answers in the back of the book.

## Across

1. Brand of cola
3. Wooden nail
5. Alt. spelling of prefix *ad,* as in _____tack
7. Meaning of root *fac*
9. Baby bear or lion
11. Exclamation of surprise
12. Abbr. for *registered nurse*
*13. Danger
15. Cooked, as a cake
16. Jacket
17. Initials for *unidentified object*
18. Stitch together
21. Past tense of *is*
23. Abbr. for *Social Security*
*24. Forbidden
26. Abbr. for *incorporated*
27. Antonym of *die*
28. Square of grass
31. Atmosphere
33. Antonym of *stop*
*34. Unimportant
*36. Regress
37. Fragrant kind of flowers
39. Antonym of *ma*
40. Small rug
41. Abbr. for *avenue*
*42. Extremist
45. Irregular verb from which we get *is, was,* etc.
46. Abbr. for *teaching assistant*
*47. Happy
48. Abbr. for *hour*
49. Petroleum
51. Where Dorothy met the wizard
53. Short written message
*55. Absurd

## Down

*1. Strong
*2. Confusion
3. High status
*4. Try hard
5. Abbr. for *Atomic Energy Commission*
6. Also
*7. Facts
8. Either, _____; neither, nor
*9. Negative
*10. Very odd
14. Animal's foot
19. Abbr. for *Lincoln's first name*
20. Abbr. for *Missouri*
*22. Evil
*25. To cast out
29. Spanish for *gold*
*30. Cheerless
32. Prefix meaning *away from,* as in _____ficient
35. Abbr. for *Vocational Education Act*
36. Abbr. for *right*
*38. Prevent
39. To turn on a point
41. Detest
42. Unbiased
43. Andrew Jackson's monogram
44. Antonym of *from*
46. Antonym of *bottom*
50. French for *the*
52. Abbr. for *Tuesday*
54. Alt. spelling for prefix meaning *in,* as in _____tice

Choose from your outside reading ten words that you would like to learn and write them in the spaces below. When you look them up in the dictionary, take a few moments to think about their synonyms and antonyms. Pronounce each word, put the definition in your own words, use the word in a sentence, make up a mnemonic, and put the word on a flash card for regular review.

1. _____

2. _____

3. _____

4. _____

5. _____

6. _____

7. _____

8. _____

9. _____

10. _____

# chapter 12

# USING WORDS CORRECTLY

© 1966 "Peanuts" is reprinted by permission of UFS, Inc.

Mark Twain once said, "The difference between the right word and the almost right word is the difference between lightning and the lightning bug." Since you started this book you have learned about 200 words, and you have gained the tools for locating additional new words and finding their definitions, their pronunciations, their etymologies, their word parts, and their synonyms and antonyms. But a word is not really mastered until you are able to use it correctly and comfortably in speech and writing.

## Shades of Meaning

Look at the thesaurus entry below.[1]

### DRINKING

*Nouns*—**1,** drinking, imbibing, potation, libation

**2, a.** drink, beverage, draft, impotation, liquor, nectar, broth, soup; potion. **b.** hard liquor, alcoholic drink, spirits, the bottle, little brown jug; home brew; brandy, cognac, applejack, hard cider; beer, ale; gin, rum, whiskey, cocktail, mixed drink, nightcap, pick-me-up; liqueur, cordial; the grape, [white, red, *or* rosé] wine, malmsey, retsina, champagne; grog, toddy, flip, punch, negus, cup, wassail. *Colloq.,* moonshine, hair of the dog [that bit one], booze. *Slang,* hooch, sauce. **c.** nonalcoholic beverage, soft drink, cola; coffee, chocolate, cocoa, tea. **d.** dram, draft, draught, nip, sip, sup, gulp, pull, swill. *Colloq.,* swig.

**3,** drunkenness, intoxication; INTEMPERANCE; inebriety, inebriation; ebriety, ebriosity; insobriety; wine bibbing; bacchanals, bacchanalia, libations; alcoholism, dipsomania, oenomania, delirium tremens, D.T.'s. *Colloq.,* bust, hangover. *Slang,* binge, tear, bat, toot, jag, bender, pink elephants; the morning after.

**4,** drunkard, drunk; alcoholic, dipsomaniac, sot, toper, tippler, bibber, wine bibber, guzzler; hard drinker; soaker, sponge, tosspot; thirsty soul, reveler, carouser; Bacchanal, Bacchanalian, Bacchante, devotee of Bacchus. *Colloq.,* boozer, barfly. *Slang,* souse, wino, lush, tank, rumhound, dipso, rummy.

**5,** tavern, inn; public house, pub (both *Brit.*); barroom, taproom, rathskeller, bar [and grill], alehouse, saloon, [cocktail] lounge; bistro, cabaret; bartender. *Slang,* gin mill.

*Verbs*—**1,** drink, imbibe, quaff, sip, lap; take a drop, guzzle, squizzle, soak, sot, carouse, tope, swill; take to drink; drink up, drink hard, drink like a fish; drain the cup, take a hair of the dog [that bit one]; wet one's whistle, crack a bottle, pass the bottle; toss off; wash down. *Colloq.,* booze, swig.

**2,** be *or* get drunk; fall off the wagon; see double. *Slang,* feel no pain; liquor up, lush, get high, hit the bottle *or* the sauce, go on a toot, paint the town red, hang one on, have an edge on, have a jag on, pass out [cold].

**3,** make drunk, intoxicate, inebriate, [be]fuddle, besot, go to one's head. *Slang,* plaster, pollute.

*Adjectives*—**1,** on the rocks, straight up, neat; potable, bibulous.

**2,** drunk, tipsy, intoxicated, inebrious, inebriate[d], in one's cups, in a state of intoxication, cut, fresh, merry, elevated, flush[ed], flustered, disguised, topheavy, overcome, maudlin, crapulous, dead *or* roaring drunk, drunk as a lord *or* an owl. *Colloq.,* boozy, mellow, high [as a kite]. *Slang,* off the wagon; boiled, soused, shellacked, fried, polluted, tanked, cockeyed, squiffed, stinko, tight, three sheets to the wind, out cold, stiff, blotto, feeling no pain, out of it.

**3,** intoxicating, heady.

All the words given in the entry are supposed to be synonyms for drinking in its various parts of speech. But does it really mean the same thing to say a person is *tipsy* as to say someone is *blotto*? Is there a difference between *mellow* and *three sheets to the wind*? The thesaurus does not deal with these differences.

In Chapter 11 you were directed to check words in the dictionary to learn more about usage. Most pocket dictionary entries don't go into usage in much detail, but larger dictionaries often do. Below is a dictionary entry for *drunk*. Note

---

[1]From *The New American Roget's College Thesaurus in Dictionary Form* by Philip D. Morehead and Andrew T. Morehead. Copyright © 1985. Revised edition prepared by Philip D. Morehead. Copyright © 1958, 1962 by Albert H. Morehead. Copyright © 1978 by Andrew T. Morehead and Philip D. Morehead. Reprinted by arrangement with The New American Library, Inc., New York, N.Y.

the discussion of shades of meaning under *SYN.* Also provided are brief sample phrases illustrating usage of some of the synonyms.

**drunk** (druŋk) *vt., vi.* [ME *dronke* < *dronken,* DRUNKEN] *pp. & archaic pt. of* DRINK—*adj.* **1** overcome by alcoholic liquor to the point of losing control over one's faculties; intoxicated **2** overcome by any powerful emotion [*drunk* with joy] **3** [Colloq.] DRUNKEN (sense 2) Usually used in the predicate—*n.* **1** [Colloq.] a drunken person **2** [Slang] a drinking spree *SYN.*—drunk is the simple, direct word, usually used in the predicate, for one who is overcome by alcoholic liquor [he is *drunk*]; **drunken,** usually used attributively, is equivalent to **drunk** but sometimes implies habitual, intemperate drinking of liquor [a *drunken* bum]; **intoxicated** and **inebriated** are euphemisms; there are many euphemistic and slang terms in English expressing varying degrees of drunkenness; e.g., **tipsy** (slight), **tight** (moderate, but without great loss of muscular coordination), **blind drunk** (great), **blotto** (to the point of unconsciousness), etc.—*ANT.* sober

If you were a foreigner learning English, this entry might prevent you from making a social blunder. For example, it might be acceptable to refer to your hostess as *slightly inebriated,* but never as *blind drunk.*

The discussion of shades of meaning shown above is not repeated under each synonym for *drunk.* Instead, the entries for these synonyms contain cross-references referring you to the main synonym, *drunk.* For example, the entry for *inebriated* refers you to *drunk.*[2]

**in-e-bri-at-ed** (-āt′id) *adj.* drunk; intoxicated—*SYN.* DRUNK

You can see from the sample above that one difference in meaning concerns *intensity.* For example, *tipsy* is only slightly drunk, whereas *tight* is moderately drunk and *blotto* is drunk to the point of unconsciousness. In addition to intensity, the word may have various other **connotations.** Connotations are any ideas or associations suggested by a word or phrase in addition to its official meaning or "denotation." For example, the word *mother* **denotes** "female parent" but **connotes** love, care, tenderness, and so on. *Tipsy* connotes innocent fun, but the connotations of *drunk* are more sinister to most people.

When a word is unfamiliar, it can be difficult to be sure you are using it correctly, since you may be unaware of its connotations. If usage is not discussed in your dictionary, about all you can do is to try to note the context in which you saw the word and use it in a similar way. If you need to memorize the word, it is wise to include a sentence showing the usage on the back of your flash card. The only way you can be positive that you are using the word correctly is to see or hear it many times in context.

## Idiomatic Usage

Idiomatic usage refers to the usual way in which words of a language are joined together to express thought. Idiomatic usage is generally part of a dictionary entry.

[2]Dictionary excerpts in this chapter are from *Webster's New World Dictionary, Third College Edition* (Victoria Neufeldt, Editor-in-Chief). Copyright © 1988 by Simon & Schuster, Inc. (New York: Simon & Schuster, 1988).

a-gree (ə grē´) *vi.* **-greed´, -gree´ing** [ME. *agreen* < OFr. *agreer*, to receive kindly < OFr. *a gre*, favorably < *a* (L. *ad*), to + *gre*, good will < L. *gratus*, pleasing] **1** to consent or accede (*to*); say "yes" **2** to be in harmony or accord [their versions *agree*] **3** to be of the same opinion; concur (*with*) **4** to arrive at a satisfactory understanding (*about* prices, terms, etc.) **5** to be suitable, healthful, etc. (followed by *with*) [this climate does not *agree* with him] **6** *Gram.* to be inflected so as to correspond in number, person, case, or gender—*vt.* to grant or acknowledge: followed by a noun clause [we *agreed* that it was true]

This entry distinguishes between *agree to, agree with, agree about, agree on,* and *agree that.* Idiomatic usage is one of the hardest things to learn when trying to master a foreign language. For example, how would you explain to a foreigner why we say "a course *of* action" rather than "a course *for* action," or "I'm going to relate *to* you" rather than "I'm going to relate *with* you"?

The dictionary provides some help, but sometimes paperback dictionary entries are too brief to explain idiomatic usage fully. That's why you sometimes hear sentences like, "My girlfriend is tangible" or "My mouth is arid." In the end, you must rely mainly on context to learn usage.

## Words That Look or Sound Alike

Some pairs of words are confused in writing because they look very similar (*comma* and *coma*) or because they sound alike (*accept* and *except*). These problems are much easier to solve than confusions that are due to shades of meaning or idiomatic usage. Simply use word parts or word histories and mnemonic devices. For example, the spellings of *accept* and *except* can be memorized based on their word parts. *Accept* comes from the Latin *ad-,* to + *capere,* to take. The word's meaning, *to receive,* comes directly from these parts. On the other hand, *except* comes from *ex-,* out + *capere, to take. Except* means to leave out or take out. Another example is *immigrate* and *emigrate.* They are easy to distinguish if you remember that *im* is an alternate spelling for *in,* meaning *in,* and *e* is an alternate for *ex,* meaning *out.* To remember the difference between *comma* and *coma,* think of a mnemonic device. An example might be the phrase "Co*mm*as are more co*mm*on than comas." To remember the difference between *serf* (*a slave*) and *surf* (*waves*), you might note that the derivation of *serf* is the Latin word *servus,* meaning slave, which is also the origin of the word *servant.* In this case, the etymology gives the clue to both meaning and spelling (*servus* and *serf*).

# REVIEW WORDS

The following Review Words are often confused with words similar to them in meaning. Read each definition, then read the dictionary excerpts describing their usage.

**excel** (ek sel′) *v.* to be better or greater than (another or others)

> **SYN—excel** implies superiority in some quality, skill, achievement, etc. over all or over the one (or ones) specified [to *excel* at chess]; **surpass** implies a going beyond (someone or something specified) in degree, amount, or quality [no one *surpasses* him in generosity]; **transcend** suggests a surpassing to an extreme degree [it *transcends* all understanding]; **ex-ceed** to go or be beyond (a limit, limiting regulation, mesure, etc.) [to *exceed* one's expectations]

**lure** (loor) *n.* 1. anything that tempts or entices 2. a bait used in fishing—*v.* to attract, tempt, entice

> **SYN—lure** suggests an irresistible force, as desire, greed, curiosity, etc., in attracting someone, esp. to something harmful or evil [*lured* on by false hopes]; **entice** implies a crafty or skillful luring [he *enticed* the squirrel to eat from his hand]; **decoy** implies the use of deceptive appearances in luring into a trap [artificial birds are used to *decoy* wild ducks]; **tempt** suggests the influence of a powerful attraction that tends to overcome morals or judgment [I'm *tempted* to accept your offer]; **seduce** implies enticement to a wrongful or unlawful act, especially to loss of chastity

**prominent** (präm′ə nənt) *adj.* 1. sticking out; projecting 2. noticeable; conspicuous 3. widely and favorably known

> **SYN—prominent** refers to that which literally or figuratively stands out from its background [a *prominent* nose, a *prominent* author]; **remarkable** applies to that which is noticeable because it is unusual or exceptional [*remarkable* beauty]; **conspicuous** applies to that which is so obvious or manifest as to be immediately perceptible [*conspicuous* gallantry]

**radical** (rad′i k'l) *adj.* 1. of or from the root; basic 2. favoring basic, rapid or sweeping change, as in the social or economic structure—*n.* person holding extreme views

> **SYN—radical** implies a favoring of fundamental or extreme change, specifically of the social structure; **left** originally referring to the position in legislatures of the seats occupied by parties holding such views implies political liberalism or radicalism; **fanatic** suggests a willingness to go to unreasonable lengths to maintain or carry out one's beliefs; **liberal** implies tolerance of others' views as well as open-mindedness to ideas that challenge tradition, established institutions, etc.; **progressive**, a relative term as opposed to *reactionary* or *conservative*, is applied to persons favoring progress and reform in politics, education, etc. and implies an inclination to more direct action than **liberal**; **advanced** specifically implies a being ahead of the times, as in science, the arts, philosophy, etc.

fat, āpe, cär; ten, ēven; is, bīte; gō, hôrn, tōol, look; oil, out; up, fʉr; get; joy; yet; chin; she; thin, *th*en; zh, leisure; ŋ, ring; ə for *a* in *ago*, *e* in *agent*, *i* in *sanity*, *o* in *comply*, *u* in *focus*; ' as in *able* (ā′b'l)

**reflect** (ri flekt′) *v.*   1. to throw back (light, heat, or sound)   2. to give back an image of   3. to bring as a result   4. to think seriously on   5. to cast blame or discredit

> SYN—**reflect** implies a turning of one's thoughts on or back on a subject and further implies deep or continued thought; **reason** implies a logical sequence of thought, starting with what is known or assumed and advancing to a definite conclusion through the inferences drawn [he *reasoned* that she would accept]; **speculate** implies a reasoning on the basis of incomplete or uncertain evidence and therefore stresses the uncertain character of the opinions formed [to *speculate* on the possibility of life on Mars]; **deliberate** implies careful and thorough consideration of a matter in order to arrive at a conclusion [the jury *deliberated* on the case]; **contemplate** implies a deep, continued mental viewing of a thing, sometimes suggesting the use of intuitive powers in envisioning something or dwelling upon it

The following Review Words are often confused with words similar to them in sound. Read each definition; then read the word or words with which the New Word is often confused.

**affect** (ə fekt′) *v.*   1. to have an effect on; influence   2. to stir the emotions of   3. to make a pretense of being, feeling, etc.

Confused with: effect

**alter** (ôl′tər) *v.*   to change; make or become different

Confused with: altar

**counsel** (koun′s'l) *n.*   1. mutual exchange of ideas, etc.; discussion   2. a lawyer or group of lawyers   3. a consultant—*v.*   1. to give advice to   2. to recommend (an action, etc.)   3. to give or take advice

Confused with: council

**personnel** (pʉr′sə nel′) *n.*   1. persons employed in any work, enterprise, service, etc.   2. a department for hiring employees, etc.

Confused with: personal

**site** (sīt) *n.*   location or scene

Confused with: sight, cite

fat, āpe, cär; ten, ēven; is, bīte; gō, hôrn, tōol, look; oil, out; up, fʉr; get; joy; yet; chin; she; thin, *then*; zh, leisure; ŋ, ring; ə for *a* in *ago, e* in *agent, i* in *sanity, o* in *comply, u* in *focus;* ′ as in *able* (ā′b'l)

Read the following list of Review Words. Then in each space below, write the word that best completes that sentence. Check your answers in the back of the book.

| affected | counsel | lure | prominent | reflects |
|----------|---------|------|-----------|----------|
| alter | excelling | personnel | radical | site |

1. The _____ of the Battle of Bunker Hill, which was the first great battle of the American Revolutionary War, is marked by a famous monument.

2. _____ aviator Amelia Earhart became famous as the first woman to pilot an airplane across the Atlantic Ocean.

3. The judge asked the _____ for the defense to explain his objection to the witness's answer.

4. Many people with arthritis claim that they are _____ by drastic changes in the weather.

5. Some companies have an annual Christmas party for their _____.

6. An unexpected rainstorm may cause you to _____ your plans to go on a picnic.

7. White _____ light; black absorbs light.

8. By _____ in the 1936 Olympic Games, an American black athlete named Jesse Owens proved that Hitler's theory of the "master" white race was false. As the dictator watched in fury, Owens captured four gold medals in track and field.

9. 1960s Black Muslim leader Malcolm X originally favored forming an all black nation, a concept that many people considered _____.

10. The _____ of "easy money" draws some young people into selling drugs.

The italicized word in each group is a Review Word for this chapter. The other two words are often confused with it. Each of the sentences can be best completed by only one of the three words. Choose the best word and fill it in the space provided. Use each word only once. If you need more help differentiating the sets of words, refer to the *synonym* entries on pp. 221–222. Check your answers in the back of the book.

A.  *excel*    surpass    transcend

1.  Professional athletes must _____ at their chosen sports.

2.  True art will _____ the time in which it was created.

3.  His goal was to _____ any previous world record.

B.  *lure*    decoy    tempt

1.  Wooden ducks are used to _____ wild ducks and draw them closer to the hunters.

2.  The promise of a large sum of money returned for a small investment is often used to _____ people into con games.

3.  The smells from a bakery often _____ customers to enter the store.

C.  *prominent*    remarkable    conspicuous

1.  Basketball star David Robinson is _____ in a crowd because of his height.

2.  President Clinton is a _____ American politician.

3.  Michael Jackson is known for his _____ ability to excite an audience.

D.  *radical*    fanatic    advanced

1.  Some _____ football fans have been known to wait in sub-zero weather for days to buy tickets for the Superbowl.

2.  Left-wing politicians consider themselves liberal, while their opponents call them _____ .

3.  Billy Mitchell was an _____ thinker who foresaw the use of the airplane as a military weapon.

E. *reflect*    speculate    contemplate

1. It is difficult for any human being to _____ his or her own death.

2. On New Year's Day, some people _____ on the year that has passed.

3. Since no one knows where inflation will stop, we can only _____ on the price of a dozen eggs in five years.

## EXERCISE 3: REVIEW WORDS—FREQUENTLY CONFUSED WORDS

Each word in italics is a Review Word for this chapter, and the other word is one that is often confused with it. Write the word that completes the sentence. Use a dictionary if you need further assistance. Check your answers in the back of the book.

1. The ash from the volcanic eruptions of Mount St. Helens _____ the weather in the Northern United States for years. (*affected*, effected)

2. It is feared that the volcanic ash will permanently _____ our weather. (altar, *alter*)

3. The city _____ decides whether utility companies can increase their rates. (*counsel*, council)

4. You should discuss your _____ problems with a trained counselor when they begin to affect your school work. (*personnel*, personal)

5. Architect Frank Lloyd Wright believed the _____ of a house should blend with its surroundings. Therefore, it was not unusual for him to have a tree growing through the ceiling of a living room or a river running underneath it. (*site*, cite, sight)

Take any five words from the ten Review Words and, using mnemonic devices or word parts, create a method of remembering the correct definition of each. Write the mnemonic next to the word. Answers will differ, so they are not in the back of the book.

1. _____          _____
   Word                                        Memory Technique
                                        _____

2. _____          _____
   Word                                        Memory Technique
                                        _____

3. _____          _____
   Word                                        Memory Technique
                                        _____

4. _____          _____
   Word                                        Memory Technique
                                        _____

5. _____          _____
   Word                                        Memory Technique
                                        _____

# NEW WORDS I

The following ten New Words are often confused with words similar to them in meaning. Read each definition, then read the dictionary excerpts describing their usage.

**assert** (ə surt´) *v.*   1. to state positively; declare; affirm   2. to maintain or defend (rights, claims, etc.)

> SYN—to **assert** is to state positively with great confidence but with no objective proof [he *asserted* that man's nature would never change]; to **declare** is to assert openly or formally, often in the face of opposition [they *declared* their independence]; **affirm** implies deep conviction in one's statement and the unlikelihood of denial by another [I cannot *affirm* that he was there]; **proclaim** implies official, formal announcement, made with the greatest possible publicity, of something of great moment or significance ["*Proclaim* liberty throughout all the land . . ."]

**confound** (kən found´) *v.*   1. to mix up or lump together; confuse   2. confuse; bewilder   3. to damn: use as a mild oath

> SYN—**confound** implies such confusion as completely frustrates or greatly astonishes one; **puzzle** implies such a baffling quality or such intricacy, as of a problem, situation, etc. that one has great difficulty in understanding or solving it; **perplex,** in addition, implies uncertainty or even worry as to what to think, say, or do; **confuse** implies a mixing up mentally to a greater or lesser degree; **bewilder** implies such utter confusion that the mind is staggered beyond the ability to think clearly; **dumbfound** specifically implies as its effect a confounded state in which one is momentarily struck speechless

**cunning** (kun´iŋ) *adj.*   skillful in deception; sly; crafty—*n.*   skill in deception; slyness; craftiness

> SYN—**cunning** suggests great skill or ingenuity, but often implies deception or craftiness [*cunning* as a fox]; **clever,** in this comparison, implies quick-wittedness as in contriving the solution to a problem [a *clever* reply]; **ingenious** stresses inventive skill, as in origination or fabrication [an *ingenious* explanation]; **shrewd** suggests cleverness accompanied by practicality [a *shrewd* understanding of the situation], sometimes verging on craftiness [a *shrewd* politician]; **astute** implies shrewdness combined with wisdom and sometimes connotes, in addition, artfulness or cunning [an *astute* politician]

**dupe** (do͞op) *n.*   a person easily tricked or fooled—*v.*   to deceive by trickery; fool or cheat

> SYN—**dupe** stresses credulity in the person who is tricked or fooled; **cheat,** the most general term in this comparison, implies dishonesty or deception in dealing with someone, to obtain some advantage or gain; **defraud,** chiefly a legal term, stresses the use of deliberate deception in criminally depriving a person of his rights, property, etc.; **swindle** stresses the winning of a person's confidence in order to cheat or defraud him of money, etc.; **trick** implies fooling somebody but does not always suggest fraudulence or a harmful motive; **hoax** implies a trick skillfully carried off simply to demonstrate how easily the victim is fooled

**impartial** (im pär´shəl) *adj.*   favoring no one side or party more than another; without prejudice or bias; fair; just

> SYN—**impartial** and **unbiased** both imply freedom from prejudice for or against any side [an *impartial* chairman, an *unbiased* account]; **fair,** the general word, implies the treating of both or all sides alike, without reference to one's own feelings or interests [a *fair* exchange]; **just** implies adherence to a standard of rightness or lawfulness without reference to one's own inclinations [a *just* decision]; **dispassionate** implies the absence of passion or strong emotion, hence, connotes cool, disinterested judgment [a *dispassionate* critic]; **objective** implies a viewing of persons or things without reference to oneself, one's feelings, interests, etc. [an *objective* newspaper]; **equitable** connotes a weighing of all sides of a question; **tolerant** connotes tolerance of others' beliefs, practices, etc.; **nonpartisan** implies lack of connection with a political party

fat, ăpe, cär; ten, ēven; is, bīte; gō, hôrn, to͞ol, look; oil, out; up, fur; get; joy; yet; chin; she; thin, *th*en; zh, leisure; ŋ, ring; ə for *a* in *ago, e* in *agent, i* in *sanity, o* in *comply, u* in *focus;* ´ as in *able* (ā´b'l)

**infer** (in fur′) *v.*   to conclude or decide from something known or assumed; derive by reasoning; draw, as a conclusion

> SYN—**infer** suggests the arriving at a decision or opinion by reasoning from known facts or evidence [from your smile, I *infer* that you're pleased]; **deduce,** in strict discrimination, implies inference from a general principle by logical reasoning [the method was *deduced* from earlier experiments]; **conclude** strictly implies an inference that is the final logical result in a process of reasoning [I must, therefore, *conclude* that you are wrong]; **judge** stresses the careful checking and weighing of premises, etc. in arriving at a conclusion; **gather** is an informal substitute for **infer** or **conclude** [I *gather* that you don't care]; **suggest** implies a putting of something into the mind either intentionally, as by way of a proposal [I *suggest* you leave now], or unintentionally, as through association of ideas [the smell of ether *suggests* a hospital]; **imply** stresses the putting into the mind of something involved, but not openly expressed, in a word, a remark, etc. and suggests the need for inference [his answer *implied* a refusal]; **hint** connotes faint or indirect suggestion that is, however, intended to be understood [he *hinted* that he would come]

**pessimistic** (pes′ə mis′tik) *adj.*   expecting the worst outcome in any circumstances; looking on the dark side of things

> SYN—**pessimistic** implies an attitude, often habitual, of expecting the worst to happen [*pessimistic* about one's chances to win]; **cynical** implies a contemptuous disbelief in human goodness and sincerity [he's *cynical* about recovering his lost watch]; **misanthropic** suggests a deep-seated hatred or distrust of people in general [a *misanthropic* hermit]—*ANT.* **optimistic**

**reimburse** (rē′im burs′) *v.*   1. to pay back (money spent)   2. to repay or compensate (a person) for expenses, damages, losses, etc.

> SYN—to **reimburse** is to pay back what has been expended [the salesman was *reimbursed* for his traveling expenses]; **pay** is the simple, direct word meaning to give money, etc. due for services rendered, goods received, etc.; **compensate** implies a return, whether monetary or not, thought of as equivalent to the service given, the effort expended, or the loss sustained [he could never be *compensated* for the loss of his son]; **remunerate** stresses the idea of payment for a service rendered, but it often also carries an implication of reward [a bumper crop *remunerated* the farmer for his labors]; **repay** implies a paying back of money given to one or it may refer to a doing or giving of anything in requital [how can I *repay* you for your kindness?]; **recompense** stresses the idea of compensation or requital

**seclusion** (si kloo′zhən) *n.*   1. the act of keeping away from others   2. isolation

> SYN—**seclusion** suggests retirement from intercourse with the outside world, as by confining oneself to one's home, a remote place, etc.; **solitude** refers to the state of one who is completely alone, cut off from all human contact, and sometimes stresses the loneliness of such a condition [the *solitude* of a hermit]; **isolation** suggests physical separation from others, often an involuntary detachment resulting from the force of circumstances [the *isolation* of a forest ranger]

**waive** (wāv) *v.*   1. to give up or forgo (a right, claim, privilege, etc.)   2. to refrain from insisting on or taking advantage of   3. to put off until later; postpone; defer

> SYN—**waive** suggests a voluntary relinquishing by refusing to insist on one's right or claim to something [to *waive* a jury trial]; **relinquish** implies a giving up of something desirable and connotes compulsion or the force of necessity [he will not *relinquish* his advantage]; **abandon,** in this connection, implies a complete and final relinquishment, as because of weariness, discouragement, etc. [do not *abandon* hope]; **forgo** implies the denial to oneself of something, as for reasons of expediency or altruism [I must *forgo* the pleasure of your company this evening]; **abdicate** most commonly refers to the formal giving up by a sovereign of his throne, but sometimes describes a surrender of any prerogative; **renounce,** often interchangeable with **abdicate,** is the more frequent usage when the voluntary surrender of any right, claim, title, practice, etc. is meant, and often suggests sacrifice [she *renounced* the pleasures of society]

---

fat, āpe, cär; ten, ēven; is, bīte; gō, hôrn, tool, look; oil, out; up, fur; get; joy; yet; chin; she; thin, *th*en; zh, leisure; ŋ, ring; ə for *a* in *ago, e* in *agent, i* in *sanity, o* in *comply, u* in *focus;* ′ as in *able* (ā′b′l)

Use the dictionary usage excerpts in the New Words list to complete the following exercise. In each sentence below, one of the four choices best completes the thought. Write in the best word. Check your answers in the back of the book.

1. The president officially _____ the month of January National Baby Month. (asserted, affirmed, proclaimed)

2. Isaac Merritt Singer was the _____ inventor of the first practical sewing machine. (cunning, shrewd, astute, ingenious)

3. A good magician will always be able to _____ her audience. (defraud, cheat, dupe, swindle)

4. Authoritarian governments are not _____ of other people's beliefs. (tolerant, nonpartisan, equitable, impartial)

5. Sherlock Holmes's ability to _____ a person's occupation, previous whereabouts, and place of residence from his or her clothing, speech, and manner was amazing. (infer, judge, gather, conclude)

6. The children were _____ when they were told their father had suffered another major heart attack. (pessimistic, cynical, misanthropic)

7. To keep some very contagious diseases from spreading, the victims are placed in _____. (seclusion, isolation, solitude)

8. Prospecting for gold becomes popular when the increased price of the metal offers prospectors the chance to be _____. (paid, reimbursed, remunerated, repaid)

9. Bob was so _____ by Dorothy's refusal of his marriage proposal that he couldn't think of anything to say. (puzzled, perplexed, confounded)

10. If you want to lose weight you must _____ high-calorie desserts. (waive, forgo, abdicate)

Write the proper word to complete each sentence below. Check your answers in the back of the book.

| assert | cunning | impartial | pessimistic | seclusion |
| confound | duped | inferred | reimburse | waive |

1. Bruce _____ that power must have been out the night before when his watch, which was accurate, was two hours ahead of all the clocks in his house.

2. If your employer plans to _____ your expenses on a business trip, you should keep receipts and good records.

3. A _____ person sees a glass as half empty while others see it as half full.

4. _____ English pickpockets in the 1800s knew that people watching the public hangings were easy prey; however, most of the thieves never seemed to think that if they were caught, they too would be hanged.

5. There is a problem trying to establish a legal case for women who _____ that they have been sexually harassed on a job, because concrete proof to support their claims is often hard to find.

6. It is difficult to make a reasonable decision on whether to end a marriage because emotions _____ the situation.

7. Although Supreme Court justices are supposed to be _____, many were appointed after having held political office.

8. From the early 1940s until her death, Greta Garbo, an American film actress born in Sweden, lived in _____ .

9. There is a long list of people who have been _____ by unscrupulous persons posing as repairmen.

10. According to the decision in the *Miranda* case, a prisoner who does not specifically _____ the right to have an attorney present during questioning is being questioned illegally, and what is said must be disregarded during the trial.

# NEW WORDS II

The following New Words are often confused with other words that have similar spellings.

**amoral** (ā môr′əl) *adj.*   1. not to be judged by criteria of morality; neither moral nor immoral   2. without moral sense or principles; incapable of distinguishing between right and wrong

Confused with: immoral

**causal** (kôz′l) *adj.*   1. indicating, relating to, or acting as a cause; causative   2. showing interaction of cause and effect

Confused with: casual

**envelop** (in vel′əp) *v.*   1. to wrap up, cover completely   2. to surround   3. to conceal; hide

Confused with: envelope

**flair** (flãr) *n.*   1. a natural talent or ability; aptitude; knack   2. [Colloq.] a sense of what is stylish and striking; dash

Confused with: flare

**locale** (lō kal′) *n.*   a place or locality, esp. with reference to events or circumstances connected with it, often as a setting for a story, play, etc.

Confused with: local

**prosecute** (präs′ə kyo͞ot′) *v.*   1. to follow up or pursue (something) to a conclusion [to *prosecute* a war with vigor]   2. to begin legal proceedings against or conduct criminal proceedings in court against, try in court

Confused with: persecute

**rite** (rīt) *n.*   1. a ceremonial or formal, solemn act, observance, or procedure in accordance with prescribed rule or custom, as in religious use [marriage *rites*]   2. any formal, customary observance, practice, or procedure [the *rites* of courtship]   3. a prescribed form or particular system of ceremonial procedure, religious or otherwise; ritual [the Scottish *rite* of Freemasonry]   4. a division of (Eastern and Western) churches according to the rituals used

Confused with: right, write

**rote** (rōt) *n.*   a fixed, mechanical way of doing something; routine—**by rote** by memory alone, without understanding or thought [to answer by *rote*]

Confused with: wrote

**tolerable** (täl′ər ə b'l) *adj.*   1. that which can be tolerated; bearable   2. fairly good; passable

Confused with: tolerant

**vice** (vīs) *n.*   1. immoral practice or habit   2. a trivial fault or failing [smoking is a common *vice*]

Confused with: vise

fat, āpe, cär; ten, ēven; is, bīte; gō, hôrn, to͞ol, look; oil, out; up, fur; get; joy; yet; chin; she; thin, then; zh, leisure; ŋ, ring; ə for a in ago, e in agent, i in sanity, o in comply, u in focus; ' as in able (ā′b'l)

## EXERCISE 7: FREQUENTLY CONFUSED WORDS

Each word in italics is a New Word, and the other word is one that is often confused with it. Fill in each blank with the correct word. Check your answers in the back of the book.

1.  There is a _____ relationship between rain and mud. (casual, *causal*)

2.  Young children running around without any clothing are usually not criticized because their actions are _____. (immoral, *amoral*)

3.  Fog often _____ San Francisco, making it difficult to see the whole Golden Gate Bridge. (*envelops,* envelopes)

4.  Most good comedians discover early that they have a _____ for telling funny stories. (flare, *flair*)

5.  To save money, movie studios will often try to find a more convenient _____ for scenes that supposedly take place in other countries. (*locale,* local)

6.  There is an ongoing attempt to _____ and convict offenders who commit crime after crime. (*prosecute,* persecute)

7.  Our Constitution guarantees us the _____ to practice any religion we choose. (*rite,* right)

8.  We learn the Pledge of Allegiance by _____. (*rote,* wrote)

9.  A democratic system of government demands that we be _____ of the practices of others. (tolerant, *tolerable*)

10. She used a _____ to hold the broken leg to the chair while the glue dried. (vise, *vice*)

Circle the letter before the word or phrase that best defines the italicized word in each sentence. Check your answers in the back of the book.

1. Young children are *amoral;* however, they will learn right from wrong as they mature.

   a. proper   b. unethical   c. without ethics   d. sensible

2. There was a *causal* relationship between early trade routes and wind currents, since it was easier for sailing ships to sail with the winds.

   a. random   b. special   c. cause-effect   d. accidental

3. Lighthouses were invented to help ships *enveloped in* fog stay off rocks that could not be seen.

   a. uncovered by   b. built in   c. enclosed in   d. threatened by

4. Mozart's *flair* for musical composition was evident almost from birth; at four, he was already composing lovely music.

   a. talent   b. compulsion   c. hatred   d. love

5. The film industry developed in Los Angeles rather than New York because the dry *locale* allowed for outdoor filming.

   a. location   b. time   c. season   d. theme

6. It was impossible to *prosecute* Lee Harvey Oswald for the murder of President Kennedy because the killer was shot dead before the trial.

   a. execute   b. expose   c. imprison   d. try

7. The sunrise Easter service is a *rite* that has been observed since the time of Christ.

   a. law   b. holiday   c. phenomenon   d. observance

8. Learning by *rote* is not as common in today's schools as it was early in the century. Nevertheless, some poetry and the multiplication tables are still taught in this way.

   a. routine   b. understanding   c. thinking   d. chance

9. The heat and humidity of Kuwait created weather conditions barely *tolerable* for many American soldiers during the Gulf War.

   a. possible   b. believable   c. bearable   d. appreciated

10. In spite of the efforts of educators and the police, most large cities usually have a certain amount of *vice.*

    a. pleasurable practice   b. immoral practice   c. harmless practice   d. humorous practice

## EXERCISE 9: TRUE-FALSE

Place a *T* or an *F* in the space provided. Check your answers in the back of the book.

_____ 1. The multiplication tables are learned by rote.

_____ 2. We should prosecute criminals whenever possible.

_____ 3. There is a causal relationship between not attending class and getting a low grade.

_____ 4. A pessimistic person does not have a cheerful outlook on life.

_____ 5. Amoral behavior is evil.

## EXERCISE 10: ANALOGIES

The analogies below are either synonyms, antonyms, classification : example, cause : effect, or part : whole. First, decide which type of comparison is used in the first pair of words. Second, fill in the type of analogy using *S* for synonym, *A* for antonym, *C* for classification : example, *C/E* for cause : effect, *P* for part : whole. Third, find a word from the choices that will make the second pair of words have the same relationship. Check your answers in the back of the book.

_____ 1. prominent : inconspicuous ::    a. argument   b. claim   c. suspect
      assert : _____           d. deny

_____ 2. prominent person : president ::    a. location   b. midwest   c. part
      locale : _____           d. world

_____ 3. radical : extreme ::    a. talent   b. clothes   c. money
      flair : _____           d. clumsiness

_____ 4. counsel : better decisions ::    a. friendship   b. confusion   c. loneliness
      seclusion : _____           d. public appearances

_____ 5. lure : fishing ::    a. vow   b. religion   c. book
      rite : _____           d. privilege

## EXERCISE 11: MATCHING MEANINGS

Write the letter of the word that means the opposite of the word in the first column. Check your answers in the back of the book.

_____ 1. impartial          a. unbearable

_____ 2. reimburse          b. clarify

_____ 3. tolerable          c. biased

_____ 4. vice               d. default

_____ 5. confound           e. goodness

## EXERCISE 12: WORD CONTRASTS

In each group below, circle the word that does not mean what the others mean. Check your answers in the back of the book.

1. waive       claim      take       accept

2. infer       deduce     assert     reason

3. cunning     clever     crafty     witless

4. envelop     expose     enclose    surround

5. dupe        hoax       outwit     educate

## EXERCISE 13: SENTENCE COMPLETION

Complete each sentence in your own words. Sample answers are provided in the back of the book.

1. Being an *amoral* person means _____
   _____.

2. When you *assert* yourself, _____
   _____.

3. Many things have *causal* relationships; for example, _____
   _____.

4. If a situation in school *confounds* you, _____
   _____.

5. Unless you are a *cunning* person, _____
   _____.

6. It is not proper to try to *dupe* another person into thinking _____

   _____ .

7. During the time heavy snow *envelops* a city, _____

   _____ .

8. A person who has a *flair* for fashion design _____

   _____ .

9. An umpire in a baseball game should be *impartial;* otherwise, _____

   _____ .

10. You can *infer* from the aroma of coffee in the air that _____

   _____ .

11. My favorite *locale* for a vacation is _____

   _____ .

12. A *pessimistic* person _____

   _____ .

13. While people are being *prosecuted* for serious crimes, _____

   _____ .

14. When you have *reimbursed* the bank for your car loan, _____

   _____ .

15. *Rites* such as funeral services are a part of any religion because _____

   _____ .

16. Children who are taught spelling by *rote* memory _____

   _____ .

17. You are most likely to want *seclusion* when _____

   _____ .

18. Some situations are not *tolerable;* for example, _____

   _____ .

19. Because *vice* is illegal _____

   _____ .

20. When you are told your tuition has been *waived,* _____

   _____ .

# ADVANCED WORDS

The following New Words are often confused with words similar to them in meaning. Read each definition, then read the dictionary excerpts describing their usage.

**circumvent** (sʉr′kəm vent′) *vt.*   1. to get the better of or prevent by craft of cleverness   2. to circle around or surround

> SYN—to **circumvent** implies getting the better of or preventing by craft or cleverness or going around instead of confronting [to *circumvent* tax laws by opening foreign offices]; **escape,** as compared here, implies a getting out of, a keeping away from, or simply a remaining unaffected by an impending or present danger, evil, confinement, etc. [to *escape* death, criticism, etc.]; to **avoid** is to make a conscious effort to keep clear of something undesirable or harmful [to *avoid* crowds during a flu epidemic]; to **evade** is to escape or avoid by artifice, cunning, adroitness, etc. [to *evade* pursuit, one's duty, etc.]; to **elude** is to escape the grasp of someone or something by artful or slippery dodges or because of a baffling quality [the criminal *eluded* the police, the meaning *eluded* him]

**impasse** (im′pas, im pas′) *n.*   1. a passage open only at one end; blind alley   2. a situation offering no escape; difficulty without solution or an argument where no agreement is possible; deadlock

> SYN—**impasse** implies a predicament with no solution; **predicament** implies a complicated, perplexing situation from which it is difficult to disentangle oneself; **dilemma** implies a predicament necessitating a choice between equally disagreeable alternatives; **plight** emphasizes a distressing or unfortunate situation; **fix** and **pickle** are both colloquial terms loosely interchangeable with any of the preceding, although more precisely **fix** is equivalent to **predicament** and **pickle,** to plight

**plausible** (plô′zə b'l) *adj.*   1. seemingly true, acceptable, etc., often implying disbelief   2. seemingly honest, trustworthy, etc., often implying distrust

> SYN—**plausible** applies to that which at first glance appears to be true, reasonable, valid, etc. but which may or may not be so, although there is no connotation of deliberate deception [a *plausible* argument]; **credible** is used of that which is believable because it is supported by evidence, sound logic, etc. [a *credible* account]; **possible** is used of anything that may exist, occur, be done, etc., depending on circumstances [a *possible* solution to a problem]; **feasible** is used of that which is likely to be carried through to a successful conclusion and, hence, connotes the desirability of doing so [a *feasible* enterprise]

**serenity** (sə ren′ə tē) *n.*   the quality or state of being serene; calmness; tranquillity

> SYN—**serenity** implies a lofty, clear peace of mind that is not easily clouded by ordinary stresses or excitements; **calmness,** basically applied to the weather, suggests a total absence of agitation or disturbance [a *calmness* of mind, weather, speech]; **peacefulness** suggests a lack of turbulence or disorder; **composure** implies the disciplining of one's emotions in a trying situation or self-possession in the face of excitement; **nonchalance** implies a casual indifference to or a cool detachment from situations that might be expected to disturb one emotionally

**synopsis** (si năp′sis) *n., pl.* **-ses**   a statement giving a brief, general review or summary

> SYN—a **synopsis** is a condensed, orderly treatment, as of the plot of a novel, that permits a quick general view of the whole; **abridgment** describes a work condensed from a larger work by omitting the less important parts, but keeping the main contents more or less unaltered; an **abstract** is a short statement of the essential contents of a book, court record, etc. often used as an index to the original material; **brief** and **summary** both imply a statement of the main points of the matter under consideration [the *brief* of a legal argument], **summary,** especially, implying a brief review; a **digest** is a concise, systematic treatment, generally more comprehensive in scope than a synopsis, and, in the case of technical material, often arranged under titles for quick reference

fat, āpe, cär; ten, ēven; is, bīte; gō, hôrn, to͞ol, look; oil, out; up, fʉr; get; joy; yet; chin; she; thin, *th*en; zh, leisure; ŋ, ring; ə for *a* in *ago, e* in *agent, i* in *sanity, o* in *comply, u* in *focus;* ′ as in *able* (ā′b'l)

The following New Words are often confused with words similar to them in sound. Read each definition; then read the word or words with which the New Word is often confused.

**complement** (käm′plə mənt) *n.*   1. that which completes or brings to perfection   2. the amount or number needed to fill or complete   3. a complete set; entirety   4. something added to complete a whole; either of two parts that complete each other

Confused with: compliment

**faze** (fāz) *v.*   disturb the composure or courage of; embarrass

Confused with: phase

**ingenuous** (in jen′yoo wəs) *adj.*   1. frank; open; candid   2. simple; artless; naive

Confused with: ingenious

**loath** (lōth) *adj.*   unwilling; reluctant (usually followed by an infinitive) [to be *loath* to depart]

Confused with: loathe

**taut** (tôt) *adj.*   1. tightly stretched, as a rope   2. showing strain; tense [a *taut* smile]   3. trim, tidy, well disciplined, efficient, etc. [a *taut* ship]

Confused with: taught and taunt

fat, āpe, cär; ten, ēven; is, bīte; gō, hôrn, tōōl, look; oil, out; up, fʉr; get; joy; yet; chin; she; thin, *th*en; zh, leisure; ŋ, ring; ə for *a* in *ago, e* in *agent, i* in *sanity, o* in *comply, u* in *focus;* ′ as in *able* (ā′b′l)

Use the Advanced Words to fill in the blanks in the sentences that follow. Check your answers in the back of the book.

circumvent        faze            ingenuous        plausible        synopsis
complement        impasse         loath            serenity         taut

1. When the school board and the teachers' union reached an _____ in their contract negotiations, the teachers decided to strike.

2. To _____ the legal requirement to list all assets in a bankruptcy proceeding, some people open secret Swiss bank accounts. If this practice is discovered, it is a serious federal offense.

3. It is helpful to see a _____ of the first episode of a three-part television miniseries, if you begin your viewing with part two.

4. She was _____ to give the beggar money because of his obvious drinking problem; instead, she brought him food and clothing.

5. The young man had _____ leg muscles from years of swimming on his school's swim team.

6. It doesn't _____ some children to be scolded by their teacher; others will remember the scolding all of their lives.

7. The butler gave a _____ alibi for his whereabouts during his master's murder; nonetheless, Scotland Yard did not rule out his involvement in the crime.

8. Most people look to the retirement years as a time of _____, but because of economic insecurity it may not be.

9. Most children are _____, so when they say they like something you can believe them.

10. To some people, a fine wine is the _____ of a good meal.

After the definitions of five of the Advanced Words is a dictionary excerpt that compares the word with others. Below are sentences that use those words. Cross out any word in parentheses that cannot properly be used in the sentence. Check your answers in the back of the book.

1. The short (brief, synopsis, abridgement, digest) of the novel's plot was easy to follow because the writer numbered his main points.

2. Hardy always told Laurel, "This is another fine mess you've gotten us into," whenever the two comedians were in another (impasse, predicament, dilemma).

3. Many movies are made in foreign countries to (circumvent, elude, evade) having to pay the crew high union wages.

4. Unless we can find a (plausible, credible, feasible) solution to the energy crisis, people won't be able to afford to drive cars.

5. Her (serenity, tranquillity, nonchalance) about turning in papers on time caused her to fail three classes.

## EXERCISE 16: ADVANCED WORDS—FREQUENTLY CONFUSED WORDS

Below are the Advanced Words that are confused with words that sound or look alike. Write in the correct word. Check your answers in the back of the book.

1. Fashions seem to go through different _____. One year clothes look similar to those in the 1940s, and the next year they look like clothes from science fiction movies. (fazes, phases)

2. Some people have difficulty accepting a _____. (compliment, complement)

3. People from small towns are usually stereotyped as being more _____ than people from large cities. (ingenious, ingenuous)

4. Some people so _____ cooking that they eat all their meals in restaurants. (loathe, loath)

5. His _____ expression showed he was uncomfortable going on a blind date. (taught, taut)

Fill in the puzzle below in pencil. Remember that the clues with an asterisk (*) refer to words from the New Words list in the previous chapters. Check your answers in the back of the book.

**Across**

*1. Irritate
8. Large body of water
10. Abbr. for *long-playing record*
11. Antonym of *import*
*13. Having respect for others' beliefs
17. Low, mournful sounds of sorrow or pain
19. Electroencephalogram
20. Abbr. for *laboratory*
21. Near
22. Suffix for past-tense verb
24. Roman numeral for 551
25. Abbr. for *Consumer Price Index*
26. Antonym of *your*
27. Rests in a chair
*28. To cut short
31. Abbr. for *northeast*
33. Abbr. for *North America*
34. Abbr. for *computer-aided instruction*
35. Roman numeral for 2
36. Prefix meaning *away, from,* as in _____dicate, _____stract
37. Idiom meaning *quietly, without others knowing* as "on the _____"
*38. Commotion
40. Afternoon
41. Abbr. for *University of Illinois*
42. The second and third vowels in English
43. Largest city in Brazil
*44. Believable
49. Brand of cola drink
50. Very slow animal
52. Abbr. for *district attorney*
53. Same as 52 Across
55. The burnt end of a cigarette
57. Abbr. for the largest city in California
*58. Hot; passionate
59. Type of inexpensive metal
*60. Against the law
61. Tom Cruise's monogram

**Down**

*1. To value highly; respect
2. Everything or everybody
3. Goes faster than the speed limit
4. Raced on foot
5. Initials of the inventor of the light bulb
6. Clearly stated
*7. Dark and gloomy
8. Wound made with a knife
9. Donkey
12. Hockey's Robert "Bobby" Orr's monogram
*14. To give up
*15. Disturbance
16. _____, tac, toe
18. Abbr. for *New York*
*23. Energetic; forceful
29. Roman numeral for 3
30. Plant with a white trumpet-shaped flower
32. Musician Eubie Blake's monogram
*34. Very important
39. Petroleum
*40. Danger
45. Actor Rob Lowe's monogram
46. Image of god used for worship
47. A rectangular piece of soap or candy
48. To make corrections on a paper before publication
51. Same as 2 Down
54. Abbr. for *Air Defense Command*
55. Abbr. for *Alcoholics Anonymous*
56. Abbr. for *South Dakota*
58. Abbr. for *tuberculosis*

## EXERCISE 18: OWN WORDS

Choose from your outside reading ten words that you would like to learn, and write them in the spaces below. When you look the words up in the dictionary, pay particular attention to their synonyms and antonyms. Pronounce each word, put the definition in your own words, use the word in a sentence, make up a mnemonic, and put the word on a flash card for regular review.

1. _____

2. _____

3. _____

4. _____

5. _____

6. _____

7. _____

8. _____

9. _____

10. _____

# FINAL REVIEW

## Review Words: Chapters 2–12

### I. Fill-in

Use the context to fill in the blanks in the following mystery story with words from the Review list below. Then solve the mystery.

| | | | |
|---|---|---|---|
| analysis | contemplate | lure | procession |
| calamity | elaborate | maneuver | prominent |
| colossal | excursion | minute | solemn |
| conspiracy | hostile | nonexistent | sympathetic |

### The Case of the Stranded Blonde

Inspector Keane was returning from a weekend _____ to a

nearby city, where he had attended the funeral of a _____ citizen,
              1
who had been a close friend.
              2

    Since he had been unsure of the directions, he had followed the long funeral

_____. After the _____ ceremony, because road
              3                              4
signs in the area were almost _____ and it was getting dark, he
                                        5
decided to stop at a local restaurant to get directions home. As soon as he entered

the bar, he saw a beautiful blonde with an _____ hairdo who came
                                                      6
over to him and exclaimed, "What a _____! I left my purse on
                                              7
the bus and have no way to get home. Please, can you help me?" Feeling

_____, the inspector agreed at once to drive her home.
              8

    They had only driven a short distance when a pair of bright headlights came

towards them on the unlighted road. The woman turned to Keane and said, "Oh,

that's my husband. Just honk your horn and stop; he'll be glad to drive me home."

    After only a _____ of careful _____, Keane
                        9                              10
decided not to stop. As he kept driving, he looked in his rear view mirror and saw a

_____, black sedan _____ to the opposite side of
              11                              12
the road and stopped. An obviously _____ man jumped out shak-
                                              13
ing his fist furiously. Keane had no need to _____ further. He
                                                      14
pressed the accelerator and sped away with the surprised blonde at his side. He

dropped the woman at the next well-lit area and safely proceeded home.

    How did he know that the whole incident had been a _____
                                                                  15
to _____ him into trouble?
              16

Keane quickly realized that it would have been impossible for the blonde to identify her husband's car at night while looking into its headlights. The woman could only have known about the car if she and her husband had prearranged the meeting. Therefore, the inspector wisely decided that this situation would mean trouble with a capital "T."

## II. Sentence Completions

Circle the word that best completes each sentence.

1. Poor students must make _____ improvements in their grades if they want to graduate with honors. (radical, passive)

2. A(n) _____ person gets things done. (efficient, deficient)

3. A _____ in a diamond lowers its value. (defect, status)

4. Abortion is a _____ topic. (controversial, decisive)

5. This postage stamp is _____; all others like it have been destroyed. (unique, subtle)

6. If you _____ in breaking the law, you will probably go to jail. (persist, generalize)

7. I ran back to _____ the bag I had left on the bus. (retrieve, saturate)

8. To catch the train, you need to go to the _____. (terminal, succession)

9. The _____ of the crime was blocked off. (site, priority)

10. It is difficult to _____ with the death of a close friend. (stabilize, cope)

11. An _____ pain can hurt a lot. (acute, absurd)

12. The woman was disturbed by the man's _____ manner. (immortal, offensive)

13. Airline _____ wear uniforms to identify themselves to the public. (personnel, media)

14. If you _____ a neighbor by kicking his dog, he may take your to court. (harass, exile)

15. A _____ task will be easier if you divide it into parts. (priceless, complex)

16. Not everyone likes _____ art. (preliminary, contemporary)

17. Your grade on a test may depend on the _____ of your errors. (prestige, frequency)

18. A _____ piece of equipment has many uses. (simultaneous, versatile)

19. A computer can help you _____ sentences in a paper. (obstruct, alter)

20. Modern medicine has developed new ways to _____ the life of premature infants. (imply, sustain)

### III. True-False

If the sentence is true, write *T* in the blank. If the sentence is false, write *F*.

_____ 1. A precise scientist will not omit important details in reports about his experiments.

_____ 2. Your ancestry determines your genetic possibilities.

_____ 3. Brutality is a trivial matter.

_____ 4. One antidote for self-pity is reflecting on the good things in your life.

_____ 5. If you excel in schoolwork, you may be eligible for a scholarship.

_____ 6. Neurotic behavior is appropriate in most situations.

_____ 7. One hundred pounds of excessive weight will rarely be a hazard to your health.

_____ 8. It would be premature to proclaim that tuberculosis has been wiped out.

_____ 9. One of the perils of doing acts of sabotage is the risk of being caught.

_____ 10. A military courier conveys information.

_____ 11. A person wants his or her legal counsel to be negligent.

_____ 12. It could be an ordeal to return home and find a vandal there.

_____ 13. As a tactic, police may pretend to negotiate with a bank robber who is holding customers at gunpoint.

_____ 14. Parallel lines intercept.

_____ 15. One aspect of being a good first grade teacher is having a patient temperament.

_____ 16. When a material decomposes it retains its shape.

_____ 17. It is abnormal to have an income tax deduction taken from your salary.

_____ 18. Treachery exemplifies what Americans want in a president.

_____ 19. It is unwise to contradict your boss in a rude manner; it may provoke him or her.

_____ 20. Some soldiers resist the enemy no matter what; they would rather be killed than submit.

## IV. Matching Meanings

Write the letter of the word that means the same as the word in the left-hand column.

| | | | |
|---|---|---|---|
| _____ | 1. lunatic | a. | unplanned |
| _____ | 2. anticipate | b. | untrue |
| _____ | 3. component | c. | undertaking |
| _____ | 4. affect | d. | joke |
| _____ | 5. verdict | e. | insane |
| _____ | 6. versus | f. | artificial |
| _____ | 7. vocation | g. | look forward to |
| _____ | 8. perspective | h. | ingredient |
| _____ | 9. synthetic | i. | judgment |
| _____ | 10. jest | j. | occupation |
| _____ | 11. corruption | k. | against |
| _____ | 12. enterprise | l. | point of view |
| _____ | 13. random | m. | act of taking bribes |
| _____ | 14. invalid | n. | influence |

Check your answers to the *Final Review: Review Words* in the back of the book.

### New Words: Chapters 2–12

## I. Multiple Choice

Circle the word that is closest in meaning to each numbered word.

1. aggravate    a. discover   b. confuse   c. worsen   d. please

2. arid    a. lost   b. waterless   c. useless   d. moist

3. antiquated    a. new   b. expensive   c. ugly   d. old

4. criterion    a. idea   b. criticism   c. measure   d. source

5. vice    a. evil act   b. honest act   c. persistence   d. assistance

6. sequential    a. random   b. conclusive   c. ordered   d. spontaneous

7. obligatory    a. mandatory   b. optional   c. systematic   d. helpful

8. thesis    a. minor thought   b. major idea   c. new discovery
     d. complicated information

9. infer    a. deny   b. reason   c. claim   d. coax

10. reimburse    a. owe   b. earn   c. repay   d. reverse

11. causal    a. sequenced   b. effective   c. random   d. causative

12. derivation    a. privilege   b. etymology   c. meaning   d. results

13. rote    a. written   b. mechanical   c. seen   d. practiced

14. attain    a. see   b. succeed   c. attempt   d. accept

15. reminiscent    a. neglectful   b. suggestive   c. temporary   d. forgetful

16. apparatus    a. motor   b. handiwork   c. skill   d. tool

17. reliance    a. trust   b. independence   c. honesty   d. uncertainty

18. proficient    a. careful   b. adequate   c. expert   d. careless

19. avocation    a. occupation   b. talent   c. livelihood   d. hobby

20. objective    a. impartial   b. shrewd   c. dishonest   d. unique

21. symmetry    a. harmony   b. smoothness   c. difference   d. measurement

22. depose    a. dethrone   b. elect   c. assist   d. hate

23. phenomenon    a. dangerous task   b. everyday happening   c. unusual event   d. test

24. subdue    a. conquer   b. kill   c. banish   d. bless

25. fluency    a. awkwardness   b. smoothness   c. spontaneity   d. deception

26. supposition    a. assumption   b. position   c. memory   d. statement

## II. Sentence Completions

Fill in the word that best completes each sentence.

1. A _____ is a ceremony. (syndicate, rite)

2. A(n) _____ sickness has affected you for a long time. (chronic, indicative)

3. A _____ politician is not controlled by a single party. (liberal, nonpartisan)

4. You can _____ payment of a bill by check. (remit, default)

5. A law that establishes future conduct sets a _____. (stigma, precedent)

6. The sun and planets _____ our solar system. (simulate, constitute)

7. When you _____ a situation, you become involved in it. (misconstrue, intervene in)

8. Behavior that is not limited by ethics is _____. (amoral, inadvertent)

9. A(n) _____ error happens by accident. (inadvertent, pessimistic)

10. If you _____ a disaster, you prevent it. (avert, depreciate)

11. A(n) _____ item lasts a long time. (durable, inconspicuous)

12. A _____ solution is extreme. (drastic, laborious)

13. If you _____ someone, you exile her. (ostracize, designate)

14. A person with an "open mind" will listen to _____ ideas on a subject. (diverse, degenerate)

15. A(n) _____ idea is hard for children to understand. (abstract, concurrent)

16. An _____ problem is complicated. (atypical, intricate)

17. It is _____ that we will never have another famous writer in the United States. (inconceivable, apprehensive)

18. A _____ of vitamins can lead to illness. (deprivation, synthesis)

19. A statement that is _____ is unclear. (ambiguous, imposing)

20. You _____ former behavior if you return to doing things as you did them before. (surpass, revert to)

21. Something that is _____ is not spicy. (bland, colloquial)

22. A _____ is an overused expression. (cliché, graphic)

### III. Synonyms and Antonyms

If the words in each pair are synonyms, write *S* in the blank. If they are antonyms, write *A* in the blank.

| | | | |
|---|---|---|---|
| _____ | 1. | compulsory | mandatory |
| _____ | 2. | abridge | curtail |
| _____ | 3. | shrewd | cunning |
| _____ | 4. | impartial | unbiased |
| _____ | 5. | implicit | explicit |
| _____ | 6. | turmoil | agitation |
| _____ | 7. | intimate | insinuate |
| _____ | 8. | exert | endeavor |
| _____ | 9. | dilemma | plight |
| _____ | 10. | pending | subsequent |
| _____ | 11. | esteem | abhor |
| _____ | 12. | disreputable | unscrupulous |
| _____ | 13. | empathy | compassion |
| _____ | 14. | deception | hoax |
| _____ | 15. | torrid | frigid |
| _____ | 16. | spontaneous | methodical |
| _____ | 17. | deficient | superfluous |
| _____ | 18. | succumb | concede |
| _____ | 19. | crucial | irrelevant |
| _____ | 20. | obsolete | archaic |

**IV. True-False**

If the sentence is true, write *T* in the blank. If the sentence is false, write *F*.

_____ 1. A foreign dignitary is exempt from most federal laws.

_____ 2. It is easy to dupe an ingenious person.

_____ 3. If you have a flair for something, you have an aptitude for it.

_____ 4. People who commit fraudulent acts try to evade the police.

_____ 5. An excerpt from a book to commemorate an actress would tell why you detested her acting.

_____ 6. An advocate has commitment to one side of an issue.

_____ 7. Before you can solve a problem, you need the pertinent data.

_____ 8. Dismal situations make people jovial.

_____ 9. When someone seeks solitude, he does not want to be accessible.

_____ 10. To be concise, you must consolidate your ideas.

_____ 11. A credible thing is irrational.

_____ 12. The light spectrum coincides with the colors of the rainbow.

_____ 13. Fanatics often incur a bad reputation as a result of their actions.

_____ 14. Under martial law, the military and the people collaborate to form the government.

_____ 15. An authoritarian person is tolerant.

_____ 16. A cynical person is skeptical about others' motives.

_____ 17. It is a fallacy that some ethnic groups are intellectually superior to others.

_____ 18. When a person abdicates an office, she waives her rights to it.

_____ 19. Something enticing is provocative.

_____ 20. A harangue is the best method of enlightening others.

_____ 21. A person will quickly relinquish an invaluable object.

_____ 22. You cannot feel apathy toward a new business venture if you are going to be successful.

_____ 23. An irrevocable law is tentative.

_____ 24. You would enjoy staying at an intriguing locale.

_____ 25. When the latest acquisition of a museum is going to be a famous painting, an expert will be called in to ascertain whether it is real or a replica.

_____ 26. Stereotypes are generalized from superficial characteristics of a cultural, ethnic, racial, or religious group.

_____ 27. We should repudiate preposterous suggestions.

_____ 28. At Christmas most people ponder who will be the recipients of gifts.

_____ 29. A robust person generally likes static activities.

_____ 30. Water in a receptacle becomes stagnant if left for a long time.

_____ 31. When a portion of a country tries to secede, it faces many obstacles.

_____ 32. Pathology is a somber field.

_____ 33. People notorious for crimes are despicable.

## V. Matching

Match the word in the first column with the definition in the second. Write the letter of the correct definition in the space provided.

_____ 1. abstain          a. forbidden

_____ 2. suffice          b. give out

_____ 3. intermittent     c. future generations

_____ 4. jurisdiction     d. stopping and starting

_____ 5. confound       e. characteristic

_____ 6. taboo          f. adjust to

_____ 7. generic         g. to be enough

_____ 8. dynamic       h. annoy

_____ 9. integrity      i. legal power over

_____ 10. posterity     j. next to

_____ 11. envelop      k. moving

_____ 12. exasperate    l. group name

_____ 13. attribute     m. do without

_____ 14. tolerable     n. surround

_____ 15. acclimate    o. call forth

_____ 16. adjacent     p. confuse

_____ 17. assert        q. bearable

_____ 18. evoke        r. claim

_____ 19. assess        s. honesty

_____ 20. emit          t. evaluate

_____ 21. flagrant      u. decay

_____ 22. deteriorate    v. firmness or thickness

_____ 23. synchronize   w. privacy

_____ 24. naive        x. innocent

_____ 25. seclusion     y. obvious

_____ 26. consistency   z. coordinate

## VI. Fill-In

Using the words below, fill in the blanks in the story.

bizarre
chaos
compensate
composure
culprits

escalating
foil
intimidated
jeopardy

monetary
nonchalant
predicament
prosecuted

recourse
recurrent
retrospect
sinister

### The Perils of Pauline the Bank Teller
by Kathy Miller

Just last year I was in a very _____ situation where even my life
was in _____. At that time I was employed as a teller in a bank while
it was held up. I'll never forget that day when a _____-looking
man came up to me and pointed a gun at my head as he said, "Give me all your small
unmarked bills, or I'll blow your head off." This really _____ me.
Meanwhile, his two assistants, who also had guns, watched the bank doors and everyone else in the bank. At first, there was much _____ in the bank,
but then people regained their _____ when the men stopped wav-
ing their guns. As for me, realizing I could not _____ the robbers
and having no intention of _____ the situation, I tried to act
_____ and I followed their orders. I realized there was really no
other _____. The man grabbed the money I handed him, and all
three of them exited very cautiously. I immediately pushed our security button, with
much relief. Luckily, two blocks away the _____ were caught when
they were stopped for speeding. All of the money was recovered and the robbers were
later _____ and found guilty. Because of my actions, I was given a
$100 bonus. But still in _____ I know the _____
reward will never _____ me for the _____ night-
mares of that awful _____.

Check your answers to the *Final Review: New Words* in the back of the book.

## Advanced Words: Chapters 2–12

### I. True-False

Mark *T* if the sentence is true and *F* if the sentence is false.

_____ 1. An irate person is difficult to appease.

_____ 2. Procrastinators tend to defer things that must be done.

_____ 3. The electorate is not always astute about choosing its leaders.

_____ 4. Reactionaries are loath to change.

_____ 5. To prevent the native Hawaiians from being completely assimilated by intermarriage into other ethnic groups, only indigenous peoples are permitted to live on the island of Niihau.

_____ 6. It facilitates your working with someone if you loathe her.

_____ 7. Agnostics are dubious about the existence of God.

_____ 8. Auspicious occasions are ominous.

_____ 9. An emissary conveys a message from one government to another.

_____ 10. Going to a desolate place is wise if you wish to elude the press and photographers.

_____ 11. It is feasible that a business partnership can end with an equitable settlement among the members.

_____ 12. Proponents of a cause are likely to equivocate when talking about it.

### II. Multiple Choice

Circle the word that is closest in meaning to each numbered word.

1. posthumous    a. before birth   b. while living   c. after death   d. after birth

2. stoic    a. frightened   b. surprised   c. unemotional   d. cruel

3. avocation    a. occupation   b. talent   c. livelihood   d. hobby

4. coherent    a. disorganized   b. logically connected   c. spontaneous   d. agreeing

5. erratic    a. surprising   b. organized   c. irregular   d. wrong

6. futile    a. useless   b. difficult   c. useful   d. future

7. integral    a. essential   b. interchangeable   c. unimportant   d. unnecessary

8. perseverance    a. fear   b. insistence   c. persistence   d. resistance

9. specious    a. new   b. false   c. dishonest   d. foolish

10. liquidate    a. acquire   b. eliminate   c. invent   d. assist

11. vindicate    a. clear   b. convict   c. arrest   d. defeat

12. contention    a. happiness   b. sorrow   c. controversy   d. peace

13. complement    a. take in   b. add to   c. withhold from   d. favor

14. collateral    a. extra   b. necessary   c. unimportant   d. unseen

15. precarious    a. careful   b. easy   c. certain   d. risky

16. arduous    a. impossible   b. difficult   c. confusing   d. ridiculous

17. juncture    a. joining   b. problem   c. division   d. overpass

18. mode    a. force   b. model   c. style   d. invention

19. incipient    a. doubtful   b. undecided   c. weak   d. beginning

20. taut    a. forgotten   b. tightly drawn   c. tasteless   d. worn

21. guise    a. thought   b. fear   c. happiness   d. appearance

22. infamous    a. respected   b. notorious   c. unknown   d. dangerous

23. perennial    a. occasional   b. long lasting   c. temporary   d. annual

24. avid    a. sad   b. eager   c. angry   d. silly

25. exuberant    a. serious   b. depressed   c. spirited   d. confused

26. transcend    a. go beyond   b. make aware of   c. postpone   d. go around

### III. Synonyms and Antonyms

If the pairs are synonyms, mark *S* in the blank. If the pairs are antonyms, mark *A*.

_____ 1. dexterous     inept

_____ 2. longevity     transience

_____ 3. emphatic     adamant

_____ 4. loathing     antipathy

_____ 5. cursory     profound

_____ 6. precursor     antecedent

_____ 7. pandemonium     serenity

_____ 8. destitute     affluent

_____ 9. adversary     proponent

_____ 10. obstinate     tenacious

**IV. Sentence Completions**

Circle the word that best completes each sentence.

1. An _____ person is unemotional. (impassive, arbitrary)

2. An unsuccessful attempt is _____. (lethal, abortive)

3. A person who says one thing but does another is a _____. (hypocrite, dissident)

4. A short story is an _____. (edict, anecdote)

5. A(n) _____ person makes mistakes. (irate, fallible)

6. Personal belongings are _____. (scruples, paraphernalia)

7. An ideal society is a _____. (utopia, denomination)

8. A(n) _____ fact is not known by most people. (obscure, tangible)

9. A(n) _____ object cannot move by itself. (inanimate, subversive)

10. When a smell penetrates everywhere in a room, it _____ it. (permeates, deluges)

11. When something is attributed to a source, we say that source has been _____. (liquidated, cited)

12. Two things that are adjacent are _____. (juxtaposed, precipitated)

13. Something that does not stop is _____. (derelict, incessant)

14. Something no longer in existence is _____. (defunct, fallible)

15. A _____ idea is untrue. (specious, negligible)

16. Money comes in a variety of _____. (imperatives, denominations)

17. When you are in a dilemma without solution, you have reached a(n) _____. (synthesis, impasse)

18. When you _____, you repay someone for something. (reciprocate, engender)

19. A _____ is a previous statement that serves as the basis for an argument. (mode, premise)

20. Someone who is _____ is inflexible. (adamant, fazed)

## V. Matching List

Match the Advanced Word in the first column with the word from the New Words list in the second column.

| | | |
|---|---|---|
| _____ | 1. plausible | a. advocate |
| _____ | 2. infamous | b. compensate |
| _____ | 3. renounce | c. abhorrence |
| _____ | 4. tantalize | d. credible |
| _____ | 5. antipathy | e. naive |
| _____ | 6. synopsis | f. chaos |
| _____ | 7. proponent | g. evade |
| _____ | 8. facsimile | h. abstract |
| _____ | 9. dubious | i. entice |
| _____ | 10. elude | j. abdicate |
| _____ | 11. ingenuous | k. replica |
| _____ | 12. cite | l. skeptical |
| _____ | 13. remunerate | m. attribute |
| _____ | 14. pandemonium | n. notorious |

Check your answers to the *Final Review: Advanced Words* in the back of the book.

# POSTTEST

Circle the word that is closest in meaning to the numbered word.

1. assess    a. measure   b. deny   c. change   d. reward

2. drastic    a. untouchable   b. difficult   c. extreme   d. obsolete

3. durable    a. lasting   b. suitable   c. useless   d. fragile

4. exert    a. surrender   b. rundown   c. increase   d. strive

5. dilemma    a. solution   b. predicament   c. impossibility   d. answer

6. exempt    a. obligated   b. involved   c. excused   d. opposed

7. intricate    a. complicated   b. plot   c. deceiving   d. simple

8. replica    a. original   b. reproduction   c. revision   d. synopsis

9. attribute    a. cheat   b. give credit   c. worry   d. attack

10. compensate    a. default   b. coax   c. pay   d. equal

11. data    a. rules   b. advice   c. ideas   d. facts

12. thesis    a. digest   b. outline   c. book   d. long paper

13. deprivation    a. excess   b. discovery   c. scarcity   d. acceptance

14. laborious    a. effortless   b. upsetting   c. difficult   d. impossible

15. emit    a. leave out   b. give forth   c. allow   d. ask for

16. venture    a. go forth   b. recede   c. avoid   d. immobile

17. adjacent    a. beside   b. related to   c. close to   d. distant

18. intervene    a. interrupt   b. surrender   c. prevent   d. return

19. designate    a. fire   b. appoint   c. pay   d. punish

20. surpass    a. seek   b. exceed   c. join   d. succumb

21. revert    a. drive away   b. lessen   c. return   d. refuse

22. inadvertent    a. quick   b. unnecessary   c. unintentional   d. purposeful

23. abdicate    a. suggest   b. embarrass   c. speak about   d. abandon

24. perpetrate    a. refuse   b. avoid   c. commit   d. pretend

25. superfluous    a. necessary   b. extra   c. useful   d. expensive

26. deficient    a. sufficient   b. plain   c. costly   d. inadequate

27. intermittent    a. temporary   b. continuous   c. periodic   d. rare

28. recourse    a. alternative   b. repeat   c. suggestion   d. certainty

29. concurrent    a. simultaneous   b. subsequent   c. related   d. unrelated

30. composure    a. talent   b. tranquillity   c. compulsion   d. emotion

| 31. | insinuate | a. insist | b. accuse | c. imply | d. forbid |
| 32. | tentative | a. doubtful | b. seemed | c. temporary | d. settled |
| 33. | taut | a. educated | b. tight | c. loose | d. clever |
| 34. | secede | a. argue | b. conform | c. annoy | d. withdraw |
| 35. | concede | a. show | b. explain | c. consent | d. decline |
| 36. | ostracize | a. exclude | b. abandon | c. seize | d. accept |
| 37. | abhor | a. hate | b. fear | c. reject | d. welcome |
| 38. | taboo | a. permitted | b. forbidden | c. unwise | d. untrue |
| 39. | site | a. view | b. place | c. time | d. event |
| 40. | intrigue | a. bore | b. tire | c. interest | d. anger |
| 41. | enterprise | a. undertaking | b. amusement | c. equalize | d. ending |
| 42. | exasperate | a. expect | b. restrict | c. annoy | d. excite |
| 43. | flagrant | a. glaring | b. unimportant | c. essential | d. elaborate |
| 44. | invaluable | a. inexpensive | b. without value | c. useful | d. of great worth |
| 45. | methodical | a. sloppy | b. rapid | c. skilled | d. careful |
| 46. | tolerable | a. serious | b. forgiving | c. fair | d. passable |
| 47. | waive | a. take | b. relinquish | c. substitute | d. defy |
| 48. | assert | a. confirm | b. restate | c. affirm | d. infer |
| 49. | synopsis | a. summary | b. outline | c. plot | d. speech |
| 50. | explicit | a. hidden | b. loud | c. hinted | d. clear |

Check your answers in the back of the book.
Fill in your score here _____.
Record your score on the Progress Chart on page 260.

## The Meaning of Your Score

If you scored:

0–39 correct:     You need to study further the words in this book.

40–50             You're ready to advance to Level II of *Keys to a Powerful Vocabulary*.

# EPILOGUE

Students completing this book usually ask, "Where do we go from here?" If a more advanced vocabulary class is not available or convenient, we offer the following suggestions for independent study:

1. Use flash cards to learn the words you missed in this book's posttest.
2. Work in a more advanced vocabulary book, such as *Keys to a Powerful Vocabulary, Level 2.*
3. Never look up a word in the dictionary without noting the part of speech, etymology, and multiple meanings.
4. Continue to study words you see in your reading, using the methods in the Own Words exercises in this book: pronounce the word, put the definition in your own words, use the word in a sentence, make up a mnemonic, and put it on a flash card.

Mark each space on the graph below with your percentile score for each test and then connect your marks to show your progress.

You calculate your percentage as follows: divide the number of correct answers by the total number of items on the test and multiply by 100.

Example: 30 correct answers on the Pretest out of a possible 50 items.

$$30 \div 50 = .60 \times 100 = 60\%$$

| | | 10 | 20 | 30 | 40 | 50 | 60 | 70 | 80 | 90 | 100 |
|---|---|---|---|---|---|---|---|---|---|---|---|
| Pretest | New Words | | | | | | | | | | |
| Chapter 2 | Review | | | | | | | | | | |
| | New Words | | | | | | | | | | |
| | Advanced | | | | | | | | | | |
| Chapter 3 | Review | | | | | | | | | | |
| | New Words | | | | | | | | | | |
| | Advanced | | | | | | | | | | |
| Chapter 4 | Review | | | | | | | | | | |
| | New Words | | | | | | | | | | |
| | Advanced | | | | | | | | | | |
| Chapter 5 | Review | | | | | | | | | | |
| | New Words | | | | | | | | | | |
| | Advanced | | | | | | | | | | |
| Chapter 6 | Review | | | | | | | | | | |
| | New Words | | | | | | | | | | |
| | Advanced | | | | | | | | | | |
| Midterm | Review | | | | | | | | | | |
| | New Words | | | | | | | | | | |
| | Advanced | | | | | | | | | | |
| Chapter 7 | Review | | | | | | | | | | |
| | New Words | | | | | | | | | | |
| | Advanced | | | | | | | | | | |
| Chapter 8 | Review | | | | | | | | | | |
| | New Words | | | | | | | | | | |
| | Advanced | | | | | | | | | | |
| Chapter 9 | Review | | | | | | | | | | |
| | New Words | | | | | | | | | | |
| | Advanced | | | | | | | | | | |
| Chapter 10 | Review | | | | | | | | | | |
| | New Words | | | | | | | | | | |
| | Advanced | | | | | | | | | | |
| Chapter 11 | Review | | | | | | | | | | |
| | New Words | | | | | | | | | | |
| | Advanced | | | | | | | | | | |
| Chapter 12 | Review | | | | | | | | | | |
| | New Words | | | | | | | | | | |
| | Advanced | | | | | | | | | | |
| Posttest | New Words | | | | | | | | | | |
| Final | Review | | | | | | | | | | |
| | New Words | | | | | | | | | | |
| | Advanced | | | | | | | | | | |

# ANSWERS

## CHAPTER 1

### Pretest (p. 5)

| | | | | |
|---|---|---|---|---|
| 1. d | 11. c | 21. c | 31. d | 41. d |
| 2. a | 12. d | 22. b | 32. c | 42. c |
| 3. a | 13. b | 23. b | 33. a | 43. a |
| 4. a | 14. b | 24. a | 34. a | 44. b |
| 5. a | 15. a | 25. d | 35. b | 45. c |
| 6. c | 16. b | 26. b | 36. b | 46. a |
| 7. c | 17. c | 27. c | 37. d | 47. a |
| 8. c | 18. a | 28. c | 38. d | 48. a |
| 9. b | 19. c | 29. c | 39. a | 49. b |
| 10. d | 20. a | 30. b | 40. b | 50. d |

## CHAPTER 2

### Proverb Pronunciation (p. 10)

a. Every cloud has a silver lining.
b. A watched pot never boils.
c. A penny saved is a penny earned.

### Exercise 1 (p. 15)

| | |
|---|---|
| 1. ordeal | 6. neurotic |
| 2. convey | 7. cope |
| 3. absurd | 8. negligent |
| 4. negotiate | 9. unique |
| 5. hostile | 10. contemplate |

### Exercise 2 (p. 15)

I.
1. a. foolish
   b. It is *absurd* to think you can become a scientist after studying in college one year.
2. a. to fight successfully or at least on equal terms; to deal with a problem
   b. Many students have difficulty *coping* with the pressures of both going to school and working.
3. a. to talk in order to come to an agreement
   b. The union representatives and employers try to *negotiate* a new contract before a strike occurs.
4. a. a difficult or painful experience
   b. It's an *ordeal* to lose someone you love.

5. a. one and only; single; sole; having no equal; unusual
   b. Each of us is *unique* in this world, even those of us who have twins.

II. Here are some sample mnemonic devices. Check yours with your instructor.
   1. People who *contemplate* might hesitate.
   2. *conveyor* belt
   3. Throwing a hot tile is *hostile.*
   4. *Negligent* people neglect things.
   5. *Neurotic* people are nervous.

### New Words I (p. 17)

These are some possible devices:
commemorate: a memorial helps us remember
default: Payments halt when you *default.*
detest: People *detest* a pest.
durable: Something *durable* lasts *during* many ages.
evade: the opposite of invade
exert: When you *exert*, you make an effort until you hurt.
frigid: A refrigerator is *frigid.*
notorious: noted in a bad way
spontaneous: *Spontaneous* people respond easily.
unscrupulous: Picture an *unscrupulous* person unscrewing your car stereo to steal it.

### Exercise 3 (p. 18)

| | |
|---|---|
| 1. durable | 6. frigid |
| 2. detest | 7. unscrupulous |
| 3. exerts | 8. commemorate |
| 4. default | 9. spontaneously |
| 5. notorious | 10. evaded |

### New Words II (p. 19)

1. Most accountants and bankers have an *aptitude* for mathematics.
2. *Arid* areas lack water.
3. A *concise* statement is usually easier to understand.
4. You should try all other solutions to a problem before trying *drastic* ones.
5. We should *endeavor* to learn new things throughout our lives.
6. Prices have *escalated* every year for the past ten years.
7. It is a *fallacy* to believe that redheaded women have bad tempers.

## Exercise 2 (p. 57)

1. in val′id
2. min′it
3. di lib′ər āt′
4. ē lab′ər it
5. ə prō′prē āt′
6. ē lab′ə rāt′
7. mī nōōt′
8. in′və lid
9. ə prō′prē it
10. di lib′ər it

## Exercise 3 (p. 58)

acute: a. 4
      b. 3
terminal: a. 3
        b. 3
contemporary: a. 1
            b. 2
parallel: a. 1
      b. 2
complex: a. 2
       b. 2

## Exercise 4 (p. 59)

1. Check your answers with your instructor.
2. a. invalidate
   b. elaborateness; elaboration
   c. minutely
   d. deliberateness; deliberation
   e. terminate
3. a. et cetera         and so forth
   b. id est            that is (to say)
   c. exempli gratia    for example
   d. et alii           and others
   e. répondez s'il vous plaît    please reply
4. a. 2
   b. see following entry
   c. 1
   d. Old Norse
   e. The plural of fiasco can be either fiascoes or fiascos.

## Exercise 5 (p. 61)

1. William
2. Scandinavian
3. cleave
4. Celts
5. Bolivia
6. self

*Mystery Saying: A Definition of Love*—A combination of two vowels, two consonants, and two fools.

## Exercise 6 (p. 63)

1. 1 aggravate
2. 1 attributed
3. 1 compensate
4. 1 intimate
5. 1 consistency
6. 1 foil
7. 1 liberal
8. 4 objective
9. 1 abstract
10. 3 intrigued

## Exercise 7 (p. 65)

1. d
2. a
3. b
4. b
5. c
6. c
7. b
8. d
9. c
10. b

## Exercise 8 (p. 66)

1. criteria
2. datum
3. theses
4. phenomena
5. apparatus or apparatuses

## Exercise 9 (p. 66)

1. F
2. T
3. T
4. F
5. T

## Exercise 10 (p. 66)

1. S, d
2. S, b
3. A, a
4. S, b
5. A, a

## Exercise 11 (p. 67)

1. d
2. a
3. e
4. b
5. c

## Exercise 12 (p. 67)

1. contemporary
2. theories
3. ending
4. assist
5. guess

## Exercise 13 (p. 67); Sample answers:

1. You might want to read an *abridged* novel if *you don't have time to read the whole thing.*
2. Whenever you look at an *abstract* painting, *you will see something different.*
3. Spicy food can *aggravate* an ulcer; however, *some people eat what they want regardless of the consequences.*
4. Modern hospitals must have expensive *apparatus;* for example, *a heart machine may cost a million dollars.*
5. The *archaic* language we find in old books sounds strange because *we no longer hear it.*
6. Beauty is an *attribute* most women fear losing; thus *many choose to have a face lift even though it costs a lot and is painful.*
7. Idioms are *colloquial;* for example, *you would not write "He's quite a guy" in a college essay.*
8. Some employers try to *compensate* their workers when *they work overtime or on weekends.*
9. If there is not *consistency* in disciplining a child, *the child will never learn rules of right and wrong.*
10. Although teachers may have specific *criteria* in mind when grading an essay test, *they can be influenced by the overall appearance of the answer.*
11. Whenever you collect *data* for a term paper, *you should be sure to organize them carefully.*
12. When you look up the *derivation* of a word, *be sure you understand the abbreviations.*
13. If you hear a burglar, you should call 911 instead of trying to *foil* the robbery because *the robber might have a weapon.*
14. You may tell your best friends your *intimate* secrets; nevertheless, *they may accidentally tell someone else.*

15. Unless a book is *intriguing, you probably will have difficulty finishing it.*
16. We want to eat a *liberal* portion from each of the four basic food groups every day because *we need the vitamins found in the different types of food.*
17. Although you may not know your specific *objectives* before you finish college, *you should have a general idea.*
18. Even though using gas for home lighting is *obsolete, we might use it in a rural area.*
19. The Beatles were a *phenomenon* in the 1960s, yet *other rock groups of the same period have been forgotten.*
20. Until you develop a *thesis* for your term paper, *you cannot begin to write.*

### Exercise 14 (p. 70)

| | | |
|---|---|---|
| 1. cited | 5. deluge | 9. perennial |
| 2. desolate | 6. precipitated | 10. defer |
| 3. denomination | 7. derelict | |
| 4. mode | 8. collateral | |

### Exercise 15 (p. 71)

### Exercise 16 (p. 72)

No answers provided.

## CHAPTER 5

### The Case of the Mysterious Call (p. 74)

| | | | | |
|---|---|---|---|---|
| 1. or | 9. ate | 17. ment | 25. ly | 33. ly |
| 2. ly | 10. ish | 18. ly | 26. ful | 34. ness |
| 3. er | 11. er | 19. en | 27. ic | 35. ly |
| 4. ly | 12. ion | 20. er | 28. y | 36. ment |
| 5. en | 13. ful | 21. cy | 29. less | 37. ate |
| 6. tion | 14. ous | 22. ive | 30. or | |
| 7. y | 15. ly | 23. er | 31. ly | |
| 8. ion | 16. ate | 24. ly | 32. ary | |

### Spelling Changes (p. 77)

1. a. solemnity
   b. omitting
   c. bitten
   d. uniqueness
   e. occurrence
2. a. acuteness
   b. futility
   c. liberalism
   d. coping
   e. precision
3. a. copier
   b. studying
   c. librarian
   d. annoyance
   e. pitiful
4. a. possible
   b. employable
   c. detestable
   d. invisible
   e. breakable
5. These are some possible mnemonic devices.
   a. brav*e* ends in *e*
   b. a secret*ary* is an *assistant*
   c. a defend*ant* needs an *attorney*
   d. adja*ce*nt means n*e*xt to
   e. coincid*e* ends in *e*

### Exercise 1 (p. 79)

| | |
|---|---|
| 1. derive | 6. cohere |
| 2. spontaneous | 7. consistent or consist |
| 3. deduce or deduct | 8. compel |
| 4. skeptic | 9. cite |
| 5. conspire | 10. object |

### Exercise 2 (p. 81)

| | |
|---|---|
| 1. frequency | 6. priority |
| 2. priceless | 7. ancestry |
| 3. stabilize | 8. exemplify |
| 4. offensive | 9. decisive |
| 5. brutality | 10. temperament |

### Exercise 3 (p. 82)

| | |
|---|---|
| 1. frequently | 6. offend |
| 2. decision or decisiveness | 7. temperamental |
| 3. price or pricelessness | 8. prior |
| 4. brutal | 9. example |
| 5. ancestral | 10. stable |

### Exercise 4 (p. 82)

1. desolation
2. attainable
3. escalator
4. conveyance
5. reliant

### Exercise 5 (p. 82)

| | |
|---|---|
| 1. preferable | 6. skinniness |
| 2. ——— | 7. ——— |
| 3. confinement | 8. propeller |
| 4. ——— | 9. civilize |
| 5. permissible | 10. ——— |

### Exercise 6 (p. 84)

| | |
|---|---|
| 1. consolidate | 6. laborious |
| 2. methodical | 7. monetary |
| 3. nonpartisan | 8. fluency |
| 4. authoritarian | 9. acquisitions |
| 5. graphic | 10. deprivation |

### Exercise 7 (p. 86)

| | |
|---|---|
| 1. a | 6. c |
| 2. c | 7. a |
| 3. c | 8. c |
| 4. b | 9. b |
| 5. c | 10. c |

### Exercise 8 (p. 87)

1. F
2. T
3. T
4. F
5. F

### Exercise 9 (p. 87)

1. S, d
2. C, b
3. C, c
4. A, d
5. C, a

### Exercise 10 (p. 88)

1. e
2. d
3. a
4. b
5. c

### Exercise 11 (p. 88)

1. careless
2. laborious
3. optional
4. random
5. companionship

### Exercise 12 (p. 88); Sample answers:

1. John was happy with his new *acquisition* at first; afterward, *he wasn't so sure.*
2. Sylvia was able to *consolidate* her loans within *one affordable payment.*
3. Employees complain of *authoritarian* bosses like *Captain Bligh.*
4. Sleep *deprivation* is quickly made up; as soon as *one gets a good night's sleep, all the symptoms go away.*
5. *Fluency* in Spanish has many advantages, whereas *fluency in Latin is much less useful.*
6. Mnemonic devices are most effective when cues are very *graphic; in fact, the more colorful they are, the better you remember them.*
7. Bookkeeping can be *laborious; moreover, it takes a lot of time.*
8. It is best to take a *methodical* approach; if you don't, *it's easier to make mistakes.*
9. *Monetary* rewards are less *satisfying than personal rewards.*
10. The bill had *nonpartisan* support; more important, *it had no opponents.*
11. The leader was *designated* after *a vote.*
12. Visiting *dignitaries* usually *get royal treatment.*
13. There have been several cases of *fraudulent* claims; accordingly, *the company has been more careful about checking claims.*
14. Soldiers want to *intimidate* the enemy so that *the enemy doesn't fight so well.*

15. Attendance is not *obligatory* even though *it would be difficult to pass the course without attending.*
16. *Reliance* on stockbrokers is another *way to lose your money.*
17. I enjoy *solitude* as long as *it doesn't go on too long.*
18. She had an *apprehensive* feeling; furthermore, *she was sorry she hadn't asked for advice before committing herself.*
19. The teacher's manner was *reminiscent* of my father although *the teacher was much younger.*
20. *Sequential* information is easy to remember, provided *that you use a mnemonic device.*

### Exercise 13 (p. 91)

| | |
|---|---|
| 1. emphatic | 6. fallible |
| 2. reactionary | 7. erratic |
| 3. abortive | 8. liquidate |
| 4. equitable | 9. electorate |
| 5. longevity | 10. insightful |

### Exercise 14 (p. 92)

### Exercise 15 (p. 93)

No answers provided.

## CHAPTER 6

### Exercise 1 (p. 98)

No answers provided.

### Exercise 2 (p. 99)

| | |
|---|---|
| 1. *ab*normal | 6. *ex*ile |
| 2. *pre*mature | 7. *pro*claim |
| 3. *contro*versial | 8. retrieve |
| 4. *non*existent | 9. *ob*struct |
| 5. *im*mortal | 10. *anti*dote |

### Exercise 3 (p. 101)

| | |
|---|---|
| 1. antidote | 6. nonexistent |
| 2. abnormal | 7. proclaim |
| 3. exile | 8. controversial |
| 4. premature | 9. obstruct |
| 5. retrieve | 10. immortal |

### Exercise 4 (p. 103)

| | |
|---|---|
| 1. unbiased | 6. irrelevant |
| 2. atypical | 7. posterity |
| 3. coincide | 8. subdued |
| 4. acclimate | 9. misconstrues |
| 5. intervention | 10. collaborated |

## Exercise 5 (p. 105)

1. b
2. a
3. d
4. a
5. a

6. b
7. c
8. b
9. b
10. c

## Exercise 6 (p. 106)

1. T
2. F
3. F

4. T
5. F

## Exercise 7 (p. 107)

1. S, b
2. C, b
3. A, c

4. S, a
5. S, c

## Exercise 8 (p. 107)

1. e
2. c
3. d
4. a
5. b

## Exercise 9 (p. 107)

1. characteristic
2. unbiased
3. distinguished
4. increase
5. succumb

## Exercise 10 (p. 107); Sample answers:

1. If you do not become *acclimated* to the thin air in most mountain resorts, *you will become tired very quickly.*
2. The two houses were on *adjacent* lots; moreover, *they were constructed with similar materials.*
3. A snowstorm in Southern California is *atypical,* yet *it has been known to happen.*
4. In case an earthquake and a power blackout *coincide,* take your flashlight and go outside.
5. When two people *collaborate* on a business deal, *they need to agree on what will be done.*
6. If the value of the dollar *depreciates, you cannot buy as much with your money.*
7. As long as some car repair shops are *disreputable, people need to be careful they are not charged for things that were not done.*
8. A general education is supposed to *enlighten* college students; however, *many students don't see the value of having to take American history and literature courses.*
9. Some people find food so *enticing* that *they eat too much and get sick.*
10. After reading an *excerpt* from the latest bestselling book, *I decided to read the whole book as soon as possible.*
11. It is not wise to try to *intervene* when two dogs are fighting; in fact, *you might get hurt more than the animals.*
12. *Irrational* behavior is often exhibited when *someone is very angry.*
13. During an argument, it is *irrelevant* to *bring up things that happened years ago.*
14. A teacher can *misconstrue* a situation; for example, *he may think you are cheating when you are just trying to think of an answer.*

15. After a person's death, that individual may live in *posterity* if *she has done things that made her famous.*
16. It is difficult to *subdue* people when *they are angry.*
17. During a heat wave, some people *succumb* to the heat, which means *they get dizzy and feel faint.*
18. One way to lose *superfluous* weight is to diet; another *is to exercise.*
19. Whenever you try to *surpass* the accomplishments of people like your friends and family, *you are taking the chance they may become jealous.*
20. A jury should be *unbiased* because *the case must be decided based on the evidence presented.*

## Exercise 11 (p. 110)

1. agnostic
2. inanimate
3. elude
4. transcends
5. remuneration

6. dissidents
7. obscure
8. posthumous
9. permeate
10. inexplicable

## Exercise 12 (p. 111)

```
R E M I N I S C E N T █ H E A R
E V E N █ █ A █ V O L T █ R Y E
L E T █ █ F L U E N C Y █ █ █ W
I S H █ █ █ █ P █ █ L I M A █
A █ O █ M O N E T A R Y █ N O R
N █ D I G N I T A R Y █ T █ D
C H I N █ █ █ █ █ T █ M I S S
E █ C █ G R A P H I C █ A M T
D A T A █ N I █ S A U D I █
S O L I T U D E █ A █ E D E N
O L █ P E P █ S E N D S █ A N T
A L L █ O R █ E █ I E █ T D
P S █ C O N S O L I D A T E
```

## Exercise 13 (p. 112)

No answers provided.

# MIDTERM REVIEW
## REVIEW WORDS: CHAPTERS 2–6 (p. 113)

### I.

1. solemnly
2. conveyed
3. ordeal
4. priceless
5. elaborate
6. minute

7. contemplating
8. deliberate
9. proclaiming
10. nonexistent
11. deduction
12. absurd

### II.

1. Parallel
2. negligent
3. ancestry
4. appropriates
5. cope with

6. priority
7. exemplify
8. unique
9. invalid
10. obstruct

## III.

1. T
2. T
3. T
4. T
5. F
6. T
7. T
8. F

## NEW WORDS: CHAPTERS 2–6 (p. 115)

### I.

1. phenomenon
2. Objective
3. drastic
4. arid
5. replica
6. apparatus
7. subdue
8. derivations
9. graphic
10. compulsory
11. coincide
12. obligatory
13. acclimate
14. atypical
15. abstract
16. apprehensive
17. adjacent
18. intimate
19. commemorates
20. colloquial

### II.

1. T
2. T
3. F
4. T
5. T
6. T
7. F
8. T
9. T
10. F
11. F
12. F
13. T
14. T
15. T
16. T
17. T
18. T
19. T
20. T

### III.

1. endeavor
2. skeptical
3. integrity
4. dilemma
5. aptitude
6. criterion
7. unscrupulous
8. exert
9. exempt
10. chronic
11. designated
12. laborious
13. methodical
14. pondered
15. spontaneously
16. authoritarian
17. entice
18. shrewdness
19. compensate
20. obsolete
21. venture

## ADVANCED WORDS: CHAPTERS 2–6 (p. 118)

### I.

1. electorate
2. fallible
3. remuneration
4. coherent
5. eludes
6. perennial
7. mode
8. derelict
9. defunct
10. imperative
11. avid

### II.

1. S
2. S
3. A
4. S

## III.

1. T
2. F
3. T
4. T
5. T
6. T
7. T
8. T
9. T
10. T

## CHAPTER 7

### Exercise 1 (p. 124)

No answers provided.

### Exercise 2 (p. 125)

1. *gen*eralize
2. per*spect*ive
3. *vers*us
4. ver*dict*
5. pro*voke*
6. *vers*atile
7. *genet*ic
8. a*spect*
9. contra*dict*
10. *voc*ation

### Exercise 3 (p. 127)

1. generalize
2. perspective
3. versus
4. verdict
5. provoke
6. versatile
7. genetic
8. aspect
9. contradict
10. vocation

### Exercise 4 (p. 129)

1. spectrum
2. syndicate
3. advocate
4. avocation
5. abdicated
6. irrevocable
7. provocative
8. inconspicuous
9. generic
10. evoke

### Exercise 5 (p. 131)

1. b
2. c
3. b
4. d
5. a
6. c
7. b
8. a
9. b
10. d

### Exercise 6 (p. 132)

1. T
2. F
3. T
4. T
5. T

### Exercise 7 (p. 132)

1. S, a
2. C/E, b
3. A, d
4. C, a
5. S, a

### Exercise 8 (p. 133)

1. d
2. c
3. a
4. e
5. b

### Exercise 9 (p. 133)

1. cause
2. revert
3. forecast
4. oppose
5. inconspicuous

## Exercise 10 (p. 133); Sample answers:

1. Gus kept trying to *abdicate* his responsibility as department chair; what is more, *he got other people to do his work for him.*
2. Joan was a strong *advocate* of such renters' rights as *contesting landlords who raise rents.*
3. Betty pursues her *avocation* of playing chess wherever *she can find another chess player.*
4. Zebras are *inconspicuous* unless *they are against a plain background.*
5. *Generic* medicines are cheaper because *there are no advertising costs.*
6. A word or gesture can *evoke* complex feelings; for instance, *the Mona Lisa's smile means different things to different people.*
7. Some decisions are *irrevocable;* hence, *we should think before we act.*
8. *Provocative* behavior can get results; however, *they may not be the results we want.*
9. It covered the entire political *spectrum* from *the extreme right to the extreme left.*
10. Real estate *syndicates* can provide excellent investments so long as *the projected returns are realistic.*
11. Stanley is *despicable;* in contrast, *Lisa is very nice.*
12. Alzheimer's disease causes brain cells to *degenerate;* as a result, *we see such symptoms as loss of memory.*
13. People from *diverse* backgrounds sometimes *get along well.*
14. The invention was *ingenious,* but *it had no practical value.*
15. In spite of Gloria's efforts to *avert* the disaster, *the train crashed.*
16. The mistake was *inadvertent;* still, *they all lost their money.*
17. The matter was under the *jurisdiction* of Judge Brown because *it was a federal offense.*
18. Her expression was *indicative* of joy, and *she jumped up and down.*
19. Things seem different in *retrospect;* besides, *we change as we grow older.*
20. Under stress, people will *revert* to such childish behavior as *temper tantrums.*

## Exercise 11 (p. 136)

| | |
|---|---|
| 1. subversive | 6. vindicated |
| 2. edict | 7. auspicious |
| 3. indigenous | 8. specious |
| 4. adversary | 9. circumspect |
| 5. engender | 10. equivocate |

## Exercise 12 (p. 137)

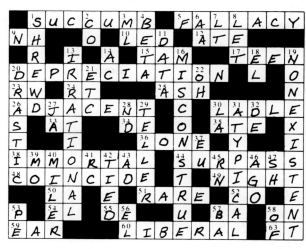

## Exercise 13 (p. 138)

No answers provided.

# CHAPTER 8

## Exercise 1 (p. 143)

No answers provided.

## Exercise 2 (p. 143)

| | |
|---|---|
| 1. per*sist* | 6. *status* |
| 2. ef*fic*ient | 7. *courier* |
| 3. *syn*thetic | 8. o *mit* |
| 4. sub*mit* | 9. *simul*taneous |
| 5. ex*cur*sion | 10. de*fect* |

## Exercise 3 (p. 145)

| | |
|---|---|
| 1. efficient | 6. status |
| 2. defect | 7. simultaneous |
| 3. excursion | 8. persist |
| 4. submit | 9. synthetic |
| 5. omit | 10. courier |

## Exercise 4 (p. 147)

| | |
|---|---|
| 1. recurrent | 6. constitute |
| 2. static | 7. symmetry |
| 3. synchronize | 8. obstacles |
| 4. recourse | 9. proficient |
| 5. superficial | 10. stagnant |

## Exercise 5 (p. 149)

| | |
|---|---|
| 1. c | 6. c |
| 2. b | 7. c |
| 3. b | 8. d |
| 4. d | 9. a |
| 5. b | 10. a |

## Exercise 6 (p. 150)

1. F
2. T
3. T
4. T
5. T

# Exercise 7 (p. 150)

1. S, c
2. C/E, d
3. C, c
4. S, d
5. A, c

# Exercise 8 (p. 151)

1. c
2. e
3. d
4. b
5. a

# Exercise 9 (p. 151)

1. significant
2. moving
3. imbalance
4. invent
5. randomly

# Exercise 10 (p. 151); Sample answers:

1. When two people make a *commitment* to each other, *they must trust each other.*
2. If two events are *concurrent*, you have to decide which one *you want to attend.*
3. Although getting a D in a class might *constitute* a passing grade in some courses, *you may not have learned enough to take the next level.*
4. Unless you are *deficient* in writing, *you should do well in English.*
5. Whenever their baby *emits* a sound, some new parents *run to see if anything is wrong.*
6. After you *incur* a large debt, *you must make a lot of money to pay back the loan.*
7. If rain is *intermittent* all night, *the ground might be wet.*
8. An *obstacle* to success in college might be *poor study habits.*
9. Until you are *proficient* in doing a task, you should not *try to show someone else how to do it.*
10. One *recourse* when you have been cheated would be to *complain to the Better Business Bureau in your city.*
11. *Recurrent* asthma attacks can exhaust you by *making you gasp for every breath.*
12. You should *remit* payment on loans as soon as they are due because *it will improve your credit rating.*
13. During a *simulated* flight, future pilots *have the chance to practice takeoffs and landings.*
14. *Stagnant* water is dangerous because *microorganisms can grow in it.*
15. When your telephone line has a lot of *static, you cannot hear what the other person is saying.*
16. If your food supply will not *suffice* on a camping trip, *you need to bring more, go shopping in the nearest town, or find wild food in the forest.*
17. After you get a *superficial* cut, *you need to clean it so it doesn't get infected.*
18. In the movies soldiers *synchronize* their watches just before *they go to blow up an enemy bridge.*
19. Although we are comfortable seeing things that have *symmetry*, artists may find them boring.
20. After you *synthesize* your thoughts about a career, *you should see your adviser or a counselor about the courses you must take.*

# Exercise 11 (p. 154)

1. assimilate
2. facsimile
3. facilitate
4. ramification
5. premise
6. cursory
7. emissary
8. obstinate
9. destitute
10. precursor

# Exercise 12 (p. 155)

# Exercise 13 (p. 156)

No answers provided.

# CHAPTER 9

## Exercise 1 (p. 160)

No answers provided.

## Exercise 2 (p. 160)

1. anti*cip*ate
2. inter*cept*
3. sus*tain*
4. sym*pathy*
5. compon*ent*
6. pro*cession*
7. de*com*pose
8. *passive*
9. re*tain*
10. suc*cession*

## Exercise 3 (p. 162)

1. anticipate
2. intercept
3. decompose
4. retain
5. procession
6. sustain
7. succession
8. components
9. passive
10. sympathy

## Exercise 4 (p. 164)

1. conceded
2. recipient
3. abstain
4. pertinent
5. precedent
6. deposed
7. deception
8. imposing
9. pathology
10. supposition

## Exercise 5 (p. 166)

1. d
2. c
3. b
4. c
5. b
6. d
7. a
8. b
9. d
10. c

270    ANSWERS

## Exercise 6 (p. 167)

1. F
2. T
3. T
4. F
5. T

## Exercise 7 (p. 167)

1. C/E, b
2. A, a
3. C, d
4. S, b
5. P, d

## Exercise 8 (p. 168)

1. c
2. d
3. e
4. b
5. a

## Exercise 9 (p. 168)

1. definite
2. ordinary
3. join
4. honesty
5. accessible

## Exercise 10 (p. 168); Sample answers:

1. Some people find it hard to *abstain* from smoking, whereas *others have less trouble.*
2. I am willing to *concede* the election whenever *the party wants me to.*
3. *Deception* leads to distrust; therefore, *you should not lie.*
4. The dictator was *deposed* after *a revolution.*
5. Chester's *imposing* manner impressed his friends, awed his enemies, and won the respect of strangers; in summary, *Chester was a winner.*
6. Her *supposition* was wrong; nevertheless, *people believed her.*
7. All were happy for the *recipient* of the award, although *they would rather have won it themselves.*
8. The case set a legal *precedent* until *a new case wiped it out.*
9. The *pertinent* data were not available due to *computer error.*
10. He was closely monitored for signs of *pathology* in case *the tumor became malignant.*
11. The conclusion is still *tentative,* yet *we should take it into account.*
12. Feelings of *apathy* can be a sign of illness, or *they could be a sign of depression.*
13. Inside the *receptacle a mold was growing.*
14. Her reaction seemed *inconceivable* at first; later, *I understood how she felt.*
15. I was surprised to find the vault so *accessible,* because *it contained the crown jewels.*
16. She usually shows *compassion,* except *for murderers.*
17. *Empathy* is a virtue; indeed, *the Golden Rule is based on it.*
18. There were good reasons to *secede;* most important, *the Union was taxing us to death.*
19. Gabrielle was known for her *composure;* in general, *she was almost impossible to upset.*
20. The motive was difficult to *ascertain;* in fact, *Sherlock Holmes failed to find it.*

## Exercise 11 (p. 171)

1. juxtapose
2. reciprocate
3. antipathy
4. tenacious
5. impassive
6. proponent
7. incessant
8. incipient
9. antecedent
10. contention

## Exercise 12 (p. 172)

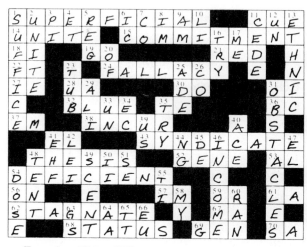

## Exercise 13 (p. 173)

No answers provided.

# CHAPTER 10

## Exercise 1 (p. 178)

1. colossal
2. sabotage
3. harass
4. jest
5. hazard
6. trivial
7. vandal
8. lunatic
9. subtle
10. prestige

## Exercise 2 (p. 179)

1. d
2. b
3. h
4. i
5. c
6. a
7. e
8. j
9. g
10. f

## Exercise 3 (p. 181)

1. d
2. g
3. f
4. e
5. b
6. i
7. h
8. j
9. c
10. a

## Exercise 4 (p. 182)

1. abhorred
2. cynical
3. bizarre
4. fanatics
5. jeopardy
6. culprit
7. harangue
8. cliché
9. chaotic
10. dismal

## Exercise 5 (p. 184)

1. jovial
2. stigma
3. preposterous
4. sinister
5. nonchalant
6. taboo
7. robust
8. martial
9. ostracize
10. stereotype

## Exercise 6 (p. 185)

1. b
2. c
3. b
4. a
5. d
6. d
7. c
8. d
9. c
10. d

## Exercise 7 (p. 186)

1. F
2. F
3. F
4. F
5. T

## Exercise 8 (p. 186)

1. C/E, b
2. A, b
3. S, a
4. P, c
5. C, a

## Exercise 9 (p. 187)

1. c
2. d
3. e
4. a
5. b

## Exercise 10 (p. 187)

1. abhor
2. logical
3. hopeful
4. delight
5. jovial

## Exercise 11 (p. 187); Sample answers:

1. I *abhor* it when *my teacher gives homework on holidays.*
2. A woman with green hair would be *bizarre* because *it is so different from normal.*
3. When a storm causes *chaos* in a town, *you should not try to drive.*
4. An example of a *cliché* I use is *"I'm cool as a cucumber."*
5. After you see a *culprit* steal something in a store, *you should tell the store manager.*
6. People in college aren't *cynical* about their futures because *they have to believe they will get good jobs and be happy.*
7. I tend to think it is a *dismal* day if *it's rainy and cold.*
8. People think you are *fanatic* when *you refuse to do anything on the weekends because there are ballgames on TV.*
9. The last time I received a long *harangue* was when *I did not tell my parents I was going to be home very late.*
10. Unless you are in *jeopardy*, you shouldn't *call the emergency telephone numbers for the police or fire departments.*
11. Because a *jovial* person is nice to be around, *happy people have many friends.*

12. During the time a country is under *martial* law, *there are usually a lot of restrictions on the people.*
13. A *nonchalant* attitude toward your job will result in *your getting fired for not doing good work.*
14. Before a club *ostracizes* one of its members, *it usually votes.*
15. A *preposterous* statement is likely to *make other people laugh at you.*
16. Because *robust* people tend to live longer, *we should exercise.*
17. Although a person may look *sinister, this impression may be wrong.*
18. An example of a *stereotype* I have seen is when *people think everyone born outside the United States can't speak English.*
19. Besides being embarrassing, a *stigma* may harm your *chances of getting the job you want.*
20. It is *taboo* in some states to *marry your first cousin.*

## Exercise 12 (p. 190)

1. pandemonium
2. utopia
3. paraphernalia
4. anecdote
5. precarious
6. scruples
7. dexterous
8. appease
9. tantalize
10. stoic

## Exercise 13 (p. 191)

1. Gr. Not given out, unpublished
2. L. *ad* = to pay *pax* = peace
3. L. right
4. Gr. all demons (used as the place where the demons lived in Milton's *Paradise Lost*)
5. Gr. bride's possessions beyond her dowry
6. L. obtained by begging or prayer
7. L. small, sharp stone
8. Gr. porch or colonnade (where Zeno preached his philosophy in Athens)
9. Gr. From the god *Tantalus,* who revealed some of Zeus's secrets and was punished by being put in water he couldn't drink and near fruit he couldn't eat
10. Gr. imaginary land in a book by Sir Thomas More; an idealized place

## Exercise 14 (p. 192)

### Exercise 15 (p. 193)

No answers provided.

## CHAPTER 11

### Proverb (p. 199)

A bird in the hand is worth two in the bush.

### Exercise 1 (p. 200)

Here are a few possible answers:

1. { Urgency
     Rush
     Hurry
     Bustle
     Precipitancy } { causes
                      creates
                      produces
                      results in } { spillages
                                     refuse
                                     unnecessary excess
                                     dissipation }

2. { Chronology
     Synchronism } { restores
                     mends
                     remedies
                     resurrects } { the totality of
                                    the aggregate
                                    the whole of } { injuries
                                                     lacerations
                                                     pains }

3. That's a { steed
              equine
              gelding
              stallion } of a { variant
                                diverse
                                diversified } { pigmentation
                                                hue
                                                tinge
                                                tint
                                                complexion
                                                tincture
                                                cast
                                                livery
                                                chroma }

### Exercise 2 (p. 200)

1. noun, adjective
2. blue chips
3. Croesus, Dives, Maecenas, Midas, Barmecide
4. noun, verb, adjective
5. temple
6. poverty
7. major
8. last
9. lettuce, cabbage, kale, beans
10. slug

### Exercise 3 (p. 202)

1. resist
2. corruption
3. enterprise
4. treachery
5. conspiracy
6. excessive
7. saturated
8. eligible
9. perils
10. tactic

### Exercise 4 (p. 202)

1. b
2. c
3. d
4. b
5. d

### Exercise 5 (p. 203)

1. c
2. b
3. a
4. d
5. a

### Exercise 6 (p. 205)

1. esteemed
2. torrid
3. flagrant
4. predicament
5. turmoil
6. tolerance
7. exasperate
8. credible
9. somber
10. insinuated

### Exercise 7 (p. 207)

1. d
2. b
3. b
4. b
5. a
6. c
7. a
8. d
9. d
10. d

### Exercise 8 (p. 208)

1. F
2. F
3. F
4. T
5. T

### Exercise 9 (p. 208)

1. C/E, c
2. P, a
3. A, b
4. S, c
5. C, b

### Exercise 10 (p. 209)

1. c
2. d
3. e
4. b
5. a

### Exercise 11 (p. 209)

1. calm
2. despise
3. dynamic
4. solution
5. pacify

### Exercise 12 (p. 209)

1. e
2. h
3. f
4. j
5. i
6. b
7. d
8. g
9. c
10. a

### Exercise 13 (p. 210)

1. b
2. g
3. a
4. f
5. i
6. h
7. d
8. j
9. c
10. e

### Exercise 14 (p. 210); Sample answers:

1. A witness must appear *credible* in order to *have an effect on a jury.*
2. Otis won not only the *esteem* of his colleagues but also *lots of money.*
3. Students can *exasperate* instructors, especially *when they don't do their assigned reading.*
4. *Flagrant* disregard of campus regulations will lead to *expulsion.*
5. Hank *insinuated* that Maria pilfered the petty cash, even though *there was no evidence against her.*
6. Her *predicament* was both embarrassing and *dangerous.*
7. An example of *somber* clothing is *a judge's robes.*
8. The boss was *tolerant* of tardiness, provided that *the work got done on time.*

9. The *torrid* affair was the most *interesting thing to happen in the community in years.*
10. Through all the *turmoil, Serena remained sure of herself.*
11. The reason for the boy's *agitation* was *mystifying.*
12. One *crucial* effect was *loss of government credibility.*
13. Willy did not *curtail* his gambling; on the contrary, *he learned a few new games.*
14. The building began to *deteriorate;* meanwhile, *the rents increased.*
15. Juliet was a *dynamic* speaker as a result of *her classes in public speaking.*
16. *Explicit* instructions were provided so that *no one would make a mistake.*
17. Attendance is *mandatory;* nevertheless, *John rarely shows up.*
18. Rather than *relinquish* his position, *he took a leave of absence.*
19. The judge made *shrewd* decisions, such as *seeing through the lawyer's maneuvers and giving a life sentence.*
20. Now that he was rich and famous, Sam *repudiated* the friends he grew up with, primarily *the ones who knew all his faults.*

### Exercise 15 (p. 213)

1. loathe
2. arduous
3. affluence
4. astute
5. renounce
6. exuberant
7. profound
8. integral
9. infamous
10. Inept

### Exercise 16 (p. 214)

| | Match | Relationship | | Match | Relationship |
|---|---|---|---|---|---|
| 1. | g | S | 6. | b | S |
| 2. | h | A | 7. | f | S |
| 3. | a | S | 8. | e | A |
| 4. | i | A | 9. | j | S |
| 5. | d | A | 10. | c | A |

### Exercise 17 (p. 215)

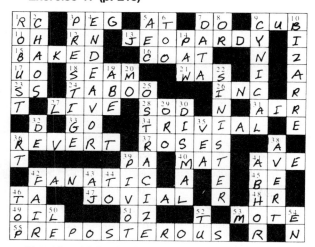

### Exercise 18 (p. 216)

No answers provided.

## CHAPTER 12

### Exercise 1 (p. 223)

1. site
2. prominent
3. counsel
4. affected
5. personnel
6. alter
7. reflects
8. excelling
9. radical
10. lure

### Exercise 2 (p. 224)

A.
1. excel
2. transcend
3. surpass

B.
1. decoy
2. lure
3. tempt

C.
1. conspicuous
2. prominent
3. remarkable

D.
1. fanatic
2. radical
3. advanced

E.
1. contemplate
2. reflect
3. speculate

### Exercise 3 (p. 225)

1. affect
2. alter
3. council
4. personal
5. site

### Exercise 4 (p. 226)

No answers provided.

### Exercise 5 (p. 229)

1. proclaimed
2. ingenious
3. dupe
4. tolerant
5. infer
6. pessimistic
7. isolation
8. remunerated
9. confounded
10. forgo

### Exercise 6 (p. 230)

1. inferred
2. reimburse
3. pessimistic
4. Cunning
5. assert
6. confound
7. impartial
8. seclusion
9. duped
10. waive

### Exercise 7 (p. 232)

1. causal
2. amoral
3. envelops
4. flair
5. locale
6. prosecute
7. right
8. rote
9. tolerant
10. vise

### Exercise 8 (p. 233)

1. c
2. c
3. c
4. a
5. a
6. d
7. d
8. a
9. c
10. b

### Exercise 9 (p. 234)

1. T
2. T
3. T
4. T
5. F

## Exercise 10 (p. 234)

1. A, d
2. C, b
3. S, a
4. C/E, c
5. P, b

## Exercise 11 (p. 235)

1. c
2. d
3. a
4. e
5. b

## Exercise 12 (p. 235)

1. waive
2. assert
3. witless
4. expose
5. educate

## Exercise 13 (p. 235); Sample answers:

1. Being an *amoral* person means *you don't know right from wrong.*
2. When you *assert* yourself, *you usually can get what you want.*
3. Many things have *causal* relationships; for example, *no money in the bank will cause your checks to bounce.*
4. If a situation in school *confounds* you, *you should see your teacher or counselor for help.*
5. Unless you are a *cunning* person, *you should not try to lie.*
6. It is not proper to try to *dupe* another person into thinking *you are rich when you are not.*
7. During the time heavy snow *envelops* a city, *school will often be cancelled.*
8. A person who has a *flair* for fashion design *will often wear interesting clothes.*
9. An umpire in a baseball game should be *impartial;* otherwise, *the game won't be judged fairly.*
10. You can *infer* from the aroma of coffee in the air that *someone is in the kitchen.*
11. My favorite *locale* for a vacation is *the mountains.*
12. A *pessimistic* person *will see problems as unending.*
13. While people are being *prosecuted* for serious crimes, *they are usually kept in jail.*
14. When you have *reimbursed* the bank for your car loan, *you no longer have to make payments.*
15. *Rites* such as funeral services are a part of any religion because *people need to believe in God at those times.*
16. Children who are taught spelling by *rote* memory *may never learn the rules.*
17. You are most likely to want *seclusion* when *you have to do some serious thinking.*
18. Some situations are not *tolerable;* for example, *hurting animals is unacceptable.*
19. Because *vice* is illegal, *people can be arrested and put in jail for it.*
20. When you are told your tuition has been *waived,* you do *not have to pay it.*

## Exercise 14 (p. 239)

1. impasse
2. circumvent
3. synopsis
4. loath
5. taut
6. faze
7. plausible
8. serenity
9. ingenuous
10. complement

## Exercise 15 (p. 240)

The following words should not be crossed out:
1. synopsis
2. predicament
3. circumvent
4. feasible
5. nonchalance

## Exercise 16 (p. 240)

1. phases
2. compliment
3. ingenuous
4. loathe
5. taut

## Exercise 17 (p. 241)

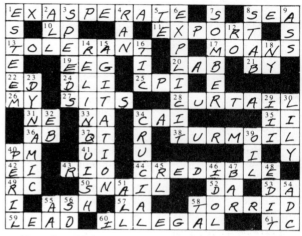

## Exercise 18 (p. 242)

No answers provided.

## FINAL REVIEW
## REVIEW WORDS: CHAPTERS 2–12 (p. 243)

**I.**

1. excursion
2. prominent
3. procession
4. solemn
5. nonexistent
6. elaborate
7. calamity
8. sympathetic
9. minute
10. analysis
11. colossal
12. maneuver
13. hostile
14. contemplate
15. conspiracy
16. lure

**II.**

1. radical
2. efficient
3. defect
4. controversial
5. unique
6. persist
7. retrieve
8. terminal
9. site
10. cope
11. acute
12. offensive
13. personnel
14. harass
15. complex
16. contemporary
17. frequency
18. versatile
19. alter
20. sustain

**III.**

| | | | |
|---|---|---|---|
| 1. T | 6. F | 11. F | 16. F |
| 2. T | 7. F | 12. T | 17. F |
| 3. F | 8. T | 13. T | 18. F |
| 4. T | 9. T | 14. F | 19. T |
| 5. T | 10. T | 15. T | 20. T |

**IV.**

| | | | |
|---|---|---|---|
| 1. e | 5. i | 9. f | 12. c |
| 2. g | 6. k | 10. d | 13. a |
| 3. h | 7. j | 11. m | 14. b |
| 4. n | 8. l | | |

## NEW WORDS: CHAPTERS 2–12 (p. 247)

**I.**

| | | | | |
|---|---|---|---|---|
| 1. c | 6. c | 11. d | 16. d | 21. a |
| 2. b | 7. a | 12. b | 17. a | 22. a |
| 3. d | 8. b | 13. b | 18. c | 23. c |
| 4. c | 9. b | 14. b | 19. d | 24. a |
| 5. a | 10. c | 15. b | 20. a | 25. b |
| | | | | 26. a |

**II.**

| | |
|---|---|
| 1. rite | 12. drastic |
| 2. chronic | 13. ostracize |
| 3. nonpartisan | 14. diverse |
| 4. remit | 15. abstract |
| 5. precedent | 16. intricate |
| 6. constitute | 17. inconceivable |
| 7. intervene in | 18. deprivation |
| 8. amoral | 19. ambiguous |
| 9. inadvertent | 20. revert to |
| 10. avert | 21. bland |
| 11. durable | 22. cliché |

**III.**

| | | | |
|---|---|---|---|
| 1. S | 6. S | 11. A | 16. A |
| 2. S | 7. S | 12. S | 17. A |
| 3. S | 8. S | 13. S | 18. S |
| 4. S | 9. S | 14. S | 19. A |
| 5. A | 10. A | 15. A | 20. S |

**IV.**

| | | | | | |
|---|---|---|---|---|---|
| 1. T | 7. T | 13. T | 19. T | 25. T | 31. T |
| 2. F | 8. F | 14. F | 20. F | 26. T | 32. T |
| 3. T | 9. T | 15. F | 21. F | 27. T | 33. T |
| 4. T | 10. T | 16. T | 22. T | 28. T | |
| 5. F | 11. F | 17. T | 23. F | 29. F | |
| 6. T | 12. T | 18. T | 24. T | 30. T | |

**V.**

| | | | |
|---|---|---|---|
| 1. m | 7. l | 13. e | 19. t |
| 2. g | 8. k | 14. q | 20. b |
| 3. d | 9. s | 15. f | 21. y |
| 4. i | 10. c | 16. j | 22. u |
| 5. p | 11. n | 17. r | 23. z |
| 6. a | 12. h | 18. o | 24. x |
| | | | 25. w |
| | | | 26. v |

**VI.**

| | | |
|---|---|---|
| 1. bizarre | 6. composure | 11. culprits |
| 2. jeopardy | 7. foil | 12. prosecuted |
| 3. sinister | 8. escalating | 13. retrospect |
| 4. intimidated | 9. nonchalant | 14. monetary |
| 5. chaos | 10. recourse | 15. compensate |
| | | 16. recurrent |
| | | 17. predicament |

## ADVANCED WORDS: CHAPTERS 2–12 (p. 253)

**I.**

| | | |
|---|---|---|
| 1. T | 5. T | 9. T |
| 2. T | 6. F | 10. T |
| 3. T | 7. T | 11. T |
| 4. T | 8. F | 12. F |

**II.**

| | | | |
|---|---|---|---|
| 1. c | 7. a | 13. b | 19. d |
| 2. c | 8. c | 14. a | 20. b |
| 3. d | 9. b | 15. d | 21. d |
| 4. b | 10. b | 16. b | 22. b |
| 5. c | 11. a | 17. a | 23. b |
| 6. a | 12. c | 18. c | 24. b |
| | | | 25. c |
| | | | 26. a |

**III.**

| | |
|---|---|
| 1. A | 6. S |
| 2. A | 7. A |
| 3. S | 8. A |
| 4. S | 9. A |
| 5. A | 10. S |

**IV.**

| | |
|---|---|
| 1. impassive | 11. cited |
| 2. abortive | 12. juxtaposed |
| 3. hypocrite | 13. incessant |
| 4. anecdote | 14. defunct |
| 5. fallible | 15. specious |
| 6. paraphernalia | 16. denominations |
| 7. utopia | 17. impasse |
| 8. obscure | 18. reciprocate |
| 9. inanimate | 19. premise |
| 10. permeates | 20. adamant |

**V.**

| | |
|---|---|
| 1. d | 8. k |
| 2. n | 9. l |
| 3. j | 10. g |
| 4. i | 11. e |
| 5. c | 12. m |
| 6. h | 13. b |
| 7. a | 14. f |

## Posttest (p. 257)

| | | | | |
|---|---|---|---|---|
| 1. a | 11. d | 21. c | 31. c | 41. a |
| 2. c | 12. d | 22. c | 32. c | 42. c |
| 3. a | 13. c | 23. d | 33. b | 43. a |
| 4. d | 14. c | 24. c | 34. d | 44. d |
| 5. b | 15. b | 25. b | 35. c | 45. d |
| 6. c | 16. a | 26. d | 36. a | 46. d |
| 7. a | 17. a | 27. c | 37. a | 47. b |
| 8. b | 18. a | 28. a | 38. b | 48. c |
| 9. b | 19. b | 29. a | 39. b | 49. a |
| 10. c | 20. b | 30. b | 40. c | 50. d |

# INDEX OF WORDS